THE
GOOD
BUSINESS

PRAISE FOR THE GOOD BUSINESS

"Good Business is the kind of story every entrepreneur should read because it is the story of actual success rather than someone's opinion. It is rare that two founders find such complete alignment, seek outside counsel but own their decisions after receiving counsel. This stands right next to Great Game of Business in my view as an authentic story that any entrepreneur can follow."

— **Greg Crabtree, CEO of CRI Simple Numbers and author of *Simple Numbers, Straight Talk, Big Profits* and *Simple Numbers 2.0: Rules for Smart Scaling***

"Too many entrepreneurs chase growth without building the foundation to sustain it. This book is a real-world example of disciplined execution, clear strategy, and values-driven leadership. It shows that you can scale past $10M without losing your soul—and without losing control. A must-read for serious builders."

— **Verne Harnish, Founder Entrepreneurs' Organization (EO), Scaling Up, and author of *Start to Scale***

"I've built my company the long way—one client at a time, one hire at a time. In my 35 years as an entrepreneur, Christian brings one of the most well-rounded viewpoints to the table when strategizing and processing ideas. This book speaks that language. It's not about hype or headlines. It's about discipline, values, and doing work you can stand behind for decades. That's the kind of business that endures."

— **Brian Benson, Founder and CEO, Benson Integrated Marketing Solutions**

"This is the kind of business book I wish I had when we were getting started. It doesn't glorify shortcuts or hype. It tells the truth about what it takes to build something real—profitably, patiently, and with your values intact. If you care about doing business the right way, this book will steady your footing."

— Gary Daemer, President & Founder, InfusionPoints

"Too many business owners miss the real tangible parts of their business - their people. Visions, missions, and culture are all vitally important but if you fail to invest in the people who steward them daily, your ship will eventually sink. This book is an excellent blueprint for anyone desiring a Good business. A must read!"

— Colonel Rob Campbell - Author, Coach, Speaker, Small Business Owner

"I've known Christian for years, and what you see in this book is exactly who he is in real life. This is an honest account of building a serious security company without shortcuts, without outside capital, and without compromising your values. In an industry that doesn't always reward patience and integrity, this is a roadmap for doing it the right way. We need more businesses like risk3sixty in our industry."

— Ross Young, Co-host CISO Tradecraft

"This book reflects the kind of leadership our industry needs more of—steady, principled, and committed to developing people. It's about building a company that serves clients well, invests in its team, and contributes to the broader security community. That mindset strengthens all of us."

— Rock Lambros, CEO and Founder of RockCyber and author of *The CISO Evolution: Business Knowledge for Cybersecurity Executives*

"Most entrepreneurs build a business that grows their bank account while shrinking their personal life. The Good Business shows you how to build and grow without selling out your freedom, your family or your people."

—Chad Willardson, Founder, Pacific Capital and ELEVATED

"A clear-eyed guide for the bootstrapped founder making the climb to $10M — and the harder climb from scrappy founder to uncapped leader. The Good Business walks the Evergreen path, treating the inner work of becoming a CEO with the same rigor, patience, and persistence as the outer work of building an enduring, profitable company."

– Dave Whorton, Founder, Tugboat Institute

Christian White & Christian Hyatt
Founders of risk3sixty

THE GOOD BUSINESS

How to Bootstrap a Business to $10m and Beyond

STONE CREST
www.stonecrestbooks.com

Stone Crest | www.stonecrestbooks.com

The Good Business
© Copyright 2026 Good Business Ventures, LLC
By Christian Hyatt, Christian White

First Edition

Published in the United States by
Stone Crest Books
www.stonecrestbooks.com
An imprint of Dinosaur House

ISBN:
978-1-961462-95-3 (hardcover)
978-1-961462-86-1 (paperback)
978-1-961462-87-8 (ebook)

Publishing Manager: Stone Crest Books
An imprint of Dinosaur House

Printed in the United States of America

DEDICATION

For Rachel, Christian, Noah, and Mikaela. Y'all are my dream team, and I love you!

—CFW

Lauren, Lily, Benjamin, and Sonora: Thank you for the life I am blessed beyond measure to share with you.

—DCH

CONTENTS

CALLED FORTH TO GREATNESS

*"Time loves **the Good Business.**"*

—Quote attributed to Warren Buffett [Emphasis added]

1

---

[1] This is the real house from this chapter. We used an AI crosshatch effect on our photos to create the art style you'll see throughout this book because we like it and feel it captures the feeling of *The Good Business*. We say this for transparency. These illustrations are the only place AI was used to generate anything in this book. Please read with confidence.

If you are considering building a business only for the money, we'd offer a word of caution:

Don't.

Money as motivation is fickle and can lead you down a path of destruction. Of course, there is great wealth to be earned as an entrepreneur, but those poor souls who begin this journey only to build their bank account just as often find that they have built a prison instead.

Peace becomes sleepless nights. Freedom is replaced with board meetings. You aren't there to send your son off to his first day of kindergarten. You miss a few dinners. Then a few more. Your face is buried in a screen checking email. Present, but not *present*. A decade goes, maybe two.

Was it worth it? You ask. *Do I even want this life? I can't quit. People are relying on me.*

We've seen it happen this way many times. But the story of your life doesn't have to be written this way.

You see, we want you to be rich. But not just rich in treasure. Instead, rich in all the things that really matter in this life: God, peace, a fifty-year marriage, a well-raised family, the freedom to pour yourself into your community, and the unbelievable privilege of enabling your team to enjoy the same.

With focus, that kind of life is yours for the taking.

That is why we wrote this book.

What Is the Good Business?

Hi, I'm Christian Hyatt, one of the two authors of this book, along with Christian White, my friend, business partner, and co-founder of risk3sixty.

Let me tell you about the view of the good life I see every day from my front porch.

Across the street is a large white brick house stretching tall behind a gray stone wall that winds around the property. The boxwoods and green lawn are all trimmed perfectly. Set at various intervals among them are statues and a large fountain. The backyard is even better: There's an infinity pool, fed by a waterfall. A large guest house sits in the shade of mature trees, with a view of the pool.

It *looks* great. The whole property is like something out of a magazine.

But what I like best about this picture of the good life is how it *feels*. I happen to know the owner, my neighbor, who is a wonderful man. For the last thirty years, he has led an elite, boutique four-person law firm with an amazing reputation. He's had the same core group working with him for over a decade because he treats them so well. And the house I have the pleasure to see every day—his home—is the *pièce de résistance* of his career.

But the thing that impresses me *most* about my neighbor? His daughter, son-in-law, and grandchildren all live next door. You *know* you've done something right when your adult daughter wants to live next door to you—especially after you've built a successful business as an entrepreneur, which can often strain relationships between business owners and their families.

And that's the good life, isn't it?

There's visible success, sure. But there's also *substance*. It's not just a life that looks good; it's a life that feels good. It's a life that *is* good, complete with integrity, love, intact relationships, an upstanding professional reputation, shared respect, and a fantastic legacy. And over the long period of time this business has been operating, there's been a wealth of profits, enough to bless his family and his team members for many years to come.

That's the kind of life worth building. And it's the kind of good life that can be fueled by building *The Good Business*: something that looks good, feels good, and *is* good.

You're going to hear us throw out that term a lot in this book: "The Good Business." So, for clarity, let's start by explaining what we mean by that term:

The Good Business is:

- **Owned by good stewards.** Closely owned businesses are best. Especially if they are owned by the founders, operators, and/or employees. Ownership must have a vested interest in the long-term success of the business, the culture, the team, and the customers.

- **Bootstrapped.** Good Businesses are free from venture capital, private equity, or other short-term investors.

- **Driven by core values.** Core values serve as a foundation for culture and expectations for how team members interact with one another.

- **Financially stable and profitable.** A Good Business generates consistent, predictable profit and maintains strong cash reserves so it can survive uncertainty, invest in its people, improve its systems, and pursue long-term growth without panic-driven decisions.

- **Self-running.** Good Businesses are not reliant on the efforts of the founder(s) to survive.

- **Invested in its primary stakeholders.** Specifically, team members and customers.

- **Earning at least $10 million in annual revenue (in 2026 dollars).** This revenue threshold represents the point at which a business can fully support professional leadership teams, robust systems and processes, competitive compensation, meaningful benefits, leadership development, and true founder independence.

One, we believe it's achievable for most entrepreneurs, given enough time—regardless of industry or starting point. Two, the size, structure, and sophistication of the team needed to achieve this level of revenue establish a minimum standard for a resilient and lasting business. And three, at this size and structure, the business has just enough scale to allow for a certain level of maturity, stability, and continuity. It's no longer solely dependent on the founders for operations. It becomes self-managing, allowing founders and other team members to focus on their best and highest use.

A Good Business also has an upstanding reputation in its industry. It's known for excellence and integrity—for treating people well. Team members love the culture, because it inspires them to do their best.

> The Good Business is profitable, known for its excellence and integrity, and fosters a high-performing culture where people thrive.

And—critically—The Good Business, as we choose to define it, is free from the encumbrances, agendas, strings, and time constraints that accompany taking venture capital or private equity.

Why does that matter?

A bootstrapped business (in other words, a business that doesn't take outside funding) has more *freedom*. The owners have freedom to make decisions that will benefit the organization and the team, to pivot on a dime and try things out. They only answer to their customers and team. They are free to prioritize long-term value creation over short-term profitability, *sustained* profitability over growth rate, and any other trade-off that creates *the triple win*—a winning environment for customers, team members, and the business. They are free to construct The Good Business without also trying to please investors who may have an entirely different vision and timeline for what the business should become.

When that *freedom* can fuel a Good Business, you've got the makings of a good life.

The World Needs You to Make a Breakthrough

The world needs more leaders to rise to the challenge of building *Good Businesses*. We need more places where people can do good work, where they can build good lives, where they are cared about and developed, and that—one by one—shape this world into something good and beautiful.

Why entrepreneurs? Because no one will care more about their own business than the owner. And God knows we need people who care, people with the moral courage, conviction, and energy to roll up their sleeves and cultivate their own land. People like us, sure, but more importantly, people like *you*.

You chose to bet on yourself and start a business. *You* took the risk, read all the business books, and committed to *building something great*. Through this effort, you are perhaps the best hope for improving your community and maybe this country.

How exciting and meaningful! As the owner of a Good Business, you are now free to build a wonderful culture. You are free to own your destiny. You are free to design the business you want.

But with that freedom comes pressure. Lots and lots of pressure.

The loneliness that comes with entrepreneurship is real—especially if you don't have a business partner. The total accountability. The heavy responsibility of continuously ensuring your clients are happy, your team is satisfied, and that you can make payroll every two weeks.

And that's just the normal, everyday pressure of owning a business. A lot else can happen along the way. For instance, maybe your growth has stalled, a common fate for founder-run startups. You're grinding yourself to the bone, yet not seeing progress. You're putting in too many hours, and you don't have a team you can delegate to. How do you get beyond that stage? Maybe you're afraid to risk what you've built to achieve a necessary breakthrough, to make a big investment to get to the next level. Heck, I'm certain some days you would give it all up if you could.

Maybe some of these thoughts keep you up at night: *How do I get other people to help? How do I make this thing work? When is all this effort going to pay off? Is it going to be like this forever? Because if it is, I'm not sure it's worth it!*

We have all felt that way, but it's time for a breakthrough.

Even if you are not sure how to scale up—or even whether you *should* scale. Even if you're unsure how to get off the ground. Even if you don't know how to get out of the treacherous cycle of working endlessly in the business, and are afraid to hire, afraid to delegate, and hesitant to make the investments it takes to get to the next level.

We wrote this book not just to encourage you to scale up, but to provide you with the playbook to do it.

My observation is that at a certain point in the life cycle of a growing business, it's easy to get stuck in what we call "the black hole." It's the stage when you're profitable and the business model *is* working, but it depends so heavily on you that you feel completely sucked into its gravitational pull. Growth has plateaued, and you haven't figured out how to scale beyond that $1 million, $3 million, or $5 million revenue range. You might be making decent money, but you can't step away from the business either. You are wearing too many hats. You are the bottleneck.

The business isn't likely to fail; it's too well established at this point (even if, sometimes, you wish it would). But you're burned out, miserable, and deeply afraid you're missing out on your kids' childhoods. You want to escape this misery, but you're questioning your every move, unsure what to do next.

At this point, "conventional wisdom" might say you should scale up and grow beyond the black hole by seeking private funding. And maybe you should—we're not against taking investment money if your business model calls for it. But in all likelihood, it doesn't make sense.

The funded model gets a lot of press, in part because there are so many monetary incentives driving that press coverage. The press releases, the selfies in front of the New York Stock Exchange, and the office parties all make getting a round of funding feel like a win. But the harsh reality is that it fundamentally changes the trajectory of your business in a way that is often counter to building The Good Business.

Why? Because the funded model is a high-risk game *of growth at all costs*: growth over culture, growth over profits, growth over family, and—often—growth over serving your customers. If you fail to play by investors' rules or secure the next round of funding, then rather than being able to help your team build a good life for themselves, you must quickly reduce that team in a series of mass layoffs. There's a wake of bodies with the funded model, one that tends to make a few winners rich while often failing to consider the people who created the value. That's why, despite all its hype, the funded model is probably wrong for more than 90 percent of the readers of this book.

We faced the possibility of taking outside capital many times throughout our own business journey. But, in hindsight, we can see with perfect clarity that *bootstrapping* was the best route for us—and a core part of building The Good Business. The bootstrapping model, in which you grow your business through the business' profits, enables strategic freedom, sustainability, and the ability to support your team in creating better lives.

> The *funded* model is a high-risk game of growth at all costs: growth over culture, growth over profits, growth over family, and—often—growth over serving your customers.
>
> The *bootstrapping* model, on the other hand, enables strategic freedom, sustainability, and the ability to support your team in creating better lives.

But in that case, how can entrepreneurs bootstrap their businesses beyond the endless grind? How do you create the Good Business so that you and your hardworking team can enjoy the good life along the journey?

It's 100 percent possible to scale your business to $10 million and beyond without taking private funding. In this book, we'll share exactly how we've done it so that you have clarity and confidence to build your own Good Business. With the compass aligned to that destination on the horizon, we'll teach you how to *set the foundation, build, and scale* the Good Business by doing the following:

Part 1: Foundations

- Picking your partner
- Setting your why and where
- Turning your mission into metrics

Part 2: Building

- Niching down
- Learning bootstrapping finance 101
- Codifying your core values and culture

Part 3: Scaling

- Scaling your leadership and teams
- Implementing systems and processes
- Unlimiting yourself
- Working *on*, not *in*

These steps won't take you on the fastest or flashiest route, but then again, most successful business stories aren't the flashy "unicorn companies" with billion-dollar valuations that show up in the news. They're just people running Good Businesses: devoting years and years to building companies with integrity, profitability, and a commitment to honoring their families and their people. We'd guess that most of the wealth in America can be found in small businesses that have followed some version of this long-term, steady growth trajectory.

> The benefit and goal of entrepreneurship is being able to do five things: Doing what you love…With people you love…Making a huge difference and impact…Being compensated appropriately…With time for other passions.
>
> —Adapted from Gino Wickman, *The EOS Life*

That's the life we've pursued, and it's the life we want to help you achieve.

We Are on This Journey with You

At this point, it's important to stress that we aren't two guys theorizing about how building The Good Business should be done. This book isn't theory. It is not a hope and a dream. It is not aspirational. It is how we have done it and how we are currently doing it today. It is real-world wisdom proven in the field. We are currently on this journey with you, shoulder-to-shoulder.

Christian White and I started risk3sixty in 2016. Although we didn't have the term for it at the time, we have always aspired to build The Good Business. We passed the $10 million milestone seven years into our journey and have been able to consistently and profitably grow the company since first launching as just two guys in a coffee shop. More importantly, we invested heavily in building a business that takes care of its people.

We have had the honor of watching our employees build good lives for themselves. Many have hit major life milestones on our watch: bought homes, made their first six-figure salary, participated in our sabbatical program, got married, and started families. (As I write this, there is currently a baby boom among our team—twenty-six babies due within twenty-four months of each other.)

To date, we have earned awards like *Consulting Magazine's* Best Firms to Work For, the *Atlanta Business Chronicle's* Hall of Fame for Fastest Growing Companies in Atlanta and 7x Best Companies to Work For. We've also received the HIRE Vets platinum medallion four times. We have also built a SaaS[2] platform, fullCircle GRC. Most new SaaS platforms are built by companies relying on external funding, because development requires extensive upfront investment. It's rare for a bootstrapped company to build one, and we're proud to have pulled it off, hit seven figures in annual recurring revenue with that product,

---

[2] SaaS stands for "software as a service." It's shorthand to describe any web portal where you'd log in, use, and pay for the service.

and done it all while earning a healthy profit. All that to say we have done our best to live by the words we say throughout this book.

But I am also not trying to pretend we are business prodigies either. We've had to learn most of these lessons the hard way. When we first launched risk3sixty, I was leaving a stable consulting job, and Christian White (or CW, as we call him around the office and in this book) was wrapping up his service as a Captain in the United States Army. We met at the MBA program at Georgia Tech and launched risk3sixty with a single $30,000 project, a prayer, and a few months of savings in the bank. I took a major pay cut, and both our backup plans were to find full time employment if risk3sixty didn't work out after a few months.

Some days I look back and wonder how we made it, almost stumbling in the dark. Truthfully, we were relying on each other, our good instinct, and a refusal to quit. Everything we give you in this book could have only been written with the benefit of hindsight—of having already done it and organized it into steps and templates, so we could hand it over to you.

I hope that is what makes this book valuable.

The Playbook We Wish We'd Had

Which brings us to The Good Business. We've worked hard to acquire the knowledge that's led to our success, and now we're on a mission to share it with other ambitious entrepreneurs. In a sense, we've tried to write the book we wish we had when we first started: one written from the perspective of, "Been there, done that. This is what works; this is how you bootstrap a Good Business and make it sustainable without relying on outside capital."

That's why we'll provide lots of stories from our own experience. In some chapters, you'll hear primarily from me in my voice and perspective. In others, you'll hear primarily from CW in his. We've been careful to note who the primary speaker is at the beginning of each chapter, but we are aligned on all the lessons, practices, and strategies we share throughout this book. They're the reason CW and I have enjoyed such enduring success—and why we see such a bright future for risk3sixty.

And while this book has *some* principles, we've tried to make it as tactical and practical as possible, with clear applicable strategies you can begin implementing today. Each tactic, strategy, or application is designed with one purpose in mind: to help small business owners like you build something special, to help you *see* the path to the Good Business, to help bring you to the intersection of maximum freedom, low risk, and true wealth.

We'll also incorporate the unique perspective we've gained by seeing inside hundreds of other businesses through our work at risk3sixty and by talking with hundreds of other business leaders along the way. We've distilled the best wisdom, crucial recommendations, and strategies for you in this book to give you the best shot at building The Good Business.

Take heed, dear reader, you are now called forth to greatness. Now go and do good things.

–   Christian Hyatt & Christian White

CHAPTER 1

THE CASE FOR BOOTSTRAPPING

Why You Should Scale *Without* Taking Private Funding

Narrated by Christian White (CW)

> You give up control. When you turn to outsiders for funding, you have to answer to them too...
>
> *Are you starting your own business to take orders from someone else? Raise money and that's what you'll wind up doing.*
>
> —Jason Fried and David Heinemeier Hansson, Rework

We thought we'd hit the jackpot.

When Jim[3] offered to invest in risk3sixty early in our entrepreneurial journey, it felt like a huge win. The former CEO of a Fortune 1000 tech company wanted to mentor *us*? He wanted to invest in *our* little company? Incredible. What powerful validation.

In the early days, we did what a lot of first-time founders do: We confused validation from investors with success. Our MBA program at Georgia Tech had largely oriented itself around a business model that involved securing outside capital. In fact, our capstone project was to pitch to various venture capitalists and private equity firms. They scored us and gave feedback. If we were really good, one of them might turn into our investor. Getting the money was the win.

By that definition, we seemed to be winning.

Jim had invited us to his office several times. He usually conducted our meetings in a large room, with several other staff members present. It was an intimidating environment that made him seem especially impressive. At this most recent meeting, he'd even had a number of mock-ups made for us, illustrating variations of a product he wanted us to build. We ended on a high note, as he verbally committed to giving us money.

There were strings attached, of course—we'd expected that. He wanted us to work out of his office space, even though doing so would mean a lengthy commute, and we could easily conduct our client meetings remotely. He wanted us to market the product he'd pitched, even though it wasn't integral to our intended business model. And he wanted some say over how we spent the money.

Up to this point, we'd been marinating in a narrative that prioritized *transactions*: raising funds, transferring equity, selling businesses, and so on. And because that narrative had been so persuasive and loud, this first transaction seemed like the route we were supposed to take.

---

[3] Not his real name

We left Jim's swanky office building feeling good. Though it was midafternoon, we decided to head to a steakhouse and celebrate.

Only after we'd toasted and dug into our meal did we start to think a little more clearly.

"So—how do you think we would spend the money?" I asked Christian after considering Jim's offer.

Christian shrugged. "Good question. I wasn't crazy about any of those mock-ups. I wasn't even thinking we'd *start* with product development. I was thinking we should focus on services first, build up our market awareness, and then start into product building."

"That approach makes more sense to me from a cash flow perspective," I mused. "But Jim wouldn't like it."

Christian cocked his head and squinted at something out the window, then looked back at me. "Did you get a weird vibe from him?"

"Yeah. I'm not sure if I trust him, honestly," I said, taking a moment to ponder my food. "You and I have worked really hard to establish this partnership. Taking Jim's money would essentially make him a third partner. He'd get a say in everything we did."

Christian shook his head. "I don't feel good about that."

"Yeah. Me neither."

By the time we paid for the check, we knew what we needed to do, even if it came with mixed emotions. Neither of us felt good about taking Jim's VC money. But neither of us felt particularly good about turning it down either.

Wasn't getting funding the whole point? Wasn't this what we were *supposed* to do?

As we soon came to discover—and relearned at so many other points along the journey—the answer was no, not at all.

It turns out there's a world of freedom, profitability, and creative autonomy available for the courageous entrepreneur who's willing to start lean and bootstrap their business, rather than accepting private funding.

Why Bootstrap? It's All About Freedom

As we learned through our negotiations with Jim, accepting outside funding means accepting the vision and strategy of your largest investor. It robs you of creative and strategic freedom. Our MBA program had taught us that outside funding was the way to go, but to us, it seemed like bad news. We chose to bootstrap our business instead.

Bootstrapping builds your business with your own money, which means you can work on your own timeline, with your own creative vision, and with no one else to answer to.

> Bootstrapping builds your business with your own money, which means you can work on your own timeline, with your own creative vision, and with no one else to answer to.

When you avoid outside capital, you get to lead your company with *the four freedoms*: **purpose, relationships, time, and money.**

We first learned about the idea of the four freedoms from entrepreneurial coach Dan Sullivan of Strategic Coach, and we've basically lived by them ever since. The best way to *magnify and retain* those four freedoms is through entrepreneurship, via bootstrapping and growing. If you take outside funding to build your business, chances are you won't own your time *or* your money. You'll be bound by someone else's agenda. For any entrepreneur who wants to build a Good Business, freedom is essential.

Here's why.

Freedom of Purpose: You Control Vision and Strategy

When you fully own your business, you own the vision and strategy for the entire entity. You're free to build your vision of The Good Business without having to answer to anyone else. You have the freedom to create, experiment, and iterate on your own timeline, all while balancing risk with what's best for your two most important stakeholders: your team and your clients.

Accepting external funding would mean ceding that freedom.

Here's an example of how this might play out. Imagine we take an investor's funding and agree to build their widget—say, a SaaS platform. We work at selling the platform for a while, but it isn't panning out. So, we go back to our investor and say, "Look—we can pay the bills by focusing on services. We'd like to pivot in that direction."

The investor says, "No, no, no—I want you to spend all the money on engineering and marketing. Make the software better and market the hell out of it. Then go raise another round of funding."

That's what the *investor* wants, because they want (1) the return on capital , and (2) the velocity of capital (to support their fund return dynamics) that come with the investor ecosystem's valuation of SaaS revenue, mostly built on hype and momentum, not the valuation that would come from a typical services company that generates a sustainable profit. Maybe we try groveling: "Um, please? We think for the overall health and long-term viability of the business, we need to balance the risk by having robust services."

The investor could easily reply, "I'm not interested in the long-term viability of the business; I'm in this for the next three to five years. Sorry. My money. My timeline. My strategy."

Do you see how the investor's interests often differ widely from yours? That limits your freedom. Consider: They manage the money of individuals and entities that have invested in their venture capital or private equity fund; all those stakeholders want their money back by an agreed-upon date—which may not align with *your* timeline to actually build the business. However, by taking their money, you don't have the freedom to pivot or control your strategy.

But you *need* this freedom. What works today in your business might not work tomorrow. As your company's leader, you must constantly make micro adjustments. You want the creative space to think and the confidence to make decisions nimbly, without pushback.

By bootstrapping our business, we haven't had to ask permission to make changes. We can spend $50,000 on an initiative—and if it doesn't work out, we can shut it down. If it does work out, we can double down and adjust as needed. This freedom is incredible. It creates an almost weightless feeling as we've honed our business model over time.

Don't underestimate the value of being free to shift your strategy. As your company's primary owner, allowing yourself infinite options to pivot reduces your overall risk. If you want to scale fast, you can. If you want to turn the whole thing into a coffee shop, it's your choice. You can do anything. On the other hand, if someone *else* is telling you what to do, you have a finite number of options, some of which may not even make sense. You must constantly meet the investors' expectations.

When we started risk3sixty, our main goal was to build something *good*. We wanted it to feel good and look good, and we wanted to *do* good. Although it took time to clearly define what "good" meant in practical terms, we weren't chiefly motivated by money. We also didn't want to prioritize growth merely for growth's sake. Silicon Valley and investor circles worship growth like a deity. We wanted to do things differently.

Goodness, quality, excellence, and building a thriving team—*those* were and still are our priorities. In other words, we wanted to build The Good Business.

Know What You Stand For

Decide up front what you're all about.

If you don't yet have a clear sense of your guiding principles, set aside some time to figure them out. By consciously identifying your nonnegotiable values, you can make sure you're proactively *living by* them. Defining your principles also creates your decision-making filter, allowing you to determine whether a given opportunity aligns with your vision—or would sell out your strategic freedom.

This insight was gained via hindsight, by the way. We mostly felt things out by instinct in those early days. Being intentional and explicit about our guiding principles up front would have saved us a lot of confusion. Rather than staring at each other uneasily over our drinks at the steakhouse, we could have confidently moved on from Jim at a quicker pace.

Freedom of Relationships: You Set the Culture and Choose Your Team

I didn't necessarily want to get out of the army. I loved being part of a high-performing team—including the clear responsibilities, the camaraderie, and the work. As I transitioned to civilian life, I would repeat to myself: *I'm going to go find a high-performing team, or I'm going to build one.* I didn't want to work for an organization where people were just "existing." I wanted to support a clear purpose and mission, collaborating with people who were all rowing in the same direction to propel themselves toward a bigger and better future.

When I had trouble finding that kind of team, I decided to build one with Christian.

For that reason, maintaining freedom over our company's culture has felt paramount from the beginning. As leaders, we set the tone for work ethic, performance, core values, camaraderie, how we invest our time, and all the fundamentals of how we relate to one another. In other words, we're free to create the culture of The Good Business.

Bootstrapping gives you this autonomy, and it's directly tied to the first freedom—purpose. If you don't own the strategy, you'll have a hard time building the culture you envision. Think about it: If your vision of holding a company retreat conflicts with the investor's deadline, you have to nix the retreat. If they tell you to take your marketing team off a brand-building project to focus on launching a new product, you have to hijack your marketing team's focus.

On the other hand, when you bootstrap and scale, you have the opportunity to create something special. *You* get to define how the team works, and what kind of work they do, and how people engage with one another. Rather than spending down investment dollars on someone else's timeline, you get to focus on *sustainable* value creation. You have the freedom to cultivate a work environment that inspires and fulfills your team, centers your core values, and ensures organizational stability. Every day, you're sending all those happy team members home to their families, who also benefit. *That's* building The Good Business—and the ripple effect is wonderful!

The freedom to design your company's culture directly influences your ability to grow and scale. In fact, we think a strong culture is the secret sauce to scaling. Culture is not just core to our strategy; culture *is* our strategy (as you'll see very clearly in the next chapter).

The two of us cared deeply about culture from the start, and we succeeded in building a good one. Because we bootstrapped, we have full freedom over what that culture looks like, and it has been the engine driving our company's fast growth.

Freedom of Time: You Determine the Timeline

Let's say the two of us had received some private equity money shortly after starting risk3sixty, and that money had a five-year timeline. To return the capital at the end of that period, we'd have needed to either sell the business or raise another round of capital, making us completely tied to others' timelines.

When you bootstrap, on the other hand, no one's dictating the timeline except you. If it takes your team an extra six months to develop your next product, that's okay. This flexibility enables your team to function with a completely different mindset. We work with a few folks who came from funded startups, and they often speak about the pressure they used to feel at those other companies. One of them recently told me, "Can I just say *thank you*? I've only been working here for about eleven months, but I've been way less stressed, and way happier as a person." He explained that he doesn't feel the same pressure he used to feel at his old company, because the timeline for his projects is determined by what makes the most sense for quality of work—not an arbitrary investor fund maturity date. The freedom we have over our timeline has been integral in creating The Good Business for our team.

That aspect of our model even gives us a hiring edge, because people want to work with companies that aren't on an aggressive timeline to achieve an outsider's goal. An oversimplified but fair representation of the venture capital agenda is to grow revenue, unprofitably, 10x in 7-10 years and then exit; the private equity agenda is to double revenue and triple profits in five years before selling to the next buyer. These are not unreasonable goals in many cases—but are they *your* goals?

Of course, we're still disciplined with our timeline—in fact, having this freedom over time makes us *more* disciplined than if we'd been funded. Often, investors don't want the business to be profitable; instead, they want you to have a managed and predictable burn rate, which essentially means spending down the money that you've raised over twelve or eighteen months on ticket items that will satisfy requirements to raise an *additional* round of funding. The emphasis is on short-term ROI for them, not long-term innovation and financial sustainability for the business. By pacing yourself based on these cobbled-together funding rounds and complex cap tables, you may never really hit your stride.

In the world of investors, companies are often treated like baseball cards—and traded like them as well. Your company is not their client; it's one of their portfolio companies. Their *investors* are their clients. You're just their ticket to generate the fees and raise the funds via the buying and selling of portfolio companies. They're in it for the money, not to support your long-term creation of The Good Business. When you understand the motives of investors and funds, you can objectively consider whether there's a fundamental alignment or misalignment in your respective strategies. If you don't recognize potential misalignment going in, you could be in for a painful time.

Sometimes this investor-funded model can work out well. The fast growth gives way to a bigger, better thing. Profitability and stability may eventually arrive (or not), along with a "unicorn" exit. When that happens, it's awesome for everyone.

But plenty of times, most times, it doesn't happen like that. There is a reason a unicorn is called a unicorn: It's rare. We've all heard of at least one "sexy startup" that seemed to have a rocket-ship trajectory—until it suddenly blew up in the atmosphere. Sometimes, even when they followed their investor's plan to a T—managing the burn rate, striving to hit their metrics—the interest for a subsequent round of funding simply wasn't there. Instead of getting more money, they heard, "We're winding down the business." Such endings are often abrupt and terrible; people lose their jobs overnight. And rather than building something special with long-term, sustainable value for your team and clients, you end up with nothing.

We've seen this happen to clients, friends, and acquaintances. It *doesn't* need to happen to you. Maintain your freedom of time through bootstrapping so that you can build a truly Good Business.

Freedom of Money: You Choose the Financial Strategy

It should be obvious by now that bootstrapping also enables freedom of money: *You* choose the best financial strategy for your company—and this freedom is integral to building The Good Business.

What comes to mind when you hear the word "profit?"

If you're like us, that word sparks warm, fuzzy feelings. It's a good word—a happy word! It describes a *desirable* thing. When a business generates profits, it is generating stability and owners can reinvest the money to grow the business and take distributions and share profits with their team. "Profit" means your business model is working to create real value for all parties involved in the ecosystem that you have created.

But that's not what a VC investor thinks when they hear "profit." No warm fuzzies there—more like the heebie-jeebies. If your company is profitable, those profits are *taxed*, and those taxes are passed on to the investment entity, based on their equity percentage, which investors don't want. They'd rather you deploy as much capital as possible, as quickly as possible, to *grow* as fast as possible and keep your tax burden low or nil, regardless of how sustainable or unsustainable that business model may be in the long run. In other words, *your* desire to create a healthy, thriving, profitable business directly conflicts with *investors'* desire to delay profits until they get bought out by the next round of investors.

That's a conflict of interest, friend. And in our opinion, it's one to avoid.

One of the best pieces of advice we ever received from our accountants came early on. They said, "A metric for business success is the size of your tax bill. If you're paying a lot in taxes, that means you're very profitable and your business is winning." The advice startled us. We'd absorbed the "conventional wisdom" that a large tax bill meant we were suckers. But we'd also observed entrepreneur acquaintances taking drastic measures to shrink their tax bills—for instance, by making huge business purchases at the end of the year, thereby draining their cash reserves and starting their first quarter stressed out and in debt. Obviously, we wanted to take appropriate measures in preparing our taxes so that we didn't pay more than we needed to—but prioritizing a lower tax bill at the expense of our business's health didn't make a whole lot of sense to us. The accountants' advice did.

They also encouraged us to occasionally pay ourselves a dividend, just as you might periodically receive a dividend from owning a portion of a publicly traded company, like Coca-Cola, by being a holder of their stock. "We've been paying ourselves way below market rate so that we can reinvest everything," we told them. "We're not paying ourselves high salaries or dividends."

One of the accountants in our meeting shrugged. "I'm not sure there's a good reason to do that," he said. "Being an entrepreneur already involves a lot of sacrifices and stress. Do you two have families?" We nodded yes. "You need to be winning along the way. *That's* one of the pleasures that will keep you going and prevent burnout. Pay yourself a market rate when you can (for what you do) and pay yourself a dividend every so often (for what you own)."

We've taken their advice—and it's been good for our morale, our budgets, and our marriages!

Many entrepreneurs focus on the promise of a big win at the end of the rainbow, when they'll sell the business and hope to get a big windfall of cash. But if you practice financial deprivation until then, you'll be miserable all along the way. You may not even enjoy the life you have left if and when that windfall comes.

Instead, think about winning financially along the entire journey. And as wiser, older folks will tell you, it was always about the journey anyway. When you bootstrap, you have the liberty to pay yourself out occasionally, instead of paying investors or dumping it all back into an unprofitable business.

Freedom over your money also ensures you can cultivate a healthy environment for your team—a key characteristic of The Good Business. We've talked about the freedom to build profits, but what about the freedom to take a *hit* with your profits, in support of your team? That's an important strategic freedom as well. While we were writing this book, for instance, we made the decision to fire a large client because they were making our team miserable. Their behavior was consistently abusive.

Firing them may not have been the "right" investment decision, but it was the right thing to do to remain aligned with our ethics and core values. We consciously chose to do something that reduced our short-term profits in order to take care of our people instead. Over the long term, we know we're going to be better for it, because our team's energy won't be sapped by that client. But we also know that we'll be feeling the loss of that income over the next six to twelve months. An external investor may not have tolerated that strategic decision, but we have the freedom to think ten years out, and not just ninety days out. That freedom enables us to consistently orient ourselves toward building The Good Business.

When we think back to Jim's offer and our ultimate decision to turn it down, the rationale all comes back to these four freedoms.

We wanted to be home for dinner with our families. We wanted to pay our people and ourselves well. We wanted to create an environment where we could build a high-performing team, do business on our terms, and treat people the way we'd want a company to treat us. We wanted to be an elite, boutique company with a great reputation for punching well above our weight, and then we wanted to be rewarded for that.

That was the sustaining vision. And that's why we elected to bootstrap.

Yes, There's a Drawback: All the Risk

In the Army, we operated by the Warrior Ethos: "I will always place the mission first; I will never accept defeat; I will never quit; I will never leave a fallen comrade." That is a winning formula whether on the battlefield or working in a business.

As Christian shares more of his story throughout the book, you'll see he grew up with a similar "whatever it takes" mindset. This mindset has always united us. Whereas we may not have had alignment with investors, we had complete alignment between the two of us—we were willing to shoulder the risk and do what it took.

Both of our experiences in life have opened us up to a certain tolerance for risk, which is key for any entrepreneur. *This* route—starting a business via bootstrapping—is not your "safe" bet. We've discussed the benefits of the four freedoms, but being free does come at a cost: You shoulder the risk alone. With investors, despite the drawbacks, you share the risk.

To bootstrap, you have to want those four freedoms enough to be okay with that tradeoff. You need a "whatever it takes" mentality. If you aren't comfortable with that, this path might not be for you. That's also okay.

It's worth considering the risks of bootstrapping head-on before committing to this path:

- Losing money
- Tarnishing your reputation
- Failing to maintain your team's livelihood
- Damaging relationships with your family as well as your early employees and clients, who may be your friends

These risks and responsibilities *do* create a mental burden—and it's one you typically wouldn't feel if you are an employee solely focused on doing a good job based on a defined role, getting a solid performance review, and collecting a healthy paycheck.

The other mental burden you commit to shouldering as a bootstrapping entrepreneur is unlimited accountability. The buck stops with you. Sometimes you have to make tough decisions that negatively impact others. You may know what the right, necessary choice is, but you also may never get the opportunity to explain *why* you made it. You simply have to live with it—and sometimes even absorb the blame for it. Leaders need to be okay with the fact that people won't always like their decisions, but they still have to be accountable for them.

In 2024, for example, we renamed our flagship platform and rebranded while bringing two new products to the marketplace. This was a huge undertaking: We reorganized the company to pull it off, got the whole team fired up, and made a ton of noise about it. We wanted everyone to buy into the vision and believe in it. If it went well, we could look like heroes. If it went poorly, we might look like complete idiots and be the subject of everyone's wrath. Either way, we needed to own the outcome—because having total autonomy means there's also no one else to blame.

When bootstrapping your company as a founder, you don't get to pass anything off to an investor partner—the blame, the financial responsibility, the outcomes. The buck stops with *you*, and it's a burden and there is risk.

When You *Shouldn't* Bootstrap

Despite all the benefits, bootstrapping won't work for every person or every business. Before you commit to it, consider whether any of the following applies to you.

If you're a reluctant entrepreneur and your heart's not fully in it, bootstrapping is probably not for you. We aren't trying to convince anyone to be an entrepreneur here; that's a different conversation. It takes a ton of grit and time to grow and scale through bootstrapping. Although we think it's the best way, it's also a long way—expect that it will be a decade-long commitment.

Some businesses need the funded model. We don't hate funded companies, and there's a place in society for those companies and their investors. In fact, for certain businesses, outside capital really works. Uber is a good example: It needed many billions of dollars' worth of outside funding in order to capture a market segment that required rapid scale and a war chest to fund engineers, lobbyists, and other staff. However, those are the unicorn situations; the majority of businesses don't need funding and may not even be considered "fundable" by typical venture capital or private equity investors.

You prefer to start, grow, exit (rinse and repeat) using other people's money. Some entrepreneurs have the magic formula for starting and selling businesses—and if that's your game, and if you haven't figured it out by now, this book isn't for you. For entrepreneurs that can do this well, the funded approach to scaling and selling a business can be a lucrative gig. Some people like the wild ride, though it's a game that most people cannot win consistently. If you genuinely enjoy the funded model, even with all its drawbacks—more power to you!

No Regrets

We've bootstrapped risk3sixty for a decade now and with real success. It's easy for us to look back at that meeting with Jim and breathe a sigh of relief that we walked away, even though we questioned ourselves at the time. Opting to bootstrap rather than take on private funding went against everything we'd been taught in our MBA program—we wondered if we were crazy.

Now, we realize that was the moment we committed ourselves to a life built around freedom: Living in that freedom has not only led to profits but also an amazing quality of life for us and our team and outsized value and stability for our clients.

Just the other day, one of our executives forwarded me an email from a well-known private equity investor. After listing their impressive credentials, it read:

> *We've been following the risk3sixty journey for a while and remain impressed with the compliance platform you and your team are scaling. Totally understand you might not be thinking about capital; however, I believe our investor network could be a strategic asset for future growth. I'd love to chat and see how we could potentially collaborate.*

I just deleted it. We get these all the time now. That's a path we *could* take—but it's not one we'd like to take. We are not quick to trade the freedom and control that we enjoy as leaders and stewards of a scaling business.

Which brings up a new point: You might be sold on bootstrapping, but why should you scale? Why not just keep things small?

We'll make our case for *that* in chapter 2.

Actions You Can Take Now

Go to a coffee shop, order your favorite drink, and reflect on the following questions:

1. What are all the pros and cons of bootstrapping vs. outside funding for my specific situation? Which list appeals to me more—and why? Which approach is more aligned with my values and goals for the business?
2. What are the downsides and potential risks for bootstrapping my business? How would I mitigate those risks? (For instance: "My spouse will be angry at me." That's a strategic consideration! You should probably discuss this with your significant other and get them on board before proceeding.)
3. Given that the bootstrapping approach is generally a time investment of at least a decade, what am I willing to put into my business, and what do I want to get out of it?
4. Get existential: What do I want for my life? If I were to envision my life five years out, does the bootstrapping approach help me get there?

If you feel confident that the bootstrapping model is right for you, tattoo it on your chest! Just kidding. But take some tangible steps to solidify that commitment. For example, when Christian signed our first client, he quit his job. Now that's commitment! Get ready to go all in.

THE CASE FOR SCALING

Amplify Your Freedom with 10X Scaling

Narrated by Christian Hyatt

> *"You don't help anyone by playing small."*

—Chad Willardson

Founder and President of Pacific Capital and

5x Best-Selling Author

Three yards at a time.

When I was playing high school football, that was the team's mantra. The idea was that if they could *just* gain three yards on every play, they'd get a first down in four tries.

Mike Alstott was the team's idol. He was a fullback for the Tampa Bay Buccaneers for eleven seasons—247 pounds of power—and *he* was the guy to send in if it was third down and three, and that first down was just a couple yards away. Mike would always find a way to get it three yards. He might not get five. He might not get ten. But dang it, he would get three yards.

Adopting this mentality, our team focused on getting three-yard plays, one after another, and making first downs. That way, we'd maintain possession of the ball—and eventually turn those gains into points on the scoreboard.

We often underestimate the incredible power of consistent incremental gains over time. Instead, our minds go to the big highlight-reel moments—the hundred-yard touchdown passes, Michael Jordan dunking from the free throw line, the hot startup celebrating a big IPO, and so on.

But those big highlights are the exception, not the rule. In the real world, great things are built by showing up every day, doing your job well, and moving the ball forward three hard-earned yards at a time.

We have adopted that same mantra with our business, where we prioritize steady, incremental gains: "Let's make progress today. Let's see what we can do. Then, we'll do that again tomorrow—and again the next day." Our focus on consistent, steady gains has managed to get us a few points on the scoreboard—$10 million to be exact, our first major target for annual revenue, which we hit within seven years of starting the business.

Despite its effectiveness, this "three yards at a time" approach to scaling is not popular. It's boring, for one thing. It doesn't make headlines. It wouldn't go viral on social media. It wouldn't even make a highlights reel.

The headlines are reserved for ninety-yard sprints into the end zone: the unicorn companies that manage to post billion-dollar valuations before ever going public (or even making a profit), thanks to their lucrative rounds of private funding and fast growth. But for every unicorn company's sprint into the end zone, there are hundreds and maybe thousands of companies that don't make it. Many fail to live up to investor expectations, fail to secure future funding rounds, or get dumped at fire-sale prices.

No team would find much success trying to throw a touchdown pass every play. That's insanity! But by focusing all their energy on securing outside capital, that's precisely the trap many founders fall into. Rather than focusing on building a Good Business, they're focused on the next round of funding, their "valuation," or how they stack up against others.

Forget that. Give us the Mike Alstott method: three yards at a time. With determination, grit, and a focus on incremental improvements, any entrepreneur can scale a bootstrapped company to $10 million in revenue and beyond.

And you *should* scale.

Only by scaling up—let's say *way* up—do you find the freedom, wealth creation, high-performing team, and impact that make the life of your dreams.

Why Scale? To Create a Bigger, Better Future

Scaling is often defined as growing revenue faster than costs, growing efficiently without a linear increase in expenses, headcount, or complexity; it is building leverage. When we talk about bootstrapped scaling, we are cognizant of the traditional definition of scaling, but we choose to define this differently.

To us, bootstrapped scaling is about growing the business without a linear increase in the founders' output. It's about empowering your team and building systems to enable the business to grow with or without you. It's about building the business to become a self-managing and sustainably growing operation that does not rely on you for its success.

Our threshold for achieving this sustainability milestone was $10 million in annual revenue. Here's why. When risk3sixty was earning between $3 million and $5 million, we finally felt like the business had some stability. But man, that was the hardest we have *ever* worked. At that point, I was still slinging invoices and executing client work—all while trying to be something called a "CEO."

Like many entrepreneurs, we had fallen into a productivity "black hole." We were afraid to take another round of risks to do the things we needed to get to the next level—things like investing in a leadership team, in sales and marketing, and in ourselves to become the leaders our team needed. Mentally, we had a hard time reconciling "risking" stability for the first time for the "dream" of getting to the next level.

Does that sound familiar?

Some entrepreneurs imagine scaling to be more trouble than it's worth. Wouldn't it be simpler, easier, and less work just to remain small? So long as you're able to pay the bills, why gamble what you've already built for anything bigger?

Here's why.

When you bootstrap *and* scale, you can create something special: long-term and sustainable value for everyone your company touches—employees and their family members, clients, partners, and yourself! And the *more* you scale, the greater the reach of that impact.

If you remain small, on the other hand, the most you can ever offer your team and clients is a *small* life: small opportunities, salaries restricted by small cash flow, and limited offerings to clients.

A leader's responsibility is to help create a bigger and better future for their team. We knew that if we could reach our original goal of $10 million in annual revenue, it would unlock a hidden law of business physics. We'd be able to offer an exciting life to our team members—chances for upward mobility, sustainability, new growth opportunities, and a healthy salary and benefits package.

On the other hand, if we didn't scale, we'd stagnate. For one thing, it would be hard to attract top performers. The best employees want to be recognized and affirmed for their high-caliber work. They want a raise every year, incentives, and promotions. If our firm plateaued and denied them those opportunities, we'd likely lose them to other companies that *could* fairly compensate them for their high performance. And if we lost top performers, we would be stuck too—captives inside a prison of our own construction. True freedom is on the other side of scaling your business and creating opportunities for other people.

A leader's responsibility is to help create a bigger and better future for the team.

Scaling Creates More Freedom

Although it seems counterintuitive, scaling your business is the only path to freedom. The bigger we got, the lighter the burden of entrepreneurship became. Not only was our company growing in stability and profitability, but our growth also forced us to build a Good Business. Only with a strong leadership team and good systems were we able to scale so successfully. Having leaders and systems in place meant *not everything depended on us*. There were other strong, capable leaders who could make decisions aligned with our vision and values, and we were all rowing in the same direction. The burden was suddenly shared—the weight lighter.

The bigger we got, the lighter the burden became.

It *seems* risky to scale—it seems like more work. But in reality, scaling forces you to build a strong team of leaders who will help carry the load. Once you do, you create freedom for yourself. You've got a self-sustaining business that doesn't require you for its existence.

Can you imagine how incredible that would be?! What would you do with your time if you could take a month off and completely step away from your business?

When you scale, you get that time off, but also so much more: More freedom. More profit. More collaborators to assist you. More opportunities for your team. And more impact for your clients.

Man, we want that for you.

Insurance Against Self-Sabotage

Some small businesses fail because of industry challenges or poor cash flow. But another major reason small businesses fail is self-sabotage.

Yes, self-sabotage.

Scaling provides you with some insurance *against* your own self-sabotage because you're surrounded by other people still pulling their oars. Even if you temporarily quit rowing because you need a moment, they're going to keep the boat moving forward.

Scaling also pushes you into communities where people think with greater abundance. Our business has achieved a level of growth that has allowed us to plug into masterminds and peer groups with other leaders who are living abundant lives. They think in terms of possibilities, not limitations. We benefit from their influence; even if we *wanted* to have a moment of self-sabotage, we couldn't. There are too many other boss individuals around us who would call us out and get us back on track.

If we'd elected to stay small, who knows if we would have ever bothered working on our own baggage? Without a supportive team providing ballast, our personal demons might have sunk the ship. We may have chosen to surround ourselves with other struggling entrepreneurs who held a scarcity mindset, rather than leaders who pushed us to rise above the clouds.

Scaling up isn't just good for your business. It's good for *you*. It forces you to grow beyond the person you've always been, to become the person you were meant to be.

And above the clouds, at cruising altitude—it's a whole new frontier!

Opportunity for Massive Growth

Setting your sights on 10X growth (growing your annual revenue by ten times) opens you to recognizing opportunities you may not have thought to look for with smaller goals. When you *know* the height you want to hit, you don't get complacent. You keep building and laying the groundwork to maintain your momentum.

Bootstrapping your way to $10 million isn't just possible for tech-based companies like ours, by the way. We're friends with people in all kinds of industries who have scaled successfully:

- The founder of a salvage company who has grown his company to $40 million in annual revenue over fifteen years.
- Two brothers who own and operate an oil-change company in Texas with multiple locations that is valuated in the tens of millions.
- A restaurateur has grown their business by over ten times.

Bootstrapping and scaling can happen in nearly any industry—provided the leadership is sound and you give it enough *time.* Your strategy, market size, and configuration may influence how *long* it takes you to get there. We hit our $10 million BHAG seven years after opening our business. A friend with a lawn-care business hit that growth milestone after thirty-five years, while a friend in the executive recruiting space did it in three years after being an industry insider for fifteen years prior to starting the business.

Even in a slower-growing industry like lawn care, though, you can find ways to speed things up—provided you've got your eyes open to those opportunities for massive growth. For instance, you might elect to acquire another company. In that move, you're essentially buying customers, dramatically sizing up your market share, and reducing your competition. You can do that with a bank loan or seller financing and never require external equity partners.

If you're not intentionally looking for scaling opportunities, though, you might miss them. Your brain filters for what you focus on. It was only because we were *looking* to scale from the start that we recognized and sought out the opportunities that helped us achieve fast paced growth.

Your Positive Impact Abounds

When you scale, you create an enormous set of opportunities for everyone in your orbit, such as:

- **Greater impact for clients**—risk3sixty is able to provide clients with many more services and products to address more complex problems than we used to, because we've become a larger, more sophisticated company.

- **Greater impact for your team**—People who started with us as interns or associates are now managers or directors, growing their careers along with our company.

- **Greater impact on your leadership**—Scaling your business forces you outside of your comfort zone as a leader, which means *personal* growth in your skills, strategies, and self-awareness and is, in turn, great for your team.

- **Greater impact on your family**—When your business scales beyond the initial challenges of entrepreneurship where everything depends on you, your take-home pay and freedom of time will noticeably increase, creating greater comfort, availability, and financial security for the people you love most. (To be clear, you shouldn't *wait* to be present for your family until your company hits a certain dollar amount, but it's certainly easier to step away from the business and be fully present with your loved ones when you have a strong leadership team in place.)

Chad Willardson, Founder and President of Pacific Capital and 5x Best-Selling Author, makes the case as well, "As an entrepreneur, it's both your duty and privilege to lead your company and your people towards a future full of growth and opportunity. You don't help anyone by playing small or by trying to preserve and protect the status quo."

Substance Over Style

Most successful bootstrapped businesses that we know of in the $10 million revenue range are understated. The business owners are not flashy. They prioritize depth and substance over flair and ego.

This concept applies to building personal wealth too. "Living modestly" doesn't sound sexy or flashy. It's definitely not the narrative pushed on social media, where influencers confuse getting rich for building wealth. In *The Millionaire Next Door*, Dr. Thomas Stanley interviewed hundreds of millionaires across the US to learn more about their strategies. He found that they're largely the unassuming "people next door" who have saved far more than they've spent. That's what real wealth looks like—not the person posting a selfie in front of a private jet.

You'll be more successful building the Good Business and your own personal wealth if you also prioritize depth and substance. Focus on the "boring fundamentals"— the real stuff that matters—instead of the flashy lifestyle that sells on Instagram.

Discipline and Patience: Crucial Practices to Scale

Aggressive scaling seemed like the key to creating the exciting future we wanted—both for us and our team. But beyond that practical conclusion, both of us also felt a *hunger* to scale. We *wanted* to build an exceptional business, with strong growth and profits, with a high-performing team, with a sterling reputation. That strong desire would have kept us moving forward even if things were teetering on the brink of failure. We wanted success badly enough that we would have pivoted and tried something else if we weren't hitting our growth targets.

Be honest with yourself about your own appetite for growth. Ask: *Do I want this badly enough to put in my blood, sweat, and tears? Do I have it in me to see this through, for as long as it takes? Do I have the real desire to grow and make a large-scale impact, so much so that I'll keep pivoting until I make my dream a reality?*

That hunger is fundamental for the long, challenging road ahead. If we only had half-hearted commitment, we would have stopped years ago when one of our myriad challenges arose. Instead, we were *all in* on day one, ready to put in a decade-long campaign to realize our dream. As Jocko Willink, retired Navy SEAL, puts it in *Discipline Equals Freedom: Field Manual,* "Getting better is a campaign. It's a daily, weekly, and hourly fight against weakness, temptation, and laziness. It's a campaign of discipline. A campaign of hard work and dedication."

To win the campaign, you *must* have discipline, patience, and staying power to achieve your goals. That's especially true for the bootstrapping and scaling entrepreneur.

So, let's talk about the specific areas where that discipline is going to be required.

Campaign of Discipline

First and foremost, you need ***disciplined, ethical decision-making***. In the earliest days of our company, our clearest filter for decision-making was, "We need to do the right thing." Whenever there was a doubt, we'd look at each other and say, "Let's just do the right thing."

As a practical example, we agreed that our accounting records should be super boring. If they were super boring, that meant they were done right. We didn't want "creative" accounting that sought to cut corners or leaned on dubious loopholes. We wanted everything to be completely aboveboard, even if it led to a big tax bill. In our eyes, that was part of doing the right thing.

Our resolution to "do the right thing" wasn't a magic wand that made life easy. The early days of hustling to get the business off the ground were hard. So, we started to add words to our guiding phrase to remind ourselves how important it was to remain consistent: "Do the right thing *over time.*" Eventually—almost to be comical—we hammered on a few more words: "Do the right thing over time, *consistently, indefinitely, forever.*"

In those early days, there were *so* many streams of input coming at us—and no shortage of interesting possibilities. In such an environment, making ethical decisions wasn't always the easiest or most lucrative choice, but we knew it would never go out of style and would eventually result in a great business.

> Do the right thing over time, consistently, indefinitely, forever.

How did we determine "the right thing"? We looked to our core values, which provide us with a valuable framework for decision-making even when we have incomplete information. Initially, we didn't have perfect clarity on what those values were. Eventually, though, we identified words for the principles we'd been living by: grit, steadfast, team, craftsmanship, and freedom. Then, we could ask a question like "Is this good for the team? If it's not good for the team, we shouldn't do it. It's not the right thing."

We'll discuss core values at greater length in chapter 4. For now, what's most important to understand is that ethical decision-making is a campaign of discipline. It's *hard.* It will be a years-long endeavor. But we knew, at the end of the day, our reputation would be built upon those ethical decisions—and we wanted that foundation to be firm.

You also need **disciplined execution**. Ideas are a dime a dozen. Some people are afraid to share their ideas out loud because they don't want anyone to "take" them, but the hard part is not the ideas. Everyone has good ideas. The hard part is *executing the ideas.* Disciplined execution is part of the secret sauce to scaling your business to $10 million and beyond. You've got to remain focused, keeping your eye on the ball even when there are shiny opportunities that could distract you.

Those shiny opportunities may come in a deluge once your business starts getting traction. It was in our $3 million to $5 million stage when we started getting emails from private equity and venture capital firms who wanted to join us for the ride. We considered those offers, multiple times, and they were tempting in the heat of our startup grind, when we felt pressure from clients and experienced challenges with employees. Ultimately, though, the opportunities never made it past the filter of our core value of freedom.

There were other distractions, outside of private funding. What about diversifying our focus and adding other services—even if they weren't relevant to our current customers? What about starting up another business? What about investing in a friend's business? Those shiny, appealing possibilities would have diverted our attention and focus from scaling risk3sixty, so we got used to saying no and kept "the main thing, the main thing," as author Stephen R. Covey emphasizes in *The 7 Habits of Highly Effective People*.

You also need **disciplined leadership**. In *Discipline Equals Freedom*, Jocko Willink writes:

> The shortcut is a lie. The hack doesn't get you there…To reach goals and overcome obstacles and become the best version of you possible will not happen by itself. It will not happen cutting corners, taking shortcuts, or looking for the easy way. THERE IS NO EASY WAY. There is only hard work, late nights, early mornings, practice, rehearsal, repetition, study, sweat, blood, toil, frustration, and discipline.

As leaders, we wanted to set the example of grit for all our employees to follow. In the first few years of risk3sixty, the two of us would be at our first meeting on Wednesday morning at 4:45 a.m. We called it our "445 Advisor Meeting," and it was just us two founders. *Why* did we elect to meet at that time? Because nobody did *anything* that early in the morning unless they were damn serious about it—and we were damn serious!

We believed embracing that level of personal discipline would extend to every aspect of our leadership and set the tone for the whole company. Those meetings were a wordless expression of our shared commitment and enabled us to solve a lot of strategic problems before most of our team was even awake. The habit also formed an internal commitment in each of us to rise to the demands of our role, whatever it might require: further training, investing in coaching, plugging into therapy, or joining a mastermind group. Years later, it no longer feels necessary to meet so early. The commitment is firmly established, and that meeting has since moved to 9:00 a.m.—but we still practice disciplined leadership by pushing our personal growth in all those other ways.

Finally, you'll need ***disciplined financial management*** if you want to scale through bootstrapping. Manage the company's finances the way you would your own household—ideally, with responsible budgeting and detailed forecasting that ensures you have more money coming in than going out.

Spending looks much different for companies that are externally funded. Taking funding can incentivize owners to buy the fancy office early in their journey, run expensive marketing campaigns, host lavish events, and intentionally spend more than they make, according to their burn rate. They may purchase things that don't add value, simply because they have extra money to spend.

The bootstrapped entrepreneur, on the other hand, needs to make every dollar count. We established the practice of doing zero-based budgeting every year—essentially, looking at *every* line item in the business and justifying why we should continue to spend money there. Especially in the early days, that practice ensured we kept our expenses lean until we were at a point with our revenue where it made sense to get the nicer office and spend more money on web design or marketing. Our disciplined approach to finances from the start helped us stay profitable and ensured good financial habits. We'll say much more about this in chapter 7.

That's the campaign of discipline you sign up for when you set your sights on scaling: discipline in ethical decision-making, execution, leadership, and finances. With those pieces in place, over time, you can consistently move the ball down the field.

Patience

There's a common saying in the business world: "Good businesses are an overnight success, ten years in the making." Your $10 million business is not something you get to teleport to. There's no big red "Easy" button that gets you overnight success. Sustainable, profitable, bootstrapped scaling takes *time*. Most businesses take the better part of a decade to scale to $10 million in annual revenue. And if you're okay with that time horizon, and are fully committed to it, we think there is a good chance that you'll get there.

Most business owners don't have that patience, and frankly, that's why many small businesses fail. It's hard to think in decades, especially when money's tight and personal stress is high. You might wonder, "Do I really want to risk a decade trying to do something that's not guaranteed?" It's tempting to use other people's money and do it faster, instead of cultivating the patience required to maintain freedom.

We often paraphrase Warren Buffett's quote "Time loves the good business," discussed in the book *Berkshire Hathaway Letters to Shareholders*. Businesses get better with time—but only if you actually *give* them time and reinvest so that they can grow and achieve their full potential. Buffett gives the example of buying shares of See's Candies in 1972. Berkshire Hathaway saw what See's could become because the fundamentals were right, knowing it would take time for the business to fully realize its potential. Fifty-some years later, that business has proven to be a fantastic investment.

If your fundamentals are solid, you're doing the right thing, and your business model is sound, then it's likely your business will be rewarded through simple *time*. We've lived by that belief, and it's proven true in our experiences. We've stuck to our priorities, kept our team and clients happy, and made decisions aligned with our core values. And—over time—we've been rewarded with growing success.

During the tough times, like an employee or a client pulling a low move, we've often said to each other, "Higher game, man." We don't let those setbacks crush us. We keep going, leveling up, getting better.

You will also have those opportunities during this long endeavor. Make up your mind now to live with patience and play the higher game. Success likely won't happen overnight; it's much more likely to be ten years in the making. But time will pass anyway, and you can choose to view this as *investing* a decade into the bigger, better future you want.

Embrace the long-term time horizon, knowing that it takes *time* for a Good Business to blossom and reveal to others what it truly is—what it has been all along.

When You Should NOT Scale

The points we've shared are true for us, and they'll be true for a lot of people. But we're not advocating for anyone to sacrifice themselves on the altar of scaling. There are some situations, some people, and some moments when "doing the right thing" means you *stop* your scaling efforts. If you fall into one of those categories, we don't recommend scaling up your business:

- **The toll of continuing is more significant than the toll of pivoting.** Some entrepreneurial realities are just too costly to continue, whether it's the cost to your family, your marriage, your integrity, your financial future, your health, or something else. In those cases, it may be better to end your efforts to scale or make a hard pivot to something else.

- **Your business model will never be profitable.** Some businesses are just bad businesses and they're never going to get to a place of sustainability or profitable growth. Our financial consultants have told us, "If you're 5 percent profitable, you're on life support. If you're 10 percent profitable, that's break even. If you're fifteen percent profitable, enjoy it while it lasts, because competition has a way of eroding margins over time." If you've hovered at that 5 percent mark or lower for years and can't support your family, it may be time to wrap things up or pivot.

- **Your business is geographically constrained.** Plenty of businesses can operate remotely at this point, but some businesses depend on a specific location. For example, if your business sells and installs widgets for horse owners, it can really only work in towns with a lot of horses. To scale, you'd need to get sales reps and travel to different parts of the country. Geography is not an *insurmountable* obstacle to scaling, but it's one that should give you pause.

- **You're limited in what you can charge.** If your business sells a commodity with a low price point and there are already big players in the marketplace, that could be a hard industry to break into and might signal that scaling isn't the best choice. For instance, it would be hard to compete with Amazon on delivering goods.

There *are* real barriers to scaling—but some may simply be perceived. Here's an example: Let's say you run a small business, and you are the main person providing services. You *love* the work you do and don't want to shift into the CEO role to run a larger business. Instead, you want to keep functioning as an individual contributor.

That's *not* a barrier to scaling. If you desire to see your business grow and bring in more revenue, simply hire for the functions you don't enjoy. For instance, you could hire an operations manager and have that person report to you. You could hire a fractional CFO or CPA to oversee the finances. With a great team around you, you get to reap the benefits of a larger, more profitable business while still doing the work you love.

Another perceived barrier might relate to a clumsy business model that trends toward unprofitability. Don't write your entrepreneurial dreams off just yet—this might be an opportunity to pivot.

Good Businesses grow and mature—*many* must pivot as the markets evolve. After a few successful years of running a successful oil-change business, our friends the Lazo brothers decided to scale. That first required an identity shift: the two brothers had to change their view of themselves from "sole proprietors" to "entrepreneurial franchise owners." Then, they needed to figure out the model for scaling. They focused on opening a second location in the general metropolitan area where they lived. After securing a bank loan with favorable terms, they opened the new location and hit their break-even point eighteen months in. They took their data back to the bank, secured another loan, and did the whole thing again. Through a disciplined approach and using prudent financial strategies, they've now opened around twenty locations—all of which are profitable.

Scale Your Freedom

Why did we choose to go on this journey?

Short answer: We wanted to be home for dinner with our families every night.

Early in my career, I worked as a consultant. I was on the road 80 to 90 percent of the time. I only saw my wife on the weekends—and I *hated* being gone.

We didn't want to do that.

We wanted those four freedoms—we wanted them on *our* terms—and we didn't want them small. We wanted the kind of strategic freedom, relational freedom, freedom of time, and financial freedom that could *only* come with building a business large enough to support a sizable, high-performing team.

It's been a campaign of discipline, and it took us seven years to reach our initial big 10X goal—but now, we're living the life we always hoped for. We're home with our families in the evenings. We provide a good life for them, and we help our parents as needs arise. People on our team feel financially secure and satisfied with their work. And—in a competitive industry—we have an elite reputation. Our clients know they receive an unparalleled standard of care with us.

That's been our sustaining vision. It's helped us stay in the fight, focus on the higher game, and keep the ball moving forward. We've bootstrapped and scaled way up so that we could experience the freedom we always wanted.

Do you have that desire? Do you have that hunger in you?

Good.

Because the rest of this book is devoted to teaching you how to do the same.

Actions You Can Take Now

Find a good spot to sit down for thirty minutes. Think deeply about the prompts below and write down your thoughts to increase clarity on your next steps.

1. Review the points under the section title, "When You Should NOT Scale." Do any of those points apply to you?
2. Envision what a bigger, better future would look like for you and your team, if you were to scale. You might even find greater power in trying to "feel" those goals in your body and picture them as an achieved reality. Then, write down the details and review them daily. This can help rewire your brain and strengthen your ability to spot opportunities that will take you in the direction of your goals.

Do you want to scale? Are you prepared to commit the time and discipline required to build a bigger, better future for you and your team? If so, write down your commitment and put it in a place you'll regularly see it.

1. SET

SET THE FOUNDATION OF THE GOOD BUSINESS

CHAPTER 3

CHOOSING A PARTNER

Think Carefully About Who You Get into Business With

Narrated by Christian Hyatt

"Happiness is only real when shared."

—Christopher McCandless, aka "Alexander Supertramp,"
quoted by Jon Krakauer in *Into the Wild*.

One of the most important decisions you will ever make is choosing a business partner. It's like getting married: You spend your time together, you confide in each other, you make big decisions together, you share a bank account, and, in many ways, you share a destiny. Getting the relationship right is crucial to every other part of the business. Getting it wrong could result in a messy and expensive divorce.

I met Christian White in a graduate school classroom on the first day of our MBA program in 2015.It is possible that CW and I would have never met, but as fate would have it, as I was choosing my seat in that first class, a name tag that matched my own caught my eye: *Christian.*

Christian White sat up straight and sported a clean haircut. A military man clearly destined for straight A's and great things. As a way to conduct introductions, the professor prompted each student to share what they were hoping to get out of the program. Most of my classmates shared aspirations along the lines of getting a promotion or a pay raise.

CW had other plans. More ambitious plans. He was the only one to say: "I'm here because I want to start a business."

It is by a shared name and a common ambition to start a business that we started the MBA program together—and finished it almost two years later. During that time, we attended class together, traveled abroad in China, and completed our capstone course, all of which provided the unique opportunity to vet each other.

Looking back now, I know there are a lot of ways to get to know another person well enough to start a business together, but those two years gave us the time and space to build a professional relationship both we and our families could trust. Over time, it also became clear that we had complementary personalities and skillsets that would lend itself to a solid business partnership. CW is a quieter guy who's good at getting things done and working on the operational side of a business, while I, through my own background, had developed a more charismatic demeanor that made me a great salesman. Further, while I had a lot of industry experience in cybersecurity, CW had raw drive and deep, broad business knowledge.

Seeing these obvious complementary traits and understanding that we could very well become business partners, we worked to learn as much about each other as we could. We made a conscious effort to ask each other the hard questions. We learned that we shared similar values, had a comparable work ethic, had similar life ambitions, similar risk profiles, and wanted the same trajectory for our business. We were also in similar life stages, each married with young families. And in getting to know each other through the MBA program, we developed an easy friendship.

You need three crucial factors when picking a business partner:

1.   Complementary skill sets
2.   Aligned values
3.   A shared vision for the business

The whole thing felt serendipitous—or, more likely, providential. And before the end of our MBA program, we launched risk3sixty together.

Speaking of Partners—Get Your Spouse on Board

Given the challenges of starting a business and the potential sacrifices your family will have to make, it's crucial to get your spouse's full buy-in on your choice of partner. In our process of considering each other as business partners, one major point of discernment was our spouses' approval.

Both of our wives have great intuition. And neither of them was ready to sign off on someone they didn't trust. In fact, in later years, they would raise red flags about other friends of ours, even going so far as to say explicitly, "If you want to hire that guy, that's fine—but do *not* make him a partner or be legally tied to him."

And they were right.

But on the "Christian and Christian" dynamic, both Rachel (CW's wife) and Lauren (my wife) gave us a green light. They also enjoyed each other's company, and we all shared similar values. The business partnership probably could have worked even if our wives didn't get along, but the fact that they did made things a lot easier.

If you're married, there's a good chance your spouse knows you better than almost anyone else. They'll have insight into people's treatment of you, which you may not be able to perceive. They want what's best for you—*and* the business. If they raise red flags about someone you're considering as a partner, particularly if your spouse is a good judge of character, take that insight seriously.

Because the risks of choosing a bad partner are catastrophic.

The Risks of Getting It Wrong

Many entrepreneurs have asked us, "How do you two make the partnership work? How do you trust each other?" Often, those questions are based on having experienced a failed partnership—or several. Not all business "marriages," we've learned, live happily ever after.

Starting a business is *exciting*. It's hypothetical and untried. It's pure potential. Those rosy expectations can extend to your choice of business partner: You ride the wave of excitement and hype—only to crash on the shore when you realize you're legally tied to the same business entity without ever having done your due diligence about this person.

It's easy to get carried away before thinking things through, but then you have to grow the business. And maintain it. And scale it. At any point, some nasty revelations may emerge: Your business partner has a completely different work ethic than you. They tend to fudge the numbers. They want to take a max dividend, rather than reinvesting most of the profits. They have a drinking problem. Their marriage is falling apart. They took out a loan against the business and never told you. *These are all things we have heard from other entrepreneurs.*

Consider carefully the ramifications if things go south with your business partner. In that case, your choices are not great:

- Navigate disagreements—which may be irreconcilable differences over selling, scaling, payouts, strategy, and more.
- Get stuck in a stalemate about any of the above.
- Go behind each other's backs—or outright betray each other—to break that stalemate.
- Buy the partner out or engage in a forced sale of the business, likely for less than its value.
- Get attorneys involved, because dissolving a business partnership is just as complex and potentially acrimonious as getting a divorce.
- Negotiate the settlement agreement over assets, employees, and clients, which can get as nasty as a custody battle.

A failed business partnership is a mess, it's expensive, and it's heartbreaking.

We've seen brothers burn their relationship down over their unraveling business partnership, and spouses teeter on the brink of divorce because the business they started together put such an enormous strain on their marriage. As this relational angst grows, so does the fallout, tanking morale and creating a toxic, dysfunctional work environment. If your partnership buckles, the business will too. Period.

On the other hand, if the partnership is successful amazing things happen. You will both decrease the risk to the business and exponentially increase its potential success. A business partnership can be an amazing asset if it's set up well—just like an amazing marriage can increase your quality of life.

> If your partnership buckles, the business will too. If the relationship is healthy, the business has a foundation on which it's likely to thrive.

So, what are some ways to ensure you get your partnership right? Let's get practical.

Risk Reduction: How to Optimize Your Partnership

A healthy working partnership becomes a force multiplier. If you have the right business partner, you not only have access to *your* skills and abilities; you have access to *theirs* as well. You also get a confidant—someone you can run ideas by and make decisions with, which can decrease the loneliness founders often feel.

> A healthy working partnership is a force multiplier.

Working alongside a trusted partner means *not everything is on you*. You don't have to make all the decisions in a vacuum; your conversations with your partner will feel like a mini mastermind, pooling your collective wisdom, experiences, and intuition.

A strong partnership can also help sustain your business's momentum, because if one founder's confidence lags, the other partner can help pull them along. When one partner lacks clarity, the other partner can help sharpen it.

Clearly, there are enormous advantages to working alongside a business partner, but there are also risks. How do you mitigate those, pick the right partner, and ensure your partnership remains healthy?

Who Do You Need in Your Foxhole?

Business can feel like battle: You're up against the rapid fire of making payroll, handling customer problems, and doing damage control when well-meaning team members commit "friendly fire" by making mistakes that cost you clients. You're also defending yourself against well-funded competitors who want to poach your business or people, and on top of it all, haters on social media might be giving you a hard time.

In those instances of heightened adversity, who do you want with you in your foxhole?

A great business partner will stand beside you, provide cover, help recognize oncoming threats, and have your back. When the stress eases up, they'll be the one to restore levity with humor, help you process what just happened, and work with you to heat up the coffee.

A *bad* business partner will force you to take the brunt of the fire. Their commitment may not match your own. They may even steal your resources, leaving you without sufficient ammo (or even dry socks). The erosion of trust will weigh heavily on your shoulders and poke holes in your confidence. Even if you do manage to find your way out of a jam, your first step might be into some other crap your partner has created.

You need someone who adds positive energy. That doesn't drain you. Who isn't work to be around every day for the next ten or twenty years.

And adversity tends to bring out people's true colors. You'll navigate many ups and downs with your business partner, and you want someone beside you who's reliable and a genuine contributor—no matter the situation.

When CW was in the military, he didn't always get to choose who was in his foxhole. As a business founder, he did—just like *you* get to choose the person you enter into partnership with. To find the right person, write down some of your desired qualities in a business partner *before* beginning a relationship.

Some qualities should be no-brainers:

- Reliable

- Strong character and integrity

- Trustworthy

- Emotionally stable

- Track record of good decision-making and financial responsibility

Other desired character qualities will be unique to your specific industry and pairing. Ideally, your business partner will have skills that *complement* your own. For instance, while I had the industry expertise and strong sales skills, CW had the team-building expertise and a passion for operations. That "yin and yang" alignment offers true force multiplication, enabling you and your partner to sync, coordinate, and chart next steps and priorities. As you and your partner learn how each other operates, you'll also learn to hone your communication, aligning more readily, and become comfortable in challenging each other's ideas.

Repeat after me: "I don't need another me; I need a *you*." Think carefully about your list of *complementary* needs that will balance your own.

For instance, CW's desired skills in a partner were as follows:

- Industry expertise
- Strong sales skills
- Wants to lead in building client relationships
- Strong visionary

While my list looked like this:

- Disciplined operator
- Turn vision into action
- Great at people management
- Unshakable

Finally, think about the desired aspects of your relational *dynamic*. For instance:

- Consistent mutual respect
- Friendship
- Relational compatibility (i.e., not driving each other crazy)
- A safe bet to be financially and legally tied to each other
- Shared values and vision for the business

If a person you're considering a partnership with doesn't meet the criteria you've set for yourself, that's a red flag that you should not go into business together. They might be a friend and good for a laugh, but do you really want to be financially and legally tied to them?

Total Transparency Required

Would you marry someone after a first date? Probably not—there are too many opportunities for incompatibility. The same is true with your business partner: *Get to know them* before hopping into business together.

Vet your potential partner even if you already know them well socially. That includes if you're starting a business with your spouse, a former coworker, a best friend, or a sibling. You've never experienced this person as a *business partner*.

It's fine to assume you can trust another person, but that is an assumption you should rigorously test before becoming business partners.

Be intentional about this process. You might even consider formally interviewing each other about sensitive topics. (We have a whole agenda to guide the conversation you can download using the QR code at the end of this chapter.)

Will that feel weird? Maybe. But there's a whole lot of forced intimacy in the foxhole of entrepreneurship, so you may as well get the awkward phase of the relationship over with as soon as possible. Your progress is on the other side of a hard conversation.

In addition to asking questions, you are also going to learn a lot about the other person by spending time together, especially in unique or uncomfortable situations.

We learned a lot about each other when we took a trip to China with our MBA program. We agreed to be roommates, which required a ton of time together in small hotel rooms with two twin beds. For instance, I learned that CW was a very *neat* packer. At our first stop, he took his *neatly* folded clothes out of his *neatly* packed suitcase and put them *neatly* away in the hotel dresser.

Worked for me. I pack stuff neatly too.

Neither of us made a mess in the hotel room. We weren't interested in partying or staying out super late. We were on the same page about how to spend our free time; usually, that meant getting coffee, grabbing a meal, or checking out the sights. Our habits lined up. We used the long train rides across the country to get to know each other better and talk through how we envisioned running a future business.

All that forced intimacy revealed that we were compatible. That's the kind of clarity you want to get about your potential partner before you commit to starting a business together.

We also suggest complete financial transparency before deciding to become business partners. Each of you requires a certain salary to maintain your living standards, you may have debt, house payments, car payments, and your kids' schooling to pay for. All of that needs to be addressed completely and accurately so you are both on the same page.

As you build a business, things like applying for loans requires putting all your financial cards on the table. You'll provide tax statements, listings of assets, bank statements, and so on to open business bank accounts, apply for lines of credit, or secure a commercial property lease. If your personal financial history becomes a blocker to progress, it will immediately erode trust. So, if you're financially constrained, disclose it. If this business will put your family in a risky position, your partner needs to know that now.

Transparency has a way of building trust, so prepare yourself to plunge in. Ask the hard questions and be fully transparent about your own situation. Dig into matters of character, habits, finances, future plans, strengths, weaknesses, emotional stability— basically, anything and everything you can think of that might come up as you build something significant together.

Create a Legally Binding Operating Agreement

When you first start a business, it may feel like spending money on an attorney to draft a partnership agreement is a waste of time and money. Practically, you just want to get started building a business and the idea of spending a day on legal documents is not very fun.

But please hear me: Do it anyway. Spending a day on an operating agreement provides two essential opportunities:

1. It forces you and your business partner to ask and answer important questions about how the business will run, and

2. It will be absolutely essential if things go south, you disagree on something important, and real money is involved.

The bottom line is that a clear, legally binding operating agreement (OA) protects both of you and leaves no doubts about the nature and workings of the relationship. As author Brené Brown says, "Clarity is kindness."

What should you include in your operating agreement? Here are some tips:

- **Work with an experienced business attorney to draft and refine the OA.** You want the OA done right and then to have it out of sight. Spend time—and money—up front and customize it to reflect your intent. Don't rely on a template you found on the internet.

- **Include financial controls.** For instance, we included a cap on the line of credit. If either of us wanted to withdraw an amount over a certain number, the other partner had to sign off. Checks and balances ensure that no one can do something nefarious without the other person knowing, which ultimately strengthens trust.

- **Clarify the equity split.** More on this in a moment, but do note: You want your equity numbers written down in black and white.

- **Outline provisions if one partner wants to shift their involvement.** Define a plan for handling situations where one partner wants to increase or decrease their input, time, or attention, including how you'd handle one partner buying the other out. And on that note...

- **Have a "divorce" plan to wind up the company.** You *hope* it doesn't come to that, but it's much healthier for everyone if you sort out those "divorce" details when the split is hypothetical than when it's a reality and the relationship has soured.

Founding a business without a strong OA leaves too many opportunities for misunderstanding between you and your business partner. Nowhere is this more important than in determining how you and your partner will split your equity. For example, while a 50/50 split might sound fair, in practice, that's a *terrible* idea.

Here's why: Let's say one day you and your business partner get the opportunity to take on a new client, but it will require you to take out a loan to finance the up-front cost of doing business. The contract would be huge, but you and your business partner are not on the same page about taking out a personal line of credit that requires your home as collateral. One partner wants to take on the project. The other says no.

Who wins? If you each have 50 percent equity, there's no tiebreaker. You're in a standoff. And a situation like that can easily derail an otherwise healthy partnership.

You *should* split the equity, but it *shouldn't* be perfectly even. And you should be crystal clear about who has the decision-making authority within your partnership should the two of you disagree. And a well written OA will help you discuss these types of things in advance.

Clarity and a shared understanding go a very long way toward a healthy long-term relationship.

Investing in a Healthy Partnership

As of this writing, I have been with my wife for more than twenty years. And I can speak with some authority when I tell you that to keep a relationship healthy, you must continue to invest in it. In a business partnership, that means frequent, high-quality communication and time together.

For example, early into starting risk3sixty, we decided we needed time set aside each week just to catch up on life. Not necessarily to process business specific issues, but just to have a good cup of coffee and stay on the same page. And over the years, as our job duties and calendars have required us to work on separate parts of the business, our weekly one-on-one remains an important tool for staying in harmony.

We also schedule an annual founders' retreat. Over the years during these retreats, we have attended CEO conferences, mastermind groups, and rented a cabin in the mountains. Changing things up beyond the norm of your day-to-day routine is a good way to shock your system and find untapped energy and creativity.

But as with any relationship, it is not perfect either. We have conflict and disagreements along the way too.

And when that happens, we tackle them head-on, enabled by the fact that we've got a lot of shared trust and goodwill. If one of us used an abrasive tone when addressing a project team in a meeting, we'd each feel freedom to say to the other privately afterward, "Hey, that was a little harsh. You might want to check on them and make sure they're okay." If one of us got upset with the other for some reason, we wouldn't let that fester over the weekend. We'd say, "Hey, man—let's chat real fast."

We have found that there's *safety* to initiate hard conversations because of the goodwill we've developed. Together, we have a track record of treating each other with respect and meeting commitments. If we didn't trust one another, it would be easy to get defensive in those moments, rather than humbly receiving feedback. We know that we're looking out for each other's interests and the good of the company, so we listen to one another, which ultimately helps us be better leaders.

That kind of trust isn't from any single event. It is from hundreds of coffees, weekly meetings, conferences, and decisions we've made along the way.

Call it compound investing over time.

Protect the Relationship

The health of your business partnership isn't just important for the two of you, or your business—it's also crucial for your team. Trust me, we have seen it go bad. If two founders are fighting, all sorts of dysfunctional patterns emerge.

For instance, we know two partners who own a windows business together. They're both very nice people, but they developed a track record of disrespecting each other. Eventually, one of the partners decided they wanted to exit the business, while the other wanted to grow it to the next milestone. The result was absentee ownership where neither partner wanted to be in the same room. The whole team felt the tension, it slowed progress, and there were two salaries on the budget who weren't contributing very much to the success of the business.

And as the founders grew apart, alliances began to form inside the business. For example, there was one incident where the CEO approved bonuses for an underperforming sales team over the wishes (and without approval) of his business partner. As you can imagine, the he-said-she-said games between teams became toxic.

The business died a slow death, and it was sad to see. And if you asked the owners, they would tell you the root cause was that they didn't invest enough in their relationship. Years of neglect turned to disrespect which evolved into resentment. That's when it was all over.

We've made it clear to our teams that this kind of behavior is unacceptable. For example, if someone brings something to me that's in CW's domain, I'll say, "Hey, you need to ask CW about that." Often, these questions aren't malicious or intentionally manipulative; someone's just trying to get information. However, because we have clear boundaries around our roles and are aligned as partners, people don't even have the opportunity to get different answers from us or play us against each other.

We also set a clear boundary that gossip about one another is off limits.

Early on, I brought on a close friend I'd grown up with. The friend started trying to use that shared history to drive a wedge between CW and me. He even wanted a third stake as a business partner. For all the reasons we've already outlined in this chapter, it wasn't a good idea to bring this person on as a partner, but I still gave him more leeway than he deserved. He might have succeeded in salting the partnership if we hadn't actively fought to protect it—which eventually led to us exiting that person from the business.

Because we prioritized our relationship as cofounders, I was eventually able to see that this friend was damaging our company culture. If you find yourself in a situation where someone tries to get between you and your partner, shut it down. When in doubt, get all parties in a room to clear the air.

Bottom line: Your relationship will be tested. Expect that and *protect* yourselves against those challenges. We say, "We can argue behind closed doors, but we should always be a united front in our messaging to the team." It's not always easy to get this right, but good communication and investing in connection will help you stay tightly aligned 90 percent of the time.

> You endanger the health of your partnership and the business if you let anything come between you and your business partner.

Align on Strategy and Cash

The final piece of advice we'll dispense here is that to align with your partner on *strategy* and *cash*.

These two things are related: Once you're profitable, decide how to spend your *cash*, and those decisions will be determined by your *strategy*. A lack of alignment on those two points can cause a huge rift. We see it all the time, and it often ruins good partnerships.

For example, here are a couple of potential paths you will have to decide between:

Big Salary, Small Reinvestment

Do you want to run a "lifestyle business" and take all of the profits to increase your personal income? If so, don't bother reinvesting money into the business. Take a large owner's draw, but know that you won't be able to scale.

Small Salary, Big Reinvestment

Are you trying to grow the business to sell? In that case, grow the thing as fast as you can. (This approach often relies on external funding.) If you're bootstrapping and pushing for a fast sale, you'll need to sacrifice your personal disbursements—living off ramen if necessary—so you can reinvest the max amount into the business. Ideally, within a few years, you'll cash in on a healthy sale, and you can start living off the proceeds.

Balanced Approach (The Good Business)

Are you trying to grow this business over the long term, bootstrapping and scaling to build *The Good Business*? In that case, *balance* the amount of cash you reinvest with the amount you pay yourselves. (Remember, you get paid last.) Your business needs to grow while preventing your own burnout. You'll need to pay yourself enough to maintain your effort and energy with the business over a decade or more.

It is important that business partners go in eyes wide open on which path is right for you before the first checks begin to roll in.

You *cannot* establish a solid foundation for your business if you and your partner are not on the same page with your strategy and finances. As financial expert Alan Miltz states, "The number one rule of business is that *growth sucks cash.*"[4] This is an absolute truth in our experience. Growing the business, therefore, will require that both of you make personal sacrifices about your take-home pay, *which requires agreement.*

---

[4] Quoted in: Harnish, Verne. *Scaling Up: How a Few Companies Make It... and Why the Rest Don't* (Rockefeller Habits 2. 0). Forbesbooks, 2014.

When we started working together, we had many conversations around the balance between personal income and reinvesting in the business. And over time, we arrived at *The Good Business* trajectory that we describe in this book. We've focused on building long-term value and being prudent and profitable along the way. And we encourage you to consider the same.

No matter your path, have these strategy conversations with your business partner early on, and ensure you've arrived at a mutual decision with full buy-in. Don't try to force your partner to align with you. If you try to win an argument, you ultimately lose—because the only way to succeed is by agreeing on the option you *both* feel is best.

Should You Just Go It Alone?

Heck, after reading this chapter, maybe you are considering just going it alone. Why go through all the trouble of partnership?

And, you know what? Maybe you are right. Maybe it is easier to do it alone.

But speaking from experience, this journey is long and this journey is hard. And doing it alone would be very difficult—maybe even impossible. There are just too many decisions, too much work to be done, and too often we find ourselves needing another pair of hands to carry the weight of building something meaningful.

So, my advice is to find a partner if you can. If you do it right, if you follow the advice in this book, you will be glad that you did.

And remember what Alexander Supertramp said in the quote at the beginning of this chapter?

"Happiness is only real when shared."

He's right.

And it makes building The Good Business a whole lot easier too.

Actions You Can Take Now

Scan the QR code below to access a Partner Work Template. Work through these interview questions and preparation prompts to set a strong foundation, both for your potential partner relationship and for your business.

CHAPTER 4

SET YOUR WHY AND WHERE

Identify Your Reason and a Compelling Vision

Narrated by Christian Hyatt

> *"A strong enough 'why' is a timeless magnet, an invisible force that pulls us forward in difficult times."*
>
> —John Soforic, *The Wealthy Gardener*

When I was ten years old, my dad found a box of old unopened cassette tapes. And while the tapes featured mostly explicit hip-hop tracks from Atlanta-area artists, cash was always short in the Hyatt household. So, it didn't surprise me when Dad sent me to a grocery store with the box and a goal to get enough money to pay an overdue electric bill.

I remember his instructions clearly. "See if you can sell any of these—and don't take less than two dollars each. They're worth a lot more than that."

So, that's what I did. I took the box down to the grocery store, helped people carry their bags to their cars, and then asked, "Hey, do you want to make a donation for some cassette tapes?" (I even remember coming up with a genius offer of three tapes for $5. Which was my earliest memory of successful product packaging.) I made it all the way through the box and came home with enough money for my parents to pay the electric bill. My dad even gave me a ten-dollar bill for my efforts.

That story is a good example of the strange dichotomy of my life in the early years: On the one hand, our household weathered crushing poverty and addiction. On the other hand, I had parents that loved and believed in me. One day, I was sent on an errand to pay the electric bill, and on another day, my dad would be my biggest fan in the stands of a football game. I was given the gift of struggle paired with self-confidence. And, somehow, by God's grace, I didn't fall into the same negative patterns as my parents and committed instead to making a better life for myself and my family.

Looking back on it now, I can see these experiences as the origin of my *why*—the reason that motivated every bit of hustle, grind, and determination I've poured into our business. My childhood taught me that betting on myself was the surest bet of all, and that taking my destiny into my own hands offered the most likely path to make things happen. My upbringing made me scrappy and resilient, and it gave me a healthy chip on my shoulder, which created nearly bottomless motivation to prove myself.

That *why* sustained me throughout the ups and downs of starting risk3sixty. And, frankly, I enjoyed the understanding that the "lows" really weren't that low. I didn't want to rely on anyone else for my family's livelihood and figured—so long as I *got after it and stayed after it*—I would probably win.

Becoming an entrepreneur is a big risk, especially if you set your sights on scaling up to $10 million in revenue or beyond through bootstrapping. There are easier, safer paths in life. Particularly with a young family, the choice to ditch a paycheck, benefits, and assured upward mobility was not what most people would call the "safe" move.

But in hindsight, I had a unique definition of "safe." I learned through hard experience that relying on myself was the best bet, and I believed starting my own business brought the biggest opportunity to create a positive future trajectory for myself, my family, and my team. I wanted to be a transitional figure for future generations and provide for my family and my parents in a way my parents hadn't been able to provide for themselves.

I was hungry for it. That *why* gnawed away at me, fueling my motivation. Come what may, I was going to make this business happen.

Most entrepreneurs have a comparable *why*. No doubt, you do too—even if it currently resides in your subconscious. There's a reason you want what you want. Isn't there? You just need to uncover it. And you will by the end of this chapter.

Because without a strong *why, where, and how*, there's a good chance you'll burn out or your business will fizzle. If you want to build a Good Business, scale way up, bootstrap the whole thing, and do it all with integrity, you'd better have a strong internal motivation sustaining you—because this is going to be a long journey.

Set Your *Why*

Narrated by Christian White

When most people think of payday, they picture bank deposits and cash in their wallets. There's a deep satisfaction in receiving a paycheck. It's comforting, it's predictable, and it makes things feel secure—provided you're on the receiving end.

Payday is a different story for the entrepreneur. You have to *make* payroll, a prospect that many entrepreneurs lose sleep over. And who knows how much money *you* get to take home? It's a scary thing not to know where your next paycheck is coming from, especially when you have a mortgage, kids, insurance, and other responsibilities. When you add *other* people to that equation—team members relying on you for their families' livelihoods—the stress is huge. Are you ready to scale that?

These are legitimately important concerns. Who would want to give up that sense of financial security and predictability to start and then aggressively grow a business? Many people decide the risk simply isn't worth it. And for those people, they're right.

Your *why* must be strong enough to overcome the risk, the insecurity, the stress, and the responsibility for your growing team's income. It must counterbalance all those burdens, while still leaving you with enough energy to push forward. Otherwise, why would you take the risk? Why would you keep going—day after day—for a decade?

The *why* is defensive: During hard times, your *why* for building the Good Business will get you through. It will help you push past your doubt and weather tough seasons. It will be your North Star even when you are so frustrated you want to quit.

But it's also going to lead your offense: It pushes you to reach for new opportunities, to take risks, and to drive your team forward and invest in team members. Not based on your business today but instead based on your *vision for your business tomorrow.*

Get after it and keep getting after it.

Similar to Christian, my *why* also began when I was young. In middle school, I decided to one day become a successful businessman to prevent the feelings of uncertainty and anxiety I experienced growing up amid financial challenges. That motivation expanded and deepened after I got out of the Army; having served with high-performing teams in the military, I wanted to find a high-performing team in the civilian world—which then evolved to a desire to *build* a high-performing team. I wanted to sleep well at night, knowing I was making a difference in my circle of influence.

In the Army, leadership is just as much about commanding, giving orders, and setting direction as it is about accountability, putting the needs of others above your own, and living a life in service to others—those to your right and left.

That is how trust is built, bonds are formed, and why camaraderie in the armed forces runs so deep. Many veterans complete their service and fear the best part of their life is over and that they will never find that camaraderie, sense of purpose, and selfless service they experienced in the military.

I also knew that I had these thoughts and fears, and a way to combat that risk was to lean in, take a calculated risk to build a high-performing team, and continue to serve others, just in a new way.

The *why* took on additional urgency for me around the time Christian and I began discussing starting a business together. At that point, Rachel and I realized that we would likely need to play a meaningful role in supporting both sets of parents, in addition to our children, in the years ahead. Without a *much* stronger financial position, that would be difficult.

Entrepreneurship seemed like the answer to all three *whys*: becoming a successful business owner, building my own team, and creating financial stability for my family's future. Ultimately, it was a no-brainer. Because Rachel was fully supportive, I knew this path was the right choice—even though it meant letting go of employer-sponsored health insurance with a one-month-old baby.

Despite it seeming like the *worst* time to start a business on paper, deep down, I knew the right opportunity was at hand.

And in the face of all that uncertainty, we were still committed to making it happen. That's the compelling draw of a strong *why*.

> "Working hard for something we don't care about is called stress; working hard for something we love is called passion." —Simon Sinek, *Start with Why*

What's your *why*? What will fuel your motivation to build and scale your business? What reason will anchor your determination to see this growth journey through? What *why* will outweigh the risk of bootstrapping your own Good Business?

Consider This: What's the Risk of Not Building the Good Business?

There's an equal or greater risk in not building and scaling the Good Business. A business that is not growing is on life support. A steady paycheck might feel more secure in the short term, but it could mean greater financial instability in the long term. That was true in our lives, at least. There may never be a perfect time to take the leap, but if you've spelled out your why, you'll need to do it anyway—and you'll have the energy to sustain your efforts long into the future.

A Shared, Strong Why

If you're starting your business with a partner, it is important that you strengthen your dynamic by coming up with a shared *why*, in addition to your personal motivations.

For example, our shared *why* is to build The Good Business.

Both of us have experience working on tight-knit teams that were incredibly meaningful. Places that set the bar for what work could look like. We also both had experiences working under bad bosses or at organizations that drained our energy. Places that, if you spent too long, would be a waste of life. We didn't like our respective experiences with previous employers or the way they did business. We didn't like the way they underserved clients or micro-managed employees. Neither of us felt our work there was *valuable*. We thought it could be done differently and much better. And we wanted that for our future team as well.

We wanted to create something special—to provide *outsized* service for our clients, build relationships with our team, deliver transformational value, and show our employees they were an integral part of that transformation. As founders, we desired to level up the care and humanity on all sides of a business relationship—we wanted The Good Business.

If our shared *why* had simply been "to make money," we probably would have quit during the first year or two when we weren't making very much of it. And we certainly would not be as unified as we are today. In and of itself, money is shallow and disconnected from values, and it provides no strategic clarity. In other words, it's not a *why*, but simply a tool and a byproduct of value creation. You need a *why* that is in itself valuable and worthy of pursuit. If you can find that, your gas tank will become bottomless.

> "You will never stick to something for the long haul if you're doing it for external applause." —Joshua Medcalf, *Chop Wood Carry Water*

With a shared *why*, arising out of our personal aims related to family, purpose, and security, we remain aligned. Our *why* guides our decision-making and informs the culture we try to build. It is a reason we invest in things that amplify our team and their families' quality of life and why we seek to create financial security for everyone in our organization. We believe our why is a worthy mission in itself and makes working hard every day a reward.

That's the difference between a strong *why* and a weak one.

Remember, The Good Business operates with integrity, is on a long-term trajectory, focuses on building lasting value for both clients and employees, and enjoys the four freedoms. It's big enough (or is in the process of scaling up) to accommodate a bigger and better future for you *and your team*, and it's profitable enough to provide robust compensation and upward mobility for everyone at the organization. A strong *why* will be aligned with helping you and your cofounder(s) achieve those aims.

> A strong *why* is personal, connected to values, and provides strategic clarity toward building the Good Business.

A strong *why*—The Good Business *why*—commands its own gravity. It stays with you. You don't have to find it or force it because it's always there, staring at you right in the face. It will cause you to grind to succeed. It's the thing that causes you to get up early and take risks you otherwise wouldn't. A strong *why* connects to the bigger, better future of the Good Business, and it's one you value so much that you're willing to put everything on the line to make it happen. In that way, it compels your commitment. Even if you don't know how you're going to build your successful business, even if the idea scares you—a strong *why* will pull you in anyway. It will be enough for you to commit to begin, trusting that you'll figure out the rest along the way.

Once you have a strong *why* in place, envision *where* you're going.

The Where: Vision

The Good Business is our shared *why*, our guiding light.

So, what did that mean in terms of strategic vision? How could that clarify *where* we were going?

In our early days, we thought of "vision" in qualitative terms. We sought to create a special culture: building the Good Business, where we could foster a high-performing team of "strange renegades." Both of us had worked for companies in the past that were full of negativity. We felt responsible for creating an oasis for our team where our people would be treated well, feel good, and have great opportunities.

We weren't totally sure how to approach vision casting, or even what to call it. Sometimes we used the term *BHAG*, which stands for "Big, Hairy, Audacious Goal." Popularized by

Jim Collins and Jerry Porras in their book *Built to Last*, BHAGs are a tool to identify an ambitious waypoint in the future that will help you make decisions, always aligned toward that long-term target. It becomes your true north.

A "BHAG" identifies a highly ambitious waypoint in the future that serves as your true north for decision-making.

At first, although we understood the concept of a BHAG, we didn't have much clarity about *how* to create one. At one of our first quarterly meetings, we summed up our core principles on a slide titled, simply, "The Main Thing":

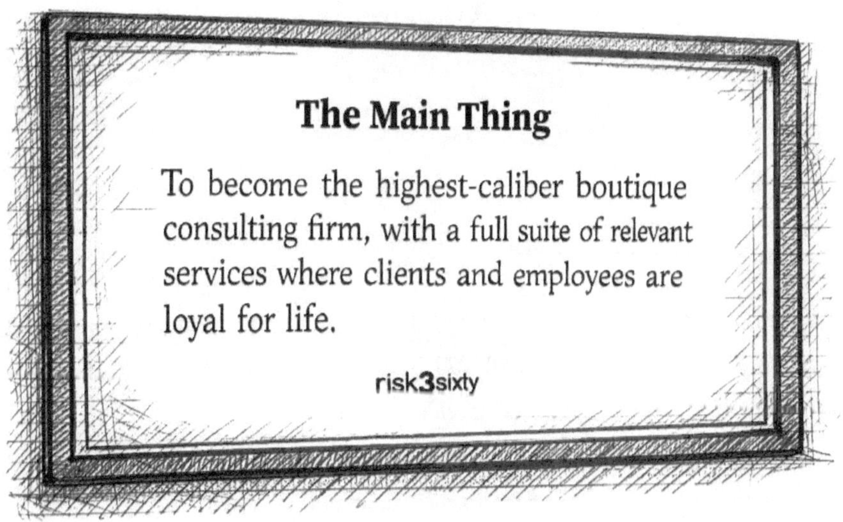

At that first annual meeting, our vision described the qualitative reality we wanted to move toward: "[To become the] highest-caliber boutique consulting firm, with a full suite of relevant services, where clients and employees are loyal for life."

Then, we started to work backward from that vision, thinking about what would need to happen to get there. We knew we needed to achieve a certain scale. We wanted enough profits to be able to invest in our marketing engine and employee benefits, enough layers to give people opportunities, and enough stability that the business wouldn't be at risk of falling apart if we lost a single client.

"We need to at *least* get to $10 million," we agreed. "That's achievable and it would give us stability and predictability."

Plus, it was a nice round number.

At our next quarterly meeting, we still described the qualitative vision, but we also had a quantitative target: $10 million in ten years. If we could achieve both the qualitative *and* quantitative elements of our BHAG, we knew we wouldn't be the only two people rowing the boat. We'd have an entire team rowing in the same direction with us. Not only would that be *awesome*, but it would also help create freedom and opportunity across the entire company.

To be honest, though, for two guys working out of a coffee shop, that number felt a little ridiculous.

Actually, we felt *completely* ridiculous.

At the time, we were just trying to figure out how to get to our first million, much less $10 million! But that's the point. A BHAG is totally beyond your current capacity; it represents a major risk to your sense of self and your comfort zone. If you shared it with certain friends or family, you suspect they might laugh at you. But in setting the goal, you anchor yourself to the belief that *it is possible*. You trust you'll figure out the "how" along the way.

A Note on Well-Intentioned "Advice"

Well-wishers, family, and advisors may give prudent advice, and you may do well to hear them out. However, remember that *you* are the entrepreneur, not them. You have the vision and are operating off a different set of principles.

You will often be misunderstood, and people won't always understand your vision. That's normal. Expect it. Entrepreneurs, by their very nature, tend to think differently. You're thinking *exponentially*, which can be hard for non-entrepreneurs to conceptualize. You likely have a higher risk tolerance than your well-wishers—and that high risk tolerance is necessary to build a successful, scaling business.

Remember: You make the decision. When you receive unsolicited advice, take it with a grain of salt. It's not that people don't want what is best for you; it's that your vision likely scares them. They don't ultimately carry the responsibility of your company. You can say, "I accept that you're concerned," without changing your plans.

And—as we discovered—once you have a clear BHAG, that "how" gets clearer. For instance, we determined the number of clients we'd need to reach $10 million, if our average contract value was $30,000. We estimated how many people we'd need to serve that many clients; based on our industry experience up to that point, we'd need a team of around fifty. In turn, we realized we'd need to build a strong organizational structure, and we started laying the groundwork for that. At every step along the way, we also continued to build toward the qualitative vision for our culture.

Slowly—over many cups of coffee and through a lot of thought work—we created a framework to achieve our goal. Even if we knew it would be hard to get there, we could envision how it was theoretically possible.

> Your BHAG should describe *qualitative* elements about culture and team dynamics, as well as *quantitative* elements that you can measure. Every part of a BHAG should be highly aspirational.

That view to scale guided every decision we made. We knew, for example, that we couldn't achieve our BHAG if we just lived off the profits. We could build a great company while taking large draws, but with no money to reinvest, it would remain a *small* company.

Our BHAG meant we chose to keep our costs low, maintain a standard of living in line with our initially very modest salaries, and reinvest the profits to facilitate our growth. It was a long-term play that required delayed gratification.

Our BHAG also guided our decisions about when to say no. If an opportunity didn't align with our long-term vision, we wouldn't push risk3sixty toward it. With time, we could see that a certain type of work wasn't helping us move toward our vision, so we began phasing out that work. The BHAG acted as a filter, enabling us to get rid of any activities that weren't congruent with our *where*.

The BHAG also informed our annual goals, which we'll talk about more in the next chapter. It helped us communicate our company's trajectory to our team. It fueled everyone's energy and belief around achieving something incredible. And the qualitative vision enabled us to create a compelling reason for people to come work with us—a "unique value proposition"—because we were building a world-class company. The BHAG was directional, aspirational, and *inspirational*. Because of our clear vision, we attracted and retained some of the best folks in the industry.

You'll experience the same kind of clarity with your BHAG in place. Filter *every* decision through your vision and core values.

And speaking of core values—we've now reached the final element of this chapter: determining the *how.*

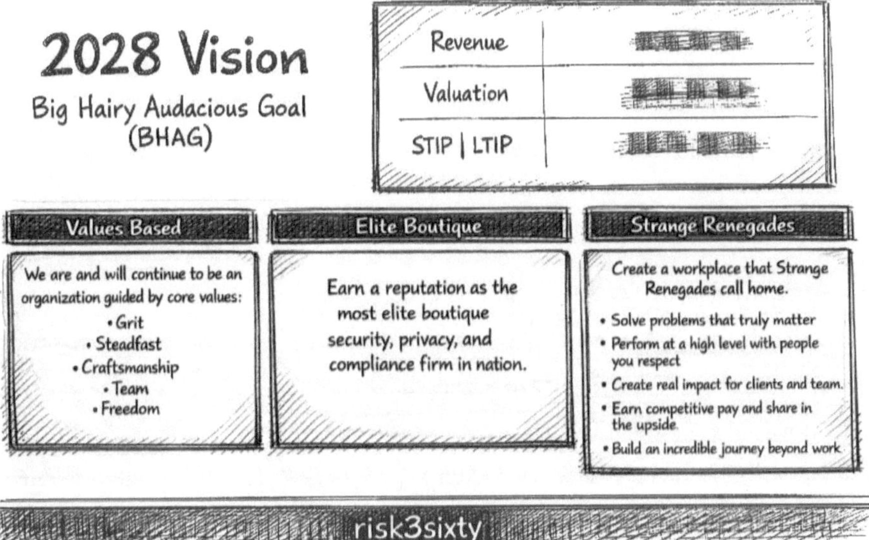

(This was the 1-page BHAG we shared with the team every opportunity we got.)

The How: Values and Philosophy

Narrated by Christian Hyatt

To be honest, the *how* is a distant third. The *why* needs to come first, because it informs the *where*—and those are the two most important elements to launch you forward. If you are clear on those, you'll figure out the *how* along the way. Your context and the market will determine most of your strategies and practical methods of implementation. You'll also continue to evolve and iterate. So, hold the *how* loosely and be willing to reinvent it often.

While the *how* is dynamic and part of the evolutionary journey of business, there are two key elements that we recommend solidifying. They'll help you make decisions and provide a reference for how your other leaders can think about making decisions. Number one, get clear on your **values**. And two, align with your partner on a shared **business philosophy**.

Values

We knew we wanted core values for risk3sixty. We didn't just want them as a formality—we wanted them to be part of our business's DNA, informing every decision. The values, we believed, should reflect the way we did business and be as bespoke as our company.

That felt like a tall order—so we took our time in developing them.

We started by floating some words that we believed were important. *Freedom* was big, as we've already shared. Another phrase we anchored ourselves to early on was *client services*. We told each other, "If we're going to accomplish the mission, our clients will never switch providers, and every client is a reference. So, we have to provide excellent client service, every time." The final phrase we landed on was *people first*. To build a high-performing team, we sought to provide our people with unmatched quality of life and plenty of opportunities for personal and professional development.

"But look, we're not going to *call* these our core values," we agreed. "Not yet. We're just going to let them bake for a while and see how they evolve."

After we'd been operating as a business for about a year and a half, we were ready to do some deeper work on clarifying our values. By then, we'd developed a clearer idea about our collective identity as a business and the things we deeply cared about.

So, CW gave me some homework. We have this habit: when one of us goes on vacation, the other person gives a homework assignment—usually a thinking exercise that's more philosophical. (This is the kind of thing we think is fun to do. Yes, even on vacation.) My homework assignment was to finish the drill on our core values.

In a tiny stone cabin on the New York side of Lake Champlain, across from Vermont, amid autumn leaves reflected in the lake, I sketched out notes about what we had been doing and then tried to assign words to those values. When I returned, the two of us knocked out the final draft—and they just felt right. We've maintained the same five core values ever since: grit, steadfast, craftsmanship, team, and freedom.

risk3sixty's Core Values

Grit: Tenacity, a relentless pursuit, passion, and persistence. Outstanding achievement is not the result of raw talent, but passionate persistence and endurance. Internal motivation, focused effort, and dogged determination.

Team: Continuity in purpose and action. Motivation beyond the self, extending beyond one's own welfare, to a group of individuals pursuing a shared vision, goals, and purpose.

Steadfast: Internally consistent, dutifully firm, and adherence to the code. Consistent and reliable in word, action, and behavior. Authentic and uncompromising values that result in lasting relationships based upon earned trust over time.

Craftsmanship: Master tradespeople who produce uncommon high quality in work product. Deliberate practice over time allows one to master the craft. As expertise forms, the resulting work product achieves uncommon quality—precision, insight, simplicity, durability, and value. Through immersive, energized focus, the craftsman finds pleasure in their trade.

Freedom: The earned opportunity to do or not to do. To forge one's path. The opportunity to innovate, to take ownership, and stand by the results. To act on opportunity and learn quickly from success or failure. To pursue a chosen craft and benefit as a member of risk3sixty.

Today, our core values are a part of everything we do. They inform how we talk and how we operate at every level. They are a filter for how we see the world. Figure out that aspect of your *how* early on, teach it to your team, make it a part of everything that you do, allowing junior leaders to "get inside your head" and make decisions the same way you would make them. The end result is alignment across the business.

Business Philosophy

We didn't really intend to develop a business philosophy as early founders—we were just reading a lot of business books. But three in particular ended up feeling *so* fundamental that we handed them to one another and basically said, "This is how we're going to do it." They came to define our shared business philosophy, guiding us as we built and scaled. They meant a lot to us, and with the hope of cutting through some of the noise, we are going to recommend them to you here.

The first book we landed on was ***Scaling Up,* by Verne Harnish**—which CW, an avid book reader, has called the best business book he's ever read. In it, Harnish focuses on the four essential priorities to scale your business: (1) strategy, (2) people, (3) execution, and (4) cash.

Those four priorities distilled the essence of what we should pay attention to and identified distractions. We agreed to focus on those four things only—and if something came up that didn't tie into one of those four categories, we weren't going to worry about it.

If CW was a passionate disciple of *Scaling Up,* I was an equally passionate proponent of ***Traction,* by Gino Wickman**. I still remember the day, I set this book down on CW's desk and said, "*This* is how we should run the business."

Wickman's book lays out what he calls "EOS," an entrepreneurial operating system, which creates discipline and cadence for a business. For example, he lays out specific recommendations for annual goal setting, and—nested within the annual goals—creating quarterly goals called "rocks." Related to those quarterly rocks, every person has individual goals called "measurables," which we refer to as key performance indicators (KPIs).

These weren't necessarily new concepts to us, but until we read *Traction,* we hadn't been consistently tracking our progress toward goals. Once we implemented our own modified cadence of goal setting and accountability, we found ourselves operating on a predictable, productive cycle—to the point that we're inspired to burst into hyperbolic metaphors. It gives every team member the same playbook! We're all playing off the same sheet of music!

Everyone's rowing in the same direction! We'll talk more about our system in Chapters 5 and 10.

The final piece came when CW read **_The Great Game of Business_, by Jack Stack and Bo Burlingham**. "I've got two more nuggets for us," he told me.

Nugget One: *open book management*, giving our team insight into the company financials. Many entrepreneurs are afraid to offer this transparency, but Stack's philosophy is that employees *want* to help the company succeed. Information about the current status and how their own efforts contribute to success enables the team to connect their own work to the company's health. By making quarterly reports available to our team—outlining how much revenue we brought in, our expenses, our profitability, and so on—our team could feel reassured of our progress and also see how their own contributions helped move the ball forward.

Nugget Two: *giving everyone a stake in our outcome*. We decided to create both a short-term incentive program, based on annual profit share, and a long-term incentive plan, based on if the company was ever sold. It took us several years to go through all the paperwork and legal review to put it together, but we ended up with something we feel great about. The incentives excite our team and help them directly benefit from the fruits of their contributions.

With those three books (and likely many more we aren't giving credit to here), we were armed with our shared business philosophy, helping us to narrow our focus on what really mattered. The books continue to hold an almost revered prominence for us—that's how fundamentally they've shaped what we've built.

> A shared business philosophy helps narrow your focus on what really matters. As a starting place for identifying your philosophy, turn to your favorite business books.

Beyond shared values and business philosophy, which are very important and must come from the founders, entrepreneurs shouldn't get too hung up on trying to know all of the *how* up front. So much is figured out in motion. You don't need to know all the answers before you begin—you'll adjust in real time, the same way you make micro adjustments all the time to your daily schedule. Allow yourself flexibility to evolve.

What's more important than having all the answers is your basic commitment to just *go for it*. Is there a market need? Can you meet that need? Are you a good fit? Do you believe in your *why* and feel clear on your *where,* and can you commit to taking the leap?

Then—jump!

When Providence Moves Too

We love this quote from W.H. Murray because it has been so true for us. He nailed it (emphasis ours):

> Until one is committed, there is hesitancy, the chance to draw back, always ineffectiveness. Concerning all acts of initiative (and creation), there is one elementary truth, the ignorance of which kills countless ideas and splendid plans: **that the moment one definitely commits oneself, then Providence moves too.** All sorts of things occur to help one that would never otherwise have occurred. A whole stream of events issues from the decision, raising in one's favor all manner of unforeseen incidents and meetings and material assistance, which no man could have dreamt would have come his way.

Murray's point is that *until* you're committed, there's always the chance you'll back out or be ineffective. But once you've made the commitment and *jumped,* all sorts of helpful and promising circumstances start to arise. When you get your company out there— propelled by your own *why*—an almost magical effect occurs. Things start to happen. Pieces fall into place. Opportunities you never could have envisioned start coming your way.

When we first started, we only had a few clients. Then, word of mouth began to spread. We got random requests to help out in different ways. We couldn't have predicted that would happen; before we started risk3sixty, we didn't even know there was a market need in some of the areas we ended up serving! (As of this writing, artificial intelligence has rapidly become a key part of our business. It didn't even exist as a need when we started risk3sixty!) It was only by putting ourselves out there—fully *committing*—that we discovered all those opportunities, just waiting for us.

Believe that something is possible, and trust that you're the team to do it. If you can believe in it—then, as Murray stresses, you must commit. Throw yourself fully into action, taking steps every day toward your *where*. Once those two pieces—belief and commitment—are in place, there's an almost invisible effect that helps propel you forward, like wind filling your sails.

Murray calls this effect Providence, and we believe it to be true. Some people might call it luck; others might credit it to positive thinking, the law of attraction, or a benevolent universe. We choose to call it faith. But regardless of where you land on the spiritual spectrum, your business' progress isn't *all* mystical. After all, even with wind filling your sails, you still need to know how to operate your boat.

In fact, now that you've considered your *why*, *where*, and *how*, we're going to get abundantly practical. Let's get down to the brass tacks of goal setting.

Actions You Can Take Now

1) Think deeply about your *why*. Brainstorm ideas, write them down, and then begin to distill them down into what rings true for you and resonates in your core. A compelling *why* can't be someone else's *why*; it must be compellingly true for *you*. Reflect:

   a. Are you an aspiring entrepreneur? Why?

   b. Are you a business founder considering whether to scale, to go big? Why?

2) Think deeply about your *where*. Based on your *why*, *where* are you trying to go? What is the compelling vision of the future that you are painting for yourself and your team? How does it fit into and support your *why*?

3) Think about the elements of your *how* that we recommended ironing out: core values and business philosophy. Maybe you don't have all these answers, but take some time to put words to paper, clarifying the values and philosophy that are important to you. These will become guiding themes and context for the tactics we'll discuss later. Your *how* will evolve in real time as a matter of normal business growth, but it should remain anchored in your values and business philosophy.

   a. Core values: _______________________________________

   b. Business philosophy: _________________________________

CHAPTER 5

MISSION TO METRICS

Use Goal Setting to Harness the Energy of Your Team

Narrated by Christian White

> *"If you could get all the people in an organization rowing in the same direction, you could dominate any industry, in any market, against any competition, at any time."*

—Patrick Lencioni

I don't remember how old I was when I heard the suggestion to identify and document my goals in life, but the concept stuck. If you were to flip through one of the notebooks I kept as a freshman in high school, you would find a page marked "<u>GOALS</u>." Underneath that all-caps and underlined title, ranked #1, would have been: "*Get into West Point.*"

Documenting my goals informed my decision-making. For instance, when I saw my friends doing things that might jeopardize my candidacy for West Point, I didn't join in. Instead, I joined student government, captained sports teams, and pursued other previously unthinkable challenges to make myself a competitive candidate. As all service academy applicants must do, I also sought out—and received—a letter of recommendation from my state representative.

When I received my West Point acceptance letter, I felt victorious. *Setting goals works!* I thought. *I achieve what I set out to do.*

Later on, when I realized how difficult it would be to *complete* my education at West Point, I wrote a new goal in my notebook: <u>*Graduate* from *West Point*</u>.

Thankfully, after navigating "Beast Barracks" (basic training), "Plebe Drowning" (Army swimming), "Plebe Beatings" (Army boxing), and everything else the "Highland Home" on the Hudson River had to offer, I managed to cross that one off the list too. Eventually, I moved away from the notebook and started logging goals in Excel spreadsheets. As I got older, I refined my process further, writing short-term, midterm, and long-term goals. In each new stage of life, I've written down my next hill to climb, shaping the actions I've taken on a yearly basis and my long-term decisions:

- Become an Infantry Officer
- Graduate from Ranger School
- Become a Company Commander
- Find the love of my life
- Have kids
- Get my MBA
- Start a business

Each achievement from this list reinforced the magic of goal setting. Identifying the goals in black and white created a filter through which I viewed the world and considered every decision. It helped clarify my direction and enabled me to track progress toward my aspirations.

By the time Christian and I were talking business, goal setting had become a way of life for both of us.

Why? To quote one of our mentors, the renowned author and CPA, Greg Crabtree, "Someone who aims at nothing hits it with amazing accuracy." This is why you set goals: When you do, you tend to hit them!

> "Someone who aims at nothing hits it with amazing accuracy." —Greg Crabtree

The last chapter guided you to identify your personal *why* and your company's *where*. A compelling vision of the future helps rally your team around the company's direction—but you still need to *get there*. Setting goals is how you get everyone "rowing in the same direction"—and, if you want to scale up quickly, it's strategically essential. Plenty of companies have *not* figured out how to get their teams aligned through effective goal setting. That means you have a massive opportunity to capture market share by gathering, motivating, and focusing your team through unified, synchronized efforts.

So, how do you do it? That's what this chapter is all about.

Clarity is the Biggest Deal

Do you know what happens when you aren't clear? It goes like this:

- Your team doesn't know its mission, so it doesn't know how to succeed.
- Since team members don't know how to succeed, they guess.
- When team members guess, they can't hold each other accountable.
- Lack of accountability creates a culture filled with nervous energy, politics, anxiety, entitlement, unclear paths to promotion, infighting, and resentment.

Without clarity, your focus is diluted. Your energy is scattered. And, worse, your teams are unintentionally working against you—and each other. That is a terrible place to be.

Fortunately, there's a solution. In *The Four Obsessions of an Extraordinary Executive*, Patrick Lencioni writes that leaders should obsess over clarity. First, be clear with yourself. Take a good, hard look and decide who you are as an organization, what you do and don't do, and who you serve. Then, work even harder to make that information clear to your team and to the market you want to serve. Clarity *focuses* your company's energy to accomplish great things.

For us, that means defining our five-year BHAG, the mission for the current year, and the goals and KPIs that will help us measure our progress, a set of targets we call "mission to metrics":

1. **BHAG**—a clear, highly ambitious five-year-plus target
2. **One-Year Plan**—an annual plan that leads us toward our BHAG but considers the short-term strategy and tactics for the year to come
3. **Clear Metrics**—quarterly goals, KPIs, and metrics attached to our annual plan across all levels of the business (company, department, and individual)
4. **Tracking to Progress**—a system of real-time data on weekly, monthly, quarterly, and annual cadences that ensure everyone knows exactly how we are performing to plan

It takes a tremendous amount of time and thoughtful energy to get this right. First, these targets will position your company for success or failure—so they'd better be strategically sound, based on your business model. Second, every target needs to be phrased clearly and simply, so there's no room for misunderstanding. Simplifying the complex is hard. And third, you have to get buy-in from your entire leadership team, which takes patience. And—most importantly—it has to be something that you truly believe in. Something that aligns to your personal principles and core values. Something worthwhile that you want to spend the next ten thousand hours fighting for.

The investment is worth it, because if you can harness the entire team's energy to accomplish a singular mission, almost nothing can stop them.

> When you harness the entire team's energy to accomplish a singular mission, almost nothing can stop them.

The Power of Focused Goals

Setting goals, especially long-term goals, is one of the most difficult things a leader must do. Why? Because it requires courage and conviction. First, it requires that you do the deep thinking to decide what it is that you really want. What do you want to spend the next decade fighting for? Clarity requires conviction.

Second, setting a vision requires you to get in front of your whole team and paint a bigger and better future for them (and for yourself). You will have to draw a line in the sand and tell people where you are going and why. You have to risk being wrong. You will have to risk that some people may not like your vision. Clarity requires courage.

But that kind of clarity is a gift to your team. It will energize the team and give them the vision they need to get on board (or not). Clarity is liberating. It clears the mind to focus on the things that need to be done and to give full effort doing it.

Clarity creates focused energy.

That is why we recommend setting a series of clear goals that help the team break your vision down into more relevant and obtainable short-term goals. This is a formal process we have used since launching risk3sixty in 2016.

Let's take a closer look at how to establish each level.

BHAG

As we discussed in the last chapter, the BHAG is an ambitious waypoint to set for your team, far off in the future. It expresses your most ambitious vision for what you want your company to become. Our BHAGs have both financial elements and cultural elements:

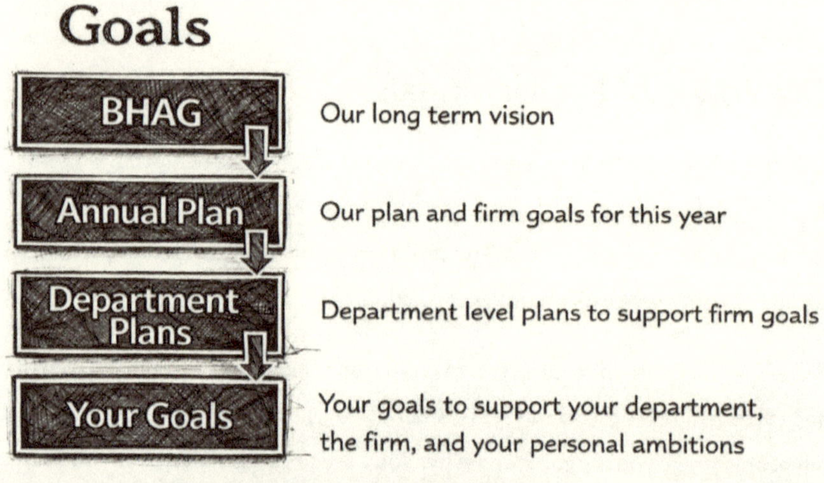

There are three main financial components: a five-year revenue target, an enterprise value target that encourages us to build a sustainable scalable company, and both a short-term incentive plan (STIP) and long-term incentive plan (LTIP) that helps ensure we reward the people who help us get there. The financial elements are specific and easily measurable.

The cultural elements of our BHAG are less tangible and harder to measure—but we believe they are more important. We often say if we had to choose, we'd be fine missing on the financial elements of our plan as long as we hit on the cultural elements. So, we identify those pieces in our BHAG as well: to remain values-based, to be an elite boutique, and to maintain our strange renegades culture.

Now, it is worth mentioning that not everyone appreciates our BHAG. We have had people along the way who were not a good fit for our culture or who encouraged us to grow faster. But the biggest advantage is that first, we were clear to ourselves, so less likely to be swayed by the opinions of others. And second, clarity about our BHAG has helped us build a team who are on board with the vision. A clear BHAG just doesn't allow for you to be all things to all people. There is a high burden of transparency and communication that comes with it.

Maybe that is why many leaders are afraid of setting BHAGs. Because it puts real skin in the game. When you set a BHAG, you plant a flag in the sand saying, "This is where I'm going"—and in so doing, you put your reputation on the line, along with your team's. That can be scary, especially because *not* getting there would be embarrassing. So, many leaders choose instead to let things happen how they happen.

That's all just negative self-talk (which we'll address in Chapter 11). Don't let fear stop you from taking this important step. Muster up your courage and conviction, cast your vision, and then get after it. Sure, you'll iterate along the way—that's expected and natural. We didn't get it perfect the first time, and we iterated a bunch. But don't let your fear of making a few mistakes stop you from setting that big vision. After all, it's often a bigger risk to *not* set the vision at all.

Once you've set your BHAG, next you'll need to break it into smaller pieces. That brings us to the next level down: annual and quarterly goals.

Annual and Quarterly Goals

Shade your eyes and look into the distance. See that BHAG? That's where you're going, but based on your priorities, you won't get there this year. You just need to figure out how to chip away at it.

For example, let's say your BHAG requires that you grow revenue 20 percent year over year for the next five years. You will need to ask questions like:

- What needs to happen next year in order to hit that number?
- What will my org chart need to look like?
- How much pipeline will I need to generate?

- How many sales need to be made? .
- What upgrades do I need to make to my culture?
- What innovations do I need to make?

Then, as with every annual plan, we suggest that you identify three to five company objectives, sorted into categories your team can focus their energy on to help you accomplish. Here is an example of what our annual plan on a page looks like:

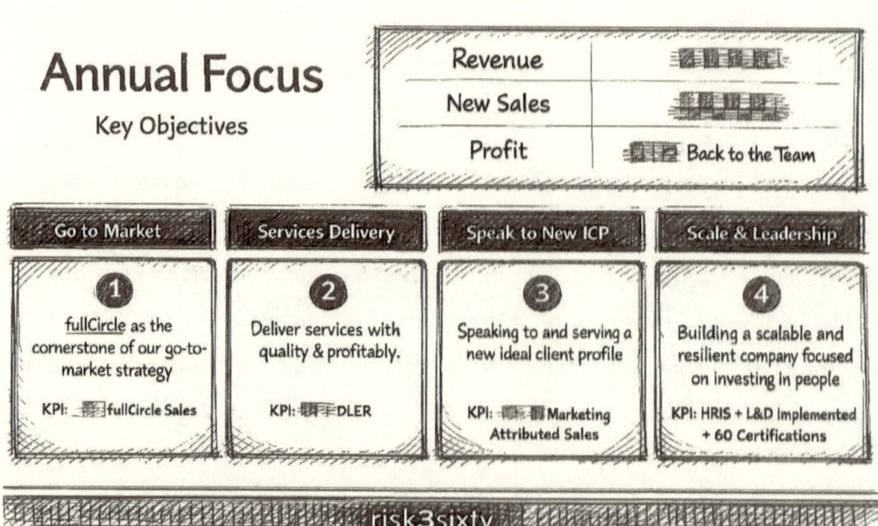

Each bucket related to different aspects of our company, each had a KPI for measuring success, and each KPI was aligned with our 2028 BHAG.

With those annual targets established, we break the goals into still smaller chunks: quarterly goals. We ask, "What kind of progress do we think we can make in the next ninety days to get us closer to that plan?" Quarterly goals are more gradual steppingstones that, when put together, will get us to the annual targets.

Each quarter, we hold an all-hands, on-site meeting to examine our progress toward our goals and make micro adjustments as needed. Sometimes we surpass what we thought we'd be able to do, and sometimes we fall short. So, we make tweaks and then head into the next ninety days. After ten years of doing this, over and over again, we've discovered this cadence works incredibly well. Quarter after quarter, we hit or exceed what we set out to do far more often than we don't.

With quarterly goals set, our departments then come together to identify each practice area's contribution.

Department-Level Goals

Can you see where this is going? Now we're at the department level, and each department is led by one or several junior leaders (which we call "practice leaders"). With the annual and quarterly plans in place, the practice leaders have clarity about where they need to go and can take initiative toward that target.

Let's look at the annual revenue goal, for example: Different departments need to come together to collectively achieve that goal, each taking a piece of the pie. The Service Delivery team needs to execute X amount of work, and the Revenue Organization needs to make Y amount in new sales. The Client Service department needs to maintain a high level of service to all those clients so that we create and maintain *raving fans* among our clients and Z numbers renew again next year.

The practice leaders get to work with individuals in their department to figure out *how* to accomplish the goals. We get freedom in deputizing that decision-making, and they get autonomy to carry out their mission. This is how we get everyone rowing in the same direction and unlock the energy and creativity of each team member.

Department goals are broken into more granular tactics and tasks. The goals are described and defined, and the criterion for success is identified. Each department goal is assigned an owner and a measurable KPI to identify how to evaluate those goals.

Individual Goals

The final piece happens at the individual level. Coaches and managers work with individual contributors to identify and document personal and professional goals that are both relevant to their own ambitions and align with the department and company's goals.

To give an example, recently I conducted a coaching session with one of our team members. We'll call him "Carter." During the session, I asked him, "What are some of your goals?"

Carter began rattling off a litany of technical certifications that he thought he should get, which in his mind were aligned with his future career ambitions. But I wanted him to think even bigger than that.

"Carter—you're a manager," I said. "Why do you think you need more technical expertise? Tell me about your *leadership* skills. What gaps do you think you have? What are you doing to level up as a leader?"

Carter seemed surprised. "I hadn't even thought about that," he said. "You mean—that's part of goal setting? Building leadership skills?"

Carter's whole body relaxed and he broke into a wide smile. He got incredibly excited about his expanded vision when he realized he could step up his game—not just as a manager, but also as a person and leader.

Individual goals should strike this balance: They should feel deeply personal to the individual, helping them achieve their dreams in life. At the same time, the goals should nest under one of the firm's annual and quarterly goal "buckets" so that they're supporting the overall trajectory of the company. We're not just talking "trips to Disneyland" or "running a personal best at the next 5K." In some instances, those sorts of goals will detract from the firm's momentum, by diffusing that individual's energy and focus, rather than sharpening it.

The sweet spot is when an individual's goals align with the firm's vision while also leveling them up in big, important ways. Carter's goals, for instance, nested directly under our 2024 annual goals' "Scale and Leadership" bucket.

We don't always get this right; we've had to find our way to this "sweet spot" of individual goal setting through some trial and error. But two things help us ensure that an individual's goals satisfy them on a personal level, while also aligning with our company's vision:

1. We hire people who are excited about our core values and the company's mission. If they're on our team, they already have huge buy-in to what we're doing.

2. When an individual works to support the business's goals, they help the business to be profitable and then share in the profits of the business through our STIP program; as a result, the business grows and thereby expands their upward mobility opportunities, and everyone enjoys more job security.

Coaching sessions are helpful in this process because coaches can affirm and challenge individuals to set their sights higher than they might have otherwise. But this is not a micromanagement strategy—it's the opposite. We can inspect goals, but since individuals know to nest their personal and professional goals under one of the firm's goal buckets, we know they'll align with the firm's overall strategy. This creates a scalable model: We've provided clarity around the target, and the individual gets to choose how they execute and contribute.

That's "mission to metrics." It's hard to do and takes a ton of effort, but when done right, the nested goals ensure we're all pulling together. No one is spinning their wheels on activities that detract from the company's mission.

Bottom line: When you set a goal and ensure your team focuses all their energy on it, you hit it. You do the right things over time to get there, and—in a way that almost feels magical—you *get* there. The energy of the team is effectively harnessed and aligned, everyone keeps those goals top of mind, and "Providence moves in" too! The goals become a reality. You're one step closer to becoming The Good Business.

The Parachute Principle

Jump out of a plane.

There was no way around it. If I wanted to become an infantry officer, I needed airborne training. That meant jumping out of a perfectly good airplane, into the open air, and relying on an intentionally designed "T-10 Delta" parachute to help rapidly descend to the ground as fast as possible without causing more than a 15 percent chance of mission-altering injuries.

None of the other stuff about my military training scared me. Repelling, Ranger School, other combat-related stuff—none of those felt like a big deal.

But I'd never liked heights and *dreaded* jumping out of a plane.

The goals you set as a company—from the BHAG all the way down to your individual goals—should be that scary. They should require that you grow far beyond your current comfort zone.

But ironically—if you want to succeed in doing the scary thing and not kill yourself in the process—you can't do it tentatively. The only safe and sure way to pursue a BHAG is to fully commit. If you try to jump out of the airplane halfway, you'll end up slamming against the side of the plane, or your parachute tether will get stuck. That's extremely dangerous! You've got to *throw* yourself out of that plane.

Airborne School was a multiweek course. First, I learned to jump off a stool and land correctly. Then, I went to the top of a little tower and jumped off while being attached to a steel cable—almost like doing a zip line.

But eventually, the progression ended up right where I had always feared: in a plane, 1,250 feet above the ground. My fellow trainees and I weren't *so* high that everything was a blur, and I could pretend I was jumping into a fluffy white blanket. No, we were just high enough that you could see *everything* laid out clearly below: All the barns I could crash into. All the fields that would catch my broken, mangled body if the chute didn't open.

All the ditches and streams where I could potentially break something. Army parachuting is not like skydiving, where you glide to the ground in what feels like slow motion using a beautiful parachute, landing at a walking pace on two feet. Army parachuting is different—think "controlled crash landing." If you don't land using the proper technique, you *will* break something, no question. It's brutal, and it hurts every time, even when you do it right.

I had been instructed to wait four seconds for the chute to deploy upon jumping. "If you don't feel a tug after four seconds, pull your reserve chute," the instructor ordered, "because you've only got a few more seconds at that point to pull your chute if you want to live. And remember what we taught you about falling. Any idiot who forgets to fall the way we taught is.going to be one of the 15 percent who breaks an ankle and becomes dead weight in combat."

See? My fears *were* justified. It was a high-risk thing to do! And you'll find the same is true in setting goals for your business. The stakes *are* high. If you hope to scale up to a Good Business, generating $10 million or more in revenue and caring for fifty-plus team members—it's a helluva drop if your chute doesn't open.

The plane climbed. "Ten minutes!" the jump master called out, over the roar of the engine.

"TEN MINUTES!" we trainees all yelled back.

The plane climbed higher. "Five minutes!"

"FIVE MINUTES!"

Then came the two-minute warning. At one minute, we all yelled, "ONE MINUTE," then stood up and began shuffling to the door. I watched the front of the line, gripping my static cord, feeling scared out of my mind. But I knew I couldn't hesitate in the doorway. For everyone to successfully land in the jump zone below, we had to jump in quick succession. If I hesitated, I'd put other people at risk. I'd also have the jump master's boot print on my fourth point of contact, to prevent me from endangering the lives of others. So, I had a choice: jump or be kicked. I didn't want to get kicked—or kicked out of Airborne School. As an officer and a leader, I knew I should set an example for the other trainees, who might or might not have been just as "excited" as me!

Three people in front...then two. The last guy in line before me disappeared out of the plane, and I stepped forward. With my heart in my throat, I got to the edge. I didn't hesitate.

I jumped.

I was fully committed.

It was a few seconds of sheer terror. Then, the chute opened—and I drifted *gently* down. When I landed, I rolled the way I'd been taught. It was over. I'd done it.

~~Jump out of plane.~~ Check.

When you set goals for your company, no one will force your hand and kick you out of the plane. But the principle of commitment stands: When conditions are right, when you've prepared for it, when the goal is a worthy objective—you jump. Even though it's scary, you jump.

Author and entrepreneurial coach Dan Sullivan emphasizes this point in his 4 C's Formula: *commitment, courage, capability,* and *confidence.* The idea is this: people are inclined to make goals that feel easily achievable, but the goals that will really change your life are probably slightly outside your current reach—which is okay, normal, and to be expected. The 4 C's Formula will guide you in making *big* goals and changes, and it starts with commitment. You may feel uncomfortable with your goal idea. You may not currently have the resources or capacity to achieve it—but you *commit* to taking the first step.

That's when the next C comes in: *courage.* You have to find the courage to actually take action—jump out of the plane and start the "doing."

As you do, you start building your *capability,* which ultimately results in more *confidence.* And that combined effect means you're ready to take on new, bigger, scarier goals. Over the years, we've become more comfortable making big commitments because of this iterative cycle. We've done this before, so now we're stacking wins and building momentum to propel the business forward.

When Christian first called me back in 2016 and said, "Hey man, I landed this client that I can't serve by myself," I felt like I was standing in the doorway of that plane again. But we'd done plenty of work to prepare ourselves up to that point. It was time. It was uncomfortable and scary, but we were ready. We knew what to do. So, we jumped.

As an entrepreneur, you'll constantly be jumping out of planes. But you can have faith in your equipment. You can have faith in your training. You can have faith in everything that got you to where you are today.

You've picked the right partner, set your why and where, and nested your goals under your BHAG. You know how to execute. In other words, you've *set the foundation* to build the Good Business.

Commit—then *jump*. Every new leap enables you to go higher and gives you the capability and confidence to build the future of your dreams.

Actions You Can Take Now

Get clear on your goals! If you can envision it, write it down, and focus on it, you can achieve it.

1. What is your BHAG for your company?
2. What are your annual goals, quarterly goals, etc.?
3. What is your process for guiding team members in making individual goals?

2. BUILD

BUILD THE GOOD BUSINESS

NICHE DOWN

The Power of Sustained Focus

Narrated by Christian Hyatt

> *"The most important lesson I can share about brand marketing is this: you definitely, certainly, and surely don't have enough time and money to build a brand for everyone. You can't. Don't try. Be specific. Be very specific."*
>
> —Seth Godin, in *This is Marketing*

"So, what are you guys doing to get business?" a former executive and solopreneur asked us early on.

"Everything," we answered truthfully. "There is *nothing* we are not doing."

From our earliest days, we embraced doing whatever we had to do to pay the bills. It was born out of necessity to keep the business alive. We did subcontracting work, we took on project management engagements, we did things so far out of our sweet spot that it almost seemed like a different company—*anything* to pay the bills and get our name out there. Not all of it worked, but in the beginning, we just wanted to live to fight another day. And that's just how things had to be.

We even invented a few company rallying cries during this time to make us feel better about the grind, such as "Take the hill!" or "Embrace the suck." These cheerful charges were a throwback to CW's cadet days at West Point, when he had to complete a smoker of a bayonet obstacle course, which started with a crawl under barbed wire through mud. Some cadets tried to avoid the mud by raising their heads up high to keep their faces clean, but not CW. He knew the whole point was to "embrace the suck," so he plunged his face right in. When he came up from the mud, it was to the cheers of his instructors. Then he sprinted up a hill, jumped over obstacles, and stabbed dummies with his bayonet to shouts of "TAKE THE HILL!"

Those are the kind of mind games we play with ourselves as young entrepreneurs eager to feel good about a hard time. So, we carried the same mentality into risk3sixty. And it was fun. As we gained reps, we trusted that better opportunities would come. Until then, we'd do anything to keep the business alive.

But then came Pittsburgh.

In the middle of *winter*.

For six weeks.

It was cold and sleeting. And the work was *terrible*.

We'd accepted a subcontracting job for another firm, a large engagement requiring several team members. It wasn't the kind of work we wanted to do in the long run—everything we did was credited to someone else's brand. Still, it offered significant revenue, and we figured it would give us a good "at bat" in an industry we were interested in exploring.

But as the project evolved and dragged on, we realized, "No—this is just *terrible*."

One morning, while we walked to the office, the sleet *hurt* as it hit our faces. There were icebergs—literal icebergs—rolling down the river. (Keep in mind, we're a couple of Georgia boys. We didn't even have clothes for this kind of weather!) And looming over us was a huge, ugly tower. Through the freezing, soggy weather, this creepy, soulless tower looked like something out of *Lord of the Rings*. I called to CW, "I feel like we're in Mordor!"

We were far from our families, freezing our tails off, doing work we weren't excited about—all to help build someone else's business instead of our own.

Suddenly, we didn't want to embrace the suck anymore. It was time to get ourselves better opportunities.

The problem was that it would require us to *stop* doing some of the subcontracting work—a scary prospect, since those checks were paying our bills. How could we turn down a six-figure project without knowing how we'd replace that revenue, and knowing that our families and our team's families were depending on us?

With the benefit of experience and hindsight, these fears help explain why we took two years to reach our first $1 million in revenue. We held ourselves back from doing what we needed to do to grow, afraid to let go of the security of our subcontracting engagements.

Every entrepreneur faces this inflection point (many times): the prospect of *giving up revenue* in order to scale. You might even need to give up the majority of your business model, which was the case for us. But we realized our one-off consulting engagements and subcontracting jobs stood in the way of the business we really wanted to grow—which would take us to the future we envisioned. Finally, I asked CW, "What part of ourselves do we have to give up to become who we need to be?"

> What part of your business do you have to give up to become what you need to be?

Here's what we learned: When you start your business, you've got to do hard things to stay alive and build momentum. This is an appropriate place to be at times—but it's *not a place you want to stay very long*. Eventually, you need to stop "embracing the suck" and lean into the identity that will propel you forward.

Figure out what you *are* and *aren't* going to do. We call this "niching down." Once you determine your business's main direction, maintain a disciplined focus and go all in on it.

How do you know when you're ready to take the leap of niching down? Here's a quick test:

- You have found something that is in high demand and can be repeatedly and profitably delivered.
- You have found something that your client needs on a recurring basis (e.g., monthly or annually) and is not a one-off.
- You have a repeatable way to identify these customers, market to them, and offer them your service.
- All of these elements are in alignment with your personal principles, your culture, and the identity of the company you want to build.

If you can check most of those boxes, you're likely ready to remove everything other than what makes your top 20 percent of revenue. *That's* niching down.

We know this is hard to do. It takes time to identify opportunities like this. It feels risky. But the only way to scale the Good Business is to stop doing *everything* and start doing one or two things really, really well.

> The only way to scale the Good Business is to stop doing *everything* and start doing one or two things really, really well.

Increasing your revenue and freedom will likely only happen if you get more *clarity* about your business's identity. As the saying goes, "What got you here won't get you there."

This chapter will provide strategies to guide you in effectively paring down your market offerings and explain the importance of disciplined execution and focus—starting with why niching down is a prerequisite for growth.

Why Niche Down?

You want the Good Business. Well, niching down is the only way forward.

Complexity Doesn't Scale

Your hustle was valuable—to a point. It forged you as a future business leader, helped you understand the marketplace, opened new doors, and established new relationships. All of that was worthwhile, and you learned a lot.

But who will you hire to keep up your level of hustle? Who can replace you in that spot and provide you with greater freedom?

That's the problem you run into when you fail to niche down. The two of us, as founders, could figure out how to do many different tasks. We had the motivation to work like crazy to make the business happen. But we couldn't ask our team members to wear all those hats. We couldn't expect them to work with the motivation of an owner, nor could we expect them to function like us in every scenario, reading our minds. As our business grew, we needed to *simplify*, establishing replicable systems and processes with a distinct, specific set of services that we could train our team on.

It's tempting to do many things and serve many types of clients, but this creates unnecessary complexity. From an operational standpoint, complexity doesn't scale. The only way to grow a business "doing everything" is to have very high-level subject matter experts in *every* aspect of the business. Not only would that be extremely expensive, it's also unrealistic.

> Complexity doesn't scale. Clarity does.

Niching down, on the other hand, provides clarity—on ideal clients, product offerings, values, and execution. It's impossible to provide that level of clarity if you're trying to do "everything," like we once bragged about. When you focus, the resulting clarity will enable you to scale.

Niching down also gives you clarity around what opportunities to say yes or no to—which, back in Pittsburgh, would have been welcome information. It's hard to say no to revenue, but not all revenue is *good* revenue in the long run. Not all revenue is profitable or supports your goals. Some revenue might require that you build up another company's brand rather than your own, or work in a place that reminds you of Mordor, or take your time and energy away from getting higher-quality clients. That's questionable revenue, friend! Niching down helps identify your ideal opportunities, ensuring that each "at bat" gets you the experience, practice, and directional momentum you want.

Another "bad" opportunity is any job that requires *you*—the founder/CEO—to deliver the work. It's one thing to do that in your early hustle days, but if you want to scale, you must delegate. Grow *beyond* your hustle. Duplicate yourself so that you can start doing higher-level tasks that employ your best and highest use: vision, hiring, sales, leadership, strategy, operations, and so on.

> Not all revenue is good revenue. Not every opportunity is the right opportunity.

Here's an example: In our early days, we did almost every task inside the business—tactical delivery, customer service, provisioning laptops, sending invoices, you name it. You could think of those tasks as being similar to an airport worker helping to de-ice a plane's wings on the runway—necessary and important, but repeatable by a team member. Even if the pilot is *really, really good* at de-icing planes, someone else could do that task.

Once we hired a team, we had more time to focus on our strategy. We could conduct high-level sales meetings, think about product offerings, and perform other more leadership-oriented jobs. Essentially, we could pilot the plane.

Once you're in a position to fly the plane, *that's* where you should focus your attention. Progress to a level of leadership where you're functioning at the highest and best use of your unique abilities.

Clearer Message = More Market Share

When you are bootstrapping, you cannot out-spend your competitors on marketing initiatives or rely on a shotgun blast approach to your messaging. If you want potential customers to hear your message, it means that you must focus on speaking clearly and loudly about a specific problem to a defined ideal client profile.

By getting extra clear on who you're serving, you can address a very specific avatar. You're able to solve their problems in a way that is specific and meaningful to them, making that ideal client more likely to choose *you* over your competition.

We know a guy named Marshall whose niche is tennis courts. Not basketball courts, not driveways—tennis courts. If there's a tennis court in the metro Atlanta area that needs to be maintained, resurfaced, or built new, there's a good chance his company's the one doing it. The key to his success is that he has spent the last thirty years understanding tennis courts better than anyone. Who buys them, when they buy them, the things they care about, maintenance schedules, color schemes, budgets—everything. Marshall is likely the world's foremost expert on outdoor tennis courts.

Marshall's sustained discipline to say no to other opportunities, like driveways, home foundations, or anything else, has enabled him to scale a very successful business. His unique niche has enabled him to corner the market. ("Do you know a tennis court guy?" "Yeah! It's Marshall. Let me give you his number.") It's also enabled him to run his company with greater efficiency. Tennis court maintenance involves processes that are focused, repeatable, and trainable—and therefore *scalable*.

Most "elite boutique" companies boast this kind of specialized expertise—including ours. Among our mastermind groups, we see the same theme among the best businesses. Christian's neighbor—the man who owns the house we described in the introduction—runs an elite boutique law firm, which *only* works on complex, class action lawsuits against large companies. He's kept his firm small and efficient because he's so specialized, while also managing to create massive value because of his expertise.

Niching down may feel like giving up opportunities—but if you try to speak to everyone, you end up speaking to no one. By speaking to your target niche clearly, you cut through the noise of your competition.

And if you want to acquire market share, that's a very important strength to have.

> If you try to speak to everyone, you end up speaking to no one.

In fact, you give up more opportunities by *not* niching down. For instance, if we offer a hundred different services on our website, our ideal client will get confused and frustrated trying to search through all that noise. They'll get the impression that we're a "jack of all trades, master of none" and will likely take their business elsewhere. On the other hand, if we make it clear that we only serve our ideal client profile, our ideal client will feel seen, recognizing us as a viable vendor and business partner. By offering a clear message to the market, we catch *only* the fish we want and reduce time attending to the fish we don't.

You want to get out of the shadow of Mordor and escape the sleet of Pittsburgh? Niche the heck down.

So, let's talk about how to do it.

Strategies for Niching Down

As you read through the following strategies, consider what you've learned already about your identity. Who are you, as a company? These recommendations can help you grow further into the *best* version of that identity.

Find Product/Market Fit

All your hard work has taught you valuable lessons about the marketplace. You should have a better understanding of where you fit in, what you do well, and who your ideal clients are. You should also have a clarified understanding of what you *don't* want to do.

Great. Now, focus on documenting your ideal client profile and ensuring everything you do is in service to that avatar. All of your marketing materials, your product, pricing, and packaging, the way you deliver—everything. Lean into the good and stop doing all the other things that aren't serving your future as you scale. Measure and double down on profitable niches.

If you are considering a niche, here is a helpful model to formally document your ideal client profile:

1. Choose an industry niche: Finance, healthcare, education, technology, etc.
2. Choose a company size: Small businesses, SMB, Middle Market, Enterprise, etc.
3. Choose a location: United States, the East Coast, New York City
4. Choose a job title: CFO, CIOs, CISOs, etc.
5. Pick a profitable and repeatable problem to solve based on the early success you have already experienced:
   a. It is profitable
   b. It is recurring or reoccurring *(ideally)*
   c. Is it repeatable and predictable
   d. Does the market size and contract value provide a path to $1M in 18 months, to $5M in 36 months

Once you answer questions like these, consider documenting your niches in a simple statement that looks something like this:

> We help **[CFOs]** at **[Enterprise]** **[Manufacturing Companies]** on **[the East Coast]** struggling with **[accurate and timely bookkeeping inside their manufacturing facilities]** by providing **[outsourced bookkeeping services]** that results in **[100% on time and accurate accounting records to support month end close]**.

Summary Ideal Client Profile

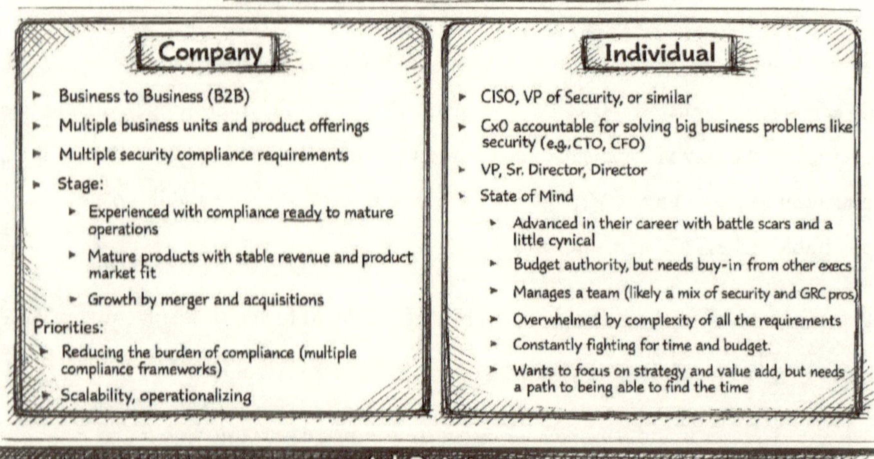

The key at this stage is that you start to pare down and focus your energy on your best clients and services and begin forming a business model around it. It may feel like you are taking a step back and saying "no" to good opportunities, but that feeling is only temporary. If you choose a good niche, you will see your win rates, revenue, and profitability rapidly increase.

We know an entrepreneur who offered thirty-seven different SKUs. But, after taking a step back and analyzing his business data, he realized that 70 percent of his profits came from only four of them. *Those* four SKUs were the obvious place for him to niche down.

Once he did, it clarified his marketing, his supply chain, and his delivery model. After about twelve months, his revenue and profits hit new heights.

At risk3sixty, we've lived this firsthand. When we first niched down, we went from subcontracting and project management for anyone who had extra work to offer to focusing on what we called "high-growth technology companies that needed help building and certifying their cybersecurity program." We even found a sub-niche for a relatively obscure cybersecurity framework and became the number one implementer within that niche, which became our flagship product offering for several years. (We later evolved our niche several times as we identified better opportunities, which is normal as you grow.) We might have initially done ten things, but we figured out that only three or four had the right combination of profitability and scalability.

> Focus all your energy on speaking to and serving your ideal client profile.

Get rid of the 80 percent you used to do so that you can focus on the 20 percent that will propel you forward.

Don't do this blindly. Continually assess your data and speak with customers (let me repeat that: SPEAK WITH CUSTOMERS) to build your understanding of what the market really wants. Once you have a clear idea of the areas where you can knock it out of the park and create great value, simplify. Begin implementing systems, processes, and training. Build a playbook so that you can easily replicate this work at a high level. Then, train and trust your teams to deliver, and turn your focus to things like growing, scaling, and recruiting—all the high-level "pilot" stuff that only you can do.

> ### The Continuous Cycle of Evolving Your Niche
>
> A decade into our journey here at risk3sixty we have come to realize that in business there is a continuous cycle of maintaining core offerings, investing in innovation to explore new opportunities, and evolving your niche when needed. The Good Business codifies this cycle into formalized processes. For example, every year during our planning process we allocate revenue toward maintenance (current niche) and investment in innovation (future niche). While you do not need to worry about this in the early days of building your business, you should feel encouraged when you find that this process never truly ends.

Make Educated Guesses and Fail Fast

But what if you get it wrong?

You will. Expect that. Take some risks. Try new things to see what lands and what doesn't. Not all investments have a positive ROI. There *is* such a thing as a sunk cost, and for all unprofitable investments, you'll need to pull the plug at some point. Scaling up a bootstrapped business is a process of trial and error, not a tightrope requiring a series of perfectly balanced steps.

Our best advice is to try low-risk experiments that test your hypothesis but leave the door open to pivot away from them if they don't work out. Our experiments usually go like this:

1. We observe a need in the marketplace.
2. We speak with clients to get their perspective (Caution: People will unintentionally lie to you and validate your ideas because they want to be nice!)
3. We try to get one to three paying customers, usually at a discount, while we figure things out.
4. We try to get five paying customers at full price.

5.   We assess if the market is large enough to support $1M in eighteen months and $5M in thirty-six months.

If the answer to these questions is yes—then we get excited about the opportunity. But the key is that if the idea starts to trend badly, we hit the eject button before too much damage is done.

For example, we once spent $20,000 (and several hundred hours of effort) to get approved as a provider for a niche cybersecurity offering. A client had asked for the service and given us inaccurate information about how much they would be willing to pay. (I told you; some clients will unintentionally lie to you!) So, we made a large investment to build up our capability to meet a certain market demand...but then we realized the market wasn't what we thought. It was a crowded, low-cost commodity service with no clear opportunity to carve out a compelling niche. So, we pulled the plug within six months of getting started. We failed and failed fast. It was the right decision, and we didn't look back, even though we'd already invested a lot of time and money. We didn't get the ROI we were after, but we did get a different ROI: clarity on what we definitely did *not* want to be doing. That knowledge was worth something. And thankfully, we arrived at that clarity pretty fast.

"Fail fast"—it's a business cliché for good reason. Some information comes only by taking shots. You've got to develop the situation enough to gather data and decide whether something is worth pursuing. But, there's a fine line between cutting something off that seems unproductive and sticking with something long enough to evaluate its full potential. That's where your judgment and conviction as an entrepreneur come in.

For example, another major investment of ours—building our SaaS platform fullCircle — took years of investment to get right. (As of this writing, we are still investing and refining it!). We experienced quite a bit of trial and error in its development, trying and then sunsetting a number of business model ideas, pricing models, and features. But the reason we kept investing is that we set progress milestones along the way that gave us confidence we were headed in the right direction. We didn't just stick with fullCircle because we had a "good gut feeling" about it. We used investment criteria to do the math and get clarity on its potential for recurring revenue. We also had a timeline that gave us a limited window to make fullCircle a success. Using data and decision-making criteria, we made our best educated guess to keep at it. In this case, the investment paid off and has become core to our business model at risk3sixty.

Take your shots, gather data, and move toward a decision on whether that shot is going to work out. If you learn that it won't, then fail fast and move on. Make educated guesses and then niche down once you discover the crown jewels.

What Isn't David?

In *10X Is Easier than 2X,* Dr. Benjamin Hardy gives the example of Michelangelo sculpting the famous *David* statue. Allegedly, when the Pope asked Michelangelo how he managed to create such a masterpiece from a block of marble, he responded, "It was easy. I just had to take away everything that wasn't *David*."

That's what you're doing when you niche down: getting rid of everything that's not the core of your business. Chisel down your offerings and wipe away the dust to unveil the masterpiece of who you are.

It's no coincidence that Hardy's analogy appears in the context of a book that is all about scaling up—*way* up. Niching down enables you to prioritize your attention on the right things and sharpen your team's focus, facilitating 10X growth. It's one of the most important steps you can take in building and scaling the Good Business.

Hone Your Message to the Market

When you clarify your identity *internally,* you can improve at communicating your identity *externally,* to the marketplace.

After getting clear on our BHAG, values, service offerings, goals, and product offering, we arrived at a clear target. Whereas before, we were simply trying to stay alive, now, we knew where we wanted to *go.* That enabled us to communicate a clear, simplified message to our ideal clients.

Some of our competitors offer a huge range of products and services. We went in the opposite direction. As part of our niching down process, we began streamlining our offerings, highlighting *only* the things that we do really, really well. With this streamlined list of offerings, we then worked to "out-teach" the competition. Even before we had a marketing team, we encouraged every member of the team to create meaningful thought leadership pieces. These white papers, blogs, and LinkedIn posts all aligned with our streamlined offerings, showing the market we were *that* elite, *that* knowledgeable, *that* dialed in to our ideal clients' needs.

We knew that we could not afford to get the exposure that our big competitors could. We couldn't afford to attend every conference, to spend hundreds of thousands of dollars on paid search or social media ads. But, what we could do was focus all of our energy on a very specific problem and address it with nuance, care, and expertise—relentlessly. So, for the last decade, that has been our strategy. And we think anyone can do the same inside their business. Anyone can be the best at one thing.

One famous example that I like is Chick-fil-A, which is headquartered right here in Atlanta, Georgia. While Chick-fil-A is famously successful now, in their early days, they pulled off the strategy of niching down better than anyone. Here are a few factors that go into their success:

- **Offering:** Small menu with offerings that are all variations on the same simple ingredients
- **Geography:** Started in the south and slowly expanded its footprint across the country
- **Delivery Model:** Chick-fil-a franchise owners are highly vetted, trained, and share an incentive model with Chick-fil-a corporate that creates loyal owners. In addition, owners are only permitted to own one to two stores and must be involved in the operations of the store.
- **Values:** Strong core values that show up in how its restaurants are run, and how it treats employees and customers.

It's easy to see how Chick-fil-A's focus has enabled it to compete and scale in a fast-food market that most folks thought had no more room for another player. Chick-fil-A is one of the fastest-growing and profitable companies in America—and they are still under private ownership. They are a wonderful example of a company applying these same principles at scale.

When we took that approach, we enjoyed outsized success too. In our third year, we began implementing the goal-setting process from the last chapter and simultaneously niched down our message to the marketplace. That was the first year we had a compound annual growth rate in excess of 40 percent. We've maintained that accelerated pace of growth every year since, essentially doubling every two years and earning a spot on Atlanta's list of Fastest 100 Growing Companies, seven years in a row. We're extremely clear on what we do. We do it very well, have built training programs around it, and have created playbooks and processes for our team. As a result, we've become highly efficient and competent within our chosen niche.

You don't have to do everything. Do *less*, and knock it out of the park—then, tell the marketplace all about it. You'll be amazed by their response.

Build Your Flywheel

As you grow your business, we encourage you not just to niche down your offerings, but also to refine your strategy. All of your company activities should support "a fan blade on the flywheel."

What do we mean by "flywheel"?

Most fans of business books are familiar with Jim Collins's *Good to Great*. But you might not know about his lesser-known forty-six-page masterpiece, *Turning the Flywheel*, about building momentum within an organization.

Jim says business is like a massive, heavy wheel: Think of a large steel fan with five long blades. It requires a lot of initial effort to set it in motion. However, as focused energy is applied toward core fundamentals—each one of the blades—the whole flywheel gains momentum. Once you have momentum, magic happens.

Our flywheel is our source of innovation and focus. It helps us understand the fundamentals of success for our business, and we focus on those fundamentals relentlessly. Day in, and day out. Forever.

As entrepreneurs, we have found it to be a helpful thinking model, and we have also found it to be a valuable communication tool for explaining to our team members how our business works and why we make certain investments. At risk3sixty, we even have a giant mural of our strategy flywheel painted on the wall in our office. It has become so core to our internal vocabulary.

The day we built it, the two of us had just finished Collins's book and had spent some time talking and drafting ideas for our flywheel. Finally, we drew our finalized flywheel on a whiteboard. Then, we sat back in our chairs, took a sip of coffee, squinted at the whiteboard, and smiled.

Through the five fundamentals of risk3sixty's flywheel, we'd achieved clarity:

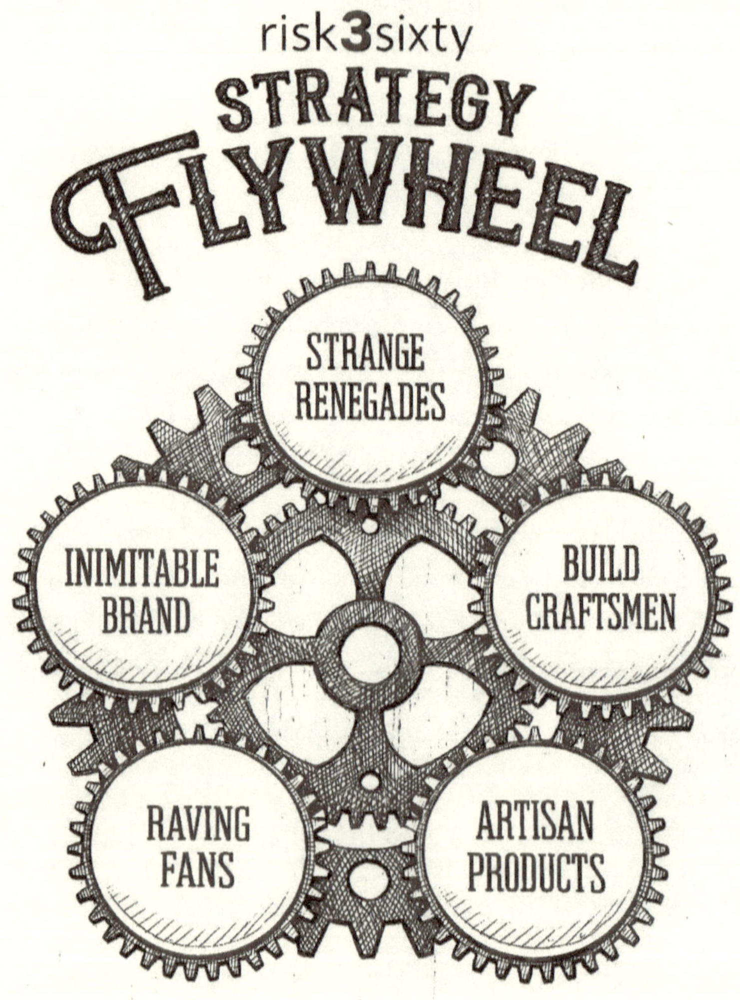

- **Recruit strange renegades**—these people are the creative, innovative, highly skilled, somewhat rebellious A-players who have character that aligns with our core values and are a clear team fit.

- **Build craftsmen**—once we hire amazing people, we develop them into uncommonly excellent craftspeople by continuously investing in a combination of customized career planning, ongoing internal training programs, and outside education.

- **Create artisan products**—our trained strange renegades create artisan products and services for our customers, helping us carve out a niche in the marketplace as a highly innovative and elite boutique company.
- **Amass raving fans**—we earn our customers' loyalty by wowing them with our artisan offerings and white-glove customer service experience. Approximately half of our new revenue every year comes from existing customers who elect to expand their business with us, and a third of our new sales come from referrals.
- **Develop an inimitable brand**—"inimitable" means something is so unique, it's impossible to copy, a difficult goal we've achieved through the combination of elements above. Our brand reputation helps us hire more strange renegades— once again, turning the entire flywheel.

When we apply pressure to the five blades of our flywheel, we build momentum for the entire business. They're not specific to services we offer but rather our framework for growth. As such, we direct all our investment to these fundamentals—building the brand, recruiting strange renegades, embracing new initiatives, and so on. If something is not aligned with the flywheel, we won't do it.

What are the blades of your flywheel? When you hone your strategy to the top five or six things that you do, you'll find enormous clarity and focus for building and sustaining growth.

Continue to Evolve and Reinvest

Finally, keep in mind that niching down is not "one and done." You will—and *should*— continue to evolve as a company. Here are just a few examples of some of risk3sixty's evolutions:

- We have redefined our ideal client profile at least three times in the last ten years.
- We have reorganized our org chart and career development models.
- We've repackaged and retooled some of our main services, requiring new marketing, different playbooks, and a lot of R&D.
- We've built new products, like fullCircle, every year in business.

The process of niching down and refining your business is continuous, and every entrepreneur must be okay with this. But the good news is that, once you've completed your first round of niching down, you'll discover that you have a bit more time as the company leader to think strategically. This is what it means to work "on the business, not in the business."

Seize that opportunity.

Begin sketching out your company's next evolution. What might be possible now? Do the analysis. Dig into the research. Imagine. Reinvent.

Keep evolving. *Keep* niching down. *Keep* growing ever more fully into your unique iteration of the Good Business.

The Secret Sauce: Discipline and Focus

I fell in love with wrestling in high school. My coach had a simple philosophy for winning: We would be in better shape than our opponent. So, what we lacked in technical ability, we made up for with the ability to go all three rounds at full speed. I used to take comfort in that idea because I often felt that if an opponent couldn't beat me in the first round, then they were in trouble. I had a chip on my shoulder that no one in the 189-pound weight class would be able to beat me in round three.

I think I've taken that same philosophy into business. The hard part is not getting started on a thing. It is doing it with quality and discipline for ten years. And I have full confidence that our team is willing and able to do that. We will get after it—and keep getting after it—forever. And there is clarity and confidence in being self-assured that you will never give up.

That mindset can be your secret sauce—your Chick-fil-A sauce, if you will—to niching down: sustained disciplined execution. The Good Business is not on anyone else's timeline. You can compete forever; you can refine your niche over a decade if you need to. Every other competitive advantage you have today is fleeting. The real differentiator is your ability to execute consistently over time. It is a structural competitive advantage most readily available to bootstrapped businesses in control of their own destiny and timeline. The competitive advantage of The Good Business.

Deliver on your brand promise effectively and with high quality.

Be *really* good at what you do.

Learn how to be efficient.

WOW your clients.

Do it as a team.

And do that all over, and over, and over again. That's how you outshine the competition.

Remember what Jocko Willink said: "Success is a campaign of discipline. It's not overnight. It's a long, grinding campaign." You need disciplined execution to successfully niche down.

Harness your entire team's energy around something specific. When two teams are in a tug of war, the trick to winning isn't having the biggest, strongest people—it's having every person on your team *pulling at the same time.* If everyone is going to town, pulling their hardest, but they're all doing it at different times, you'll *lose.* You win if the team leader harmonizes and coordinates that energy: "3, 2, 1, PULL! 3, 2, 1, PULL!"

The strategies we've taught you will enable you to coordinate and synchronize your team's energy.

And you can win any battle simply by *persevering.*

We used to tell each other, "We just have to *last.* If we can just stick around long enough, people will begin to know who we are, and we can build something great."

We got there through hard work and focus. And so can you. Your ability to scale as a company means saying no to good opportunities that are not aligned with your main focus. Niching down gives you that clarity. Focus your energy and attention on your core fundamentals as a company, and then do it again the next year.

With that laser focus, you can do incredible things.

Actions You Can Take Now

Use the link below to download and complete the following:

1. Complete the niche definition exercise.
2. Define your business flywheel.
3. Define your investment criteria for innovation.

BOOTSTRAPPING FINANCE 101

10 Rules for Managing Cash to Fund Growth

Narrated by Christian White

"Revenue is vanity, profit is sanity, but cash is king."

—Alan Miltz

"Well—on paper, it looks like we're winning," I said.

"Yes!" Our accountant, Dan, nodded encouragingly. "You're running a profitable business. Your financial statements look great."

"But it doesn't *feel* like we're winning," I noted.

Looking grim, Christian added, "I'm literally going to make half of what I would have made if I'd stayed at the accounting firm."

"We could distribute more…" I began halfheartedly, but Christian shook his head. We both knew any extra cash needed to go toward shoring up our reserves or our next hire, not our own bank accounts.

We stared at our profit and loss statements again. "We invoiced over $150,000 in the past three months," I said, trying to focus on the positive.

"Yes, the accrual perspective. That's your highest profit number," Dan agreed.

"But…from a *cash* perspective, we've actually received less than $120,000, and once we pay all of our expenses," Christian continued, "after taxes and our own small distributions, we have $10,000 left in the bank account."

Ten thousand dollars. It seemed like a pathetically small number. We had *made* $150,000. How was it possible we only had $10,000 in cash to deploy?

"This number here—" Christian tapped our tax bill. "This number pisses me off a little: *40* percent? Do we seriously have to set aside *40* percent of our profits for taxes? There's got to be a way to bring down that number."

"You may not like hearing this," Dan said, "but a hallmark of a healthy business is how much you're paying in taxes. This large number is a sign that you're *profitable*. The sooner you can come to terms with that, the better."

We tried to come to terms with it.

Reluctantly, we signed the check for our fat IRS bill.

"You guys are making good money," Dan reminded us.

"The *business* is making good money," I said.

"—on paper," Christian interjected.

"Give it a few more years," Dan said cheerfully. "You guys are on a great trajectory."

We stared at the papers. Neither of us felt nearly as cheerful as Dan. "It's funny," I said, not feeling funny. "We learned about all this in business school. We both worked in an accounting firm. And we've been tracking our numbers religiously for thirty, sixty, and ninety days—literally, by the penny. But there is still such a huge difference between what we made and the cash we have left."

"Sort of feels like we're getting screwed somewhere," Christian said.

Dan shook his head. "You're doing everything right. But getting a business up and running is expensive. And the tax man wants his share." He smiled, brightly, and tapped the first number—our highest. "This is a great number!"

We left Dan's office feeling less than thrilled. We'd always known that there was a meaningful difference between what we invoiced, what we collected, and what was actually left in the bank, after taxes and our distributions.

We'd just never *felt* it like this before.

Dan was right; it was tough getting started, but we were on a good trajectory.

This chapter isn't about finance theory; it's a boots-on-the-ground, practical application of key points of financial discipline. This is how we did it, and how we continue to build the Good Business.

Growth Sucks Cash

Listen: If you've made the decision to grow through bootstrapping, you've got to watch your cash flow like a hawk. Remember what finance expert Alan Miltz says: "Growth sucks cash." For an entrepreneur who wants to scale through self-funding, cash is the lifeblood of your business—and you need a lot of it. We would argue that you can never delegate accountability for cash flow; yes, you can eventually find a responsible party to manage it, but you are always accountable for it, and you can never take your eye off of it...ever!

> Cash is the lifeblood of your business.

The bootstrapping model is a great model. Despite all its perks, though, it requires operating with lean finances for a while, especially in the early days.

It's easy to grow faster than your cash flow, which means scaling right into bankruptcy. More companies have gone out of business due to mismanaging cashflow than probably anything else. We've seen it happen multiple times with friends and clients.

We want to help you prevent that! So, we're here to teach you our ten essential rules for bootstrapping finance. This is part science, part art, part strategy, part numbers. There are key leading and lagging indicators to watch and manage that will enable you to grow confidently—*without* the need for external cash infusions. That right there is peace of mind.

Before getting into KPIs and measuring tools, we want to give you some foundational financial principles for operating as a Good Business — the first five rules — what we call "priorities of work."

Priorities of Work: Do This *First*

In the military, I got used to directing troops according to priorities of work. For instance, on foot patrols in wooded terrain, we might pause somewhere to rest for a few hours. As soon as we stopped, we immediately began addressing the most important steps to take, done in order, according to their priority:

1. Establish security of the area.
2. Leaders meet for a planning huddle.
3. Concurrently, junior leaders build sector sketches and establish fields of fire.

The priorities went on from there, the next task beginning once the previous had been completed:

4. Rotate and clean the crew-served weapons while everyone else pulls security.
5. Rotate and clean individual weapons.
6. Conduct hygiene.
7. Establish bivouac positions behind the line.
8. Slit trenches.
9. Chow.
10. Rest with 30 to 50 percent security.

In other words, stopping to hunker down for the night didn't mean "resting"—at least, not until all the priorities of work were completed first.

You've got a similar list as a business owner. If you want to scale, paying yourself a hefty paycheck does not come first. Sorry, but that's much further down the list. There are other priorities to attend to *first* if you want to build a good business and keep up a healthy level of growth. Here are our five priorities of work and an additional five tactical rules for growing profitably:

1. Grow Profitably

A bootstrapped business stays alive and grows only because of its profits.

Ideally, you'll be profitable from day one and fund your business's growth with the profits. Self-funding requires a slower initial approach and closer monitoring than the funded model. If you're not profitable yet, you must focus on getting profitable, because it only makes sense to grow and scale a profitable business.

> A bootstrapped business stays alive and grows only because of its profits.

Here are a few pro tips to growing profitably:

- **Watch your margins.** In order to *grow* and *scale* your business, aim for revenue that exceeds your costs by 15 percent or more. For a bootstrapped business, 10 percent profit is akin to break even.

- **Operate cheaply.** The easiest way to build your margins is to just...not spend money. Obviously, you need to pay your bills—including taxes—but whereas pricing is subject to market dynamics and negotiation, many costs are yours to control and approve. When we started, we didn't have an office. When we got one later on, everything was cheap, used, or DIY. Today, we spend more on things of value, like team training, but not on frivolous stuff like an in-office beer tap. Margin *can* be found in your operational costs (OpEx)—keep an eye on that number!

- **Spend money on things that *make* you money.** Ensure costs pay for themselves (i.e., have an ROI), whether they are people, products, software, vendors, or buildings. For instance, in our early days, we didn't hire a salesperson—we hired an intern. Once he proved he could pay for himself by generating revenue with his sales, we moved him up to full-time. If anything was going to drain on our precious and modest cashflow, it needed to have a clear ROI.

- **Value-based pricing is the way to go for most businesses.** There are at least two ways to price your product or service: *cost-plus* or *value-based*. In general, cost-plus pricing—marking up your cost a little—does not lend itself to long-term value creation, because there's no incentive to deliver truly outstanding service. *Value-based pricing*, on the other hand, is based on the value of your product or service. If you're known as the best practitioner in your field—which is more likely if you niche down in your area of expertise—then your prices should be higher than those offering commodity products and services.

Bottom line: If you can't grow profitably, you can't grow. Be cheap to begin with and watch those profit margins. You'll need to be flexible, iterate, and evolve as the market does, in order to maintain or increase your margins over time. Invest in things that will generate new revenue and do the hard work of niching down to command a higher price point.

2. Build Your Capital Reserves

After ensuring that you're growing with healthy profit margins, you want to build up at least two months' worth of operating expenses in your business bank account. This is your working capital and your **capital reserves**: the cash available to draw on as the cash flow of the business fluctuates.

> Your working capital and your capital reserves should together be two months' worth of operating expenses in liquid accounts (e.g., checking and savings).

Why is this priority number 2? Because—if you *don't* want to unexpectedly run out of cash—you need a certain amount of capital in reserve, available to fund the business as it experiences typical ebbs and flows. For instance, let's say you take on a larger customer who has ninety days to pay their invoice (as opposed to your typical thirty-day terms) and typically pays fifteen days late. You need to fund the servicing of that customer, even during the bad cash conversion cycle for that account. Can you keep the lights on until the payment comes through? Yes—*provided* you've built up your capital reserves to sustain your operational expenses.

Our financial consultants coached us to hold two months' worth of operating expenses in the business. (Notably, this is also the amount the US government offered to businesses with the PPP loan during the COVID-19 pandemic.) You want that capital reserve fund to be essentially liquid—easily accessible, as needed. But, in our opinion, you don't want to be sitting on much *more* than those two months' worth of operating expenses in the business, because any easily liquidated fund won't produce much of a return. Beyond your "emergency fund," we recommend investing any additional profits into higher-yield investment vehicles and/or back into the business. As your margins improve, put excess cash to work in the business or distribute it to invest elsewhere. Don't let it sit idle, or inflation will erode it.

Some people opt to lean on a line of credit in order to keep less cash in the business, but we'd advise against that. While having a line of credit is prudent, you're in a much better position if you can fund yourself through responsible cash management and only draw on that line in an emergency.

Granted, this isn't easy. Especially in your early days, you'll need to be disciplined in building your capital reserve fund and then be consistent in growing it over time, in step with the growth of the business. There will always be other tempting avenues where you could spend that money, particularly as you're building your team.

But this is the second priority for a reason. Most startups fail because they run out of cash.

3. Pay Yourself a Market Rate

Are you growing with healthy profit margins, and have you built up your working capital reserve? Good. Then it's time to pay yourself a market rate for your role in the business.

For any founder who's had a disappointing moment like we did with our accountant, this is good news!

But we also know there are plenty of entrepreneurial martyrs out there. You'd rather keep your earnings miniscule because you're so intent on growing the business. This is well intended—but unwise.

Here's why: You're in this for the *long haul.* Some entrepreneurs get so used to sacrificing for their business that they actually feel guilty paying themselves adequately. We've seen entrepreneurs splurge on all sorts of stuff for their business while paying themselves well below market rate, but paying yourself fairly is insurance against resentment, burn out, blow-ups, and/or self-sabotage.

There's another practical reason to pay yourself a market wage: Until you do, your profit margin will appear artificially inflated. Sure, you could pay yourself peanuts, improving your profit margin to 30 percent—but if you actually paid yourself a market rate, you might only be 3 percent profitable. Be a W-2 for the work that you do *in the business* and operate with a clear picture of your business' health.

It may take time to reach a fair market salary for the role that you hold in your business. When we were starting, we set our salaries at what would pay our bills personally—but they weren't much higher than that. As we worked to establish priorities 1 and 2, we paid ourselves a mere *living wage.* We got paid last: after the capital reserve, after the tax man, and after reinvesting money into the business. That was necessary for growth, even though it sucked.

Around year three, we'd checked the first two priorities off the list. At that point, we gave ourselves a raise in better alignment with a *market wage* for our industry and the size of the business. Our personal pay was now competitive. Not only was that great personally, it also enabled us to have clean financial statements and get a clear picture of our real profitability numbers.

Over time, we've gradually increased our salaries—pegging them to the market rate and what it would take to replace us with comparable talent. This helps us to maintain an accurate financial picture as we grow. We're not "subsidizing" the business via our own low pay to make it look better than it actually is.

4. Tax Planning

Next up: Do some strategic tax planning. When we were working with Dan, he outlined a few smart strategies we could use to bring down our tax bill. For instance, we created retirement accounts that reduced our overall tax burden, and we also took advantage of the Georgia film tax credits program to reduce our state taxes.

We knew of some entrepreneurs who went on massive December spending sprees every year so they could expense those purchases, reduce their profitability, and thereby reduce their tax bill—but that strategy seemed questionable to us. Dan agreed, saying, "Don't spend a dollar to save forty cents. That's insane."

It did sort of seem insane.

"If you have legitimate purchases to make as a business that align with your overall business strategy—of course, make those and deduct the expenses," he said. "But don't reduce your profits just to save money on your taxes."

There are few options for most businesses to meaningfully reduce taxes. By all means, utilize the legitimate ones available. But don't waste mental energy trying to avoid paying taxes. It's a dilution of your focus and a waste of your time.

Just pay the man and get back to building!

5. Decide How to Handle Profits

Once your business has extra cash beyond the first four priorities, it's time to figure out what to do with it.

We like Greg Crabtree's **40/30/30 model** for allocating capital. We have proven it out over many years, and it works well:

- **40 percent goes to the tax man.** Set this amount aside quarterly; if you are based in California or other higher-tax jurisdictions, the tax savings rate may need to be higher.

- **30 percent gets reinvested in the business.** This money is earmarked for growth, innovation, increasing capital reserves, and making other investments in the business.
- **30 percent goes to the owners/founders as a distribution.** There are three reasons for this:

  1. It shores up your personal financial protection. Most of your net worth is tied up and locked in the business, so it's wise to hold additional cash reserves outside the business. We recommend working to build an additional four months of operating expenses as a reserve outside the business.

  2. It blesses your family members, who have had to sacrifice right along with you from day one.

  3. You are the lender of last resort. In a worst-case scenario if the business needs more cash—beyond its reserves, lines of credit, and other debt facilities you might employ—the founders are prepared to step in as an emergency option. This layered approach helps to manage financial risk.

The 40/30/30 rule for allocating profits: 40 percent goes to the IRS, 30 percent is for reinvestment, and 30 percent goes to the owner(s).

Those are the five priorities of work! As in the military, there may be times when you have to *pick* one priority at the expense of the other. For instance, there were times in Ranger School when the instructor told us, "Pick eating or sleeping. You get to do one or the other, but we don't have time for you to do both." I would always eat, because I was a hungry Ranger, not a sleepy one.

You get to make the executive decision about how you approach these priorities and the specific numbers or percentages that will guide your decisions. At every stage of growth, keep revisiting them and shoring them up, in order of their importance.

Your Two Roles

As an entrepreneur, you have two roles. You are an *employee* of the business and have a key role to play in its health and growth. You receive a market-based salary for this role and what you do in the business. In theory, if you found someone better suited for your role, you could replace yourself and pay them your salary.

Your other role in the business is as *an employer/business owner*. You do not receive a salary for being a business owner, but you do get compensated for what you own if the business is profitable, in the form of an owner's distribution. We highly recommend, from a personal financial management perspective, that you keep your salary and distributions separate. Live on your salary, *not your distributions*.

Why? The buck stops with you, and there is a price to pay for that responsibility—lender of last resort. You are the last to get paid, and if the business needs capital, all eyes are on you. One of the best ways that you can put yourself, the business, and your family in a healthy financial situation is by saving and investing the predominance of your distributions.

Strategies: The Art and Science of Bootstrapping Finance

We've told you what the priorities of work *are,* but we've got a lot more to say about how to *execute* the plan for bootstrapping finance. These remaining five rules cover both the strategy and actual measurement of the numbers. Some of you will read these strategies and feel immediately ready to dive deeper into measuring tools to evaluate them. Others may need to absorb the strategies more slowly. For that reason, we've provided QR links to relevant KPI measuring tools at the end of each section. Refer to these when you're ready for that deeper dive.

We should note this is *not* a comprehensive list of everything you'll eventually need to know. But our goal is to give you a great, big, fat head start. Your CPA should be able to help you with all these concepts as well.

6. Obsess Over Your Cash Flow

People like to boast about their revenue: "Oh yeah, we're doing $50 million in revenue this year." Maybe that sounds impressive, but what about their spending? If they're spending $47.5 million for every $50 million they make, that's not a $50 million business—that's only a $2.5 million business! Hence the epigraph of this chapter: "Revenue is vanity."

Profit, or "net income," is a better measurement of success. Take the business just described—if they're running at just 5 percent profit margins, they're on life support; more than likely, they cannot self-fund their growth. If instead, you still have healthy profitability (>10%) when your costs are factored in, you are better able to self-fund your growth. Profitability is a more realistic picture of the size and success of your company versus a topline vanity number.

Still, there could be a massive delta between the profits you've billed for (e.g., paper profits on the accrual P&L) and the cash you have actually received. If you've invoiced a hefty amount but your clients aren't paying you on time, you might end up with more costs than money in your bank account. Even with healthy profitability, without sufficient cash *on hand* to cover all your obligations, you still risk going under.

For that reason, the most important strategy for bootstrapping finance is to *obsess over your cash flow*. It is easy to get upside down, and if you run out of cash, you risk bankruptcy or losing control of the business.

So, how do you manage your cash?

Strategic Tool: Learn Your Business's Particular Economics

Your business and industry will have its own unique economics. Learn the rhythms of those economics so that you can project your cash flow. These are almost like laws of physics determining the ebb and flow of your financial numbers.

Our initial economic model was consulting, and we were paid at an hourly rate. In a spreadsheet, we tracked exactly how much we were going to invoice, on a monthly basis—by the hour. We also tracked exactly how much we were going to spend to stay alive, by the week. Those numbers, side by side, enabled us to ensure we remained viable. We were granular about our projections, studying the numbers like a cardiac doctor studies an EKG. Our survival depended on them!

At no point do you want to find yourself simply *hoping* things will work out. Operate off real numbers—and be meticulous about it. Do the math:

- How will you price the services/products you are providing?
- What are the payment terms you are agreeing to with customers and suppliers?
- How does that translate into invoicing?
- When will you actually receive the money? How will those invoice dates work with the due dates of your bills?
- Will you have enough cash on hand to pay your vendors?

Your cash management will depend on your type of business. For instance, retail businesses will need to spend money to purchase and carry inventory until a customer walks into the store and makes a purchase. While they get paid right away at the point of sale, they have inventory storage and carrying costs. Understand *your* economic model and then build a forecast to help guide your decisions. Bonus recommendation: Once you understand the model, optimize the levers to create additional value. For example, as you will see, we optimize our cash conversion cycle to better self-fund the business.

If you're ready to get even more granular, scan the QR code below to learn about two measuring tools that can help you track your cash: P&L statements and cash flow report.

7. Get Paid

Every business has its own *cash conversion cycle (CCC)*. Once a dollar leaves your business, it will take a certain amount of time to return. If you're paying a dollar on an employee's salary, how fast do they then create a dollar that gets invoiced, collected, and put into the bank account? That timing is all incredibly important, because your CCC is a limiting or enabling factor for growth.

How so? Let's say your CCC is ninety days. So, Harry works on June 1 and invoices it on July 1; then, your client has sixty-day terms by which to pay that invoice before those dollars end up in your bank account (assuming they pay on time). You're not getting any of Harry's revenue until September 1, ninety days later. If that's your situation, you have to monitor and moderate your growth to avoid outgrowing your available cash. If you have a *fast* cash conversion cycle, you are better able to self-fund growth at a faster pace.

Want a list of pro tips to optimize your CCC? Scan the QR code below.

Strategic Tool: Establish Proactive Financial Cadences

You want to be able to *predict* your cash conversion cycle. Do that by monitoring the rhythms of your cash flow through a series of proactive financial cadences:

- Monitor cash on at least a *weekly* basis.
- Report your finances to the executive leadership team on a *monthly* basis.
- If a customer is a *day* late paying an invoice, they get an email (this is a documented and automated procedure).
- If a customer is a *week* late paying an invoice, they get a phone call (this is a documented procedure).

We're proactive, monitoring collections and closely staying on top of invoice due dates. In fact, in our startup days, Christian was the one to send those reminder emails, manually, as the CEO. That's how important it is to keep your cash conversion cycle as tight as possible.

We've got two incredibly helpful tools to share for staying on top of this: the aging A/R report and days sales outstanding (DSO). To learn more, scan the QR code below.

8. Control Costs

"Operate cheaply." We gave you this advice under priority 1. Now we'll double-click on it, giving you strategies to practice discipline in your expenses.

Strategic Tool: Zero-Based Budgeting

Zero-based budgeting is a strategy we use to justify *every* dollar we spend and ensure it gets an ROI. When we sit down once a year to write up our annual forecast, we start at zero. There's no automatic approval of last year's budget. That way, every line item on the budget has an owner, and every owner has made a case for why continued spending is necessary. This helps to reduce spend creep that inevitably accompanies growth.

Zero-based budgeting means you write your annual budget starting at zero, every year. Every cost must be justified.

Zero-based budgeting also means we're regularly cleaning the books of any obsolete costs. Costs are like entropy—unless actively managed, things can quickly get disordered. We'd caution you against things like company credit cards, company cars, and other such perks. Those can easily lead to a lack of the fiscal discipline needed to bootstrap growth. If there is not a clear ROI, deny the spend.

Strategic Tool: Annual Forecasting

Annual forecasting is related to your BHAG and business plan—and also to *budgeting*.

Your annual plan should have specific quarterly and monthly financial targets. Ground it in real numbers by doing the math: "If our average contract value is X, and we think we can get five new customers every month enabling us to do Y, then let's make Z our annual forecast."

In your early years, you won't have much data to base these numbers on, and you'll also be growing fast—which means you'll need to modify the monthly targets as the year progresses. Think of the numbers as scaffolding: They can support growth but are also easily shifted. Once you're a few years in, you'll have more data to help guide your forecasting and your annual targets will likely be more predictable.

Use these targets to create accountability and motivation for your team, and—once again—to control costs, so that you're ideally hitting or exceeding your targets. Our number one cost, by a long shot, is people. Each year we forecast number of hires to help us with annual planning, but we do not make those hires until specific thresholds are met that would merit the hire. After all, a forecast is only a forecast; if our sales numbers are short of the mark, we throttle back the hiring plan to keep in line with sales and overall firm performance.

Strategic Tool: Budget Spending Checks and Balances

Once you reach a size and complexity to where you lose span of control and rely upon others to make key decisions within the company, we recommend implementing an **initiative review board** to approve previously unapproved/unforecasted purchases over a specified threshold. As we gradually grew as a company, we needed to decentralize decision making, empowering our junior leaders to make spending decisions. However, we still wanted to keep a handle on costs. We decided anything higher than $5,000 needed to have a formal proposal and be presented to the monthly board. That gate helps us remain disciplined about spending money, while still enabling us to move forward and operate at scale.

It serves at least two purposes, (1) forcing people to really think through and document the business case and justify the request to a group of their peers and leaders, and (2) educating our junior leaders on how we think about investment and return on invested capital.

9. Invest Strategically

To grow your business, you invest in new people, new products and services, and new tools. But the last thing you want to do is spend your precious cash on a bad investment. How can you make sure your investment dollars are put to good use?

There's no hard and fast guarantee; some trial and error is inevitable. However, these tools will optimize your likelihood of success.

Strategic Tool: Set a Threshold for Return on Invested Capital (ROIC)

In *Simple Numbers 2.0: Rules for Smart Scaling*, Greg Crabtree argues that any investment spend in the company should give you a return of 150 percent within twelve to twenty-four months. Easy, clean, simple—you can modify the numbers to whatever works for you, but this is a good starting point.

Let's say you're thinking of hiring a new head of marketing. That person's generated contribution should not only cover their own compensation but also *add* an additional 50 percent of their compensation to the net pre-tax margin of the business as ROIC. So, if you hire a head of marketing for $100,000, they should generate $150,000 in value within twelve months: $100,000 to cover their compensation and $50,000 in contribution as ROIC.

By setting a threshold for investment returns, opportunities are assessed and prioritized against this standard, and investment dollars consistently produce an ROIC in line with that standard.

Use this threshold of 150 percent as a guide to decide whether to hire and to hold hires accountable. If a director wants to spend a one-time $100,000 to stand up a new service line, consider whether or not they're likely to bring in $150,000 over the next one to two years. If the answer is no, you probably shouldn't make the investment. If the answer is maybe, then think about what conditions will enable them to meet that requirement. If the answer is yes, go for it!

This ROIC threshold will help you make smart financial investment decisions within the business and give your team the metrics and language they need to filter investment opportunities.

Learning to analyze certain key ratios can help you level up with evaluating your ROIC. Check out the link below for an explanation.

10. Confidently Forecast

The last rule of bootstrapping finance is to confidently forecast. Successfully scaling with confidence requires clarity around whether or not you can *continue* to grow and how *fast* you should grow.

It's incredibly common for businesses to abruptly grow beyond their cash reserves—and when they do, CEOs often act like they didn't see the end coming. Yet scaling aggressively to meet demand *does* require fast growth and confident commitments from the executive leadership team. How can you lead with confidence without risking viability?

You need to *predict* what's coming, using forecasting tools to get clarity on how you're doing. We do this monthly.

Luckily for you, we have some: the "Rule of 40" and your trade capital percentage. Learn more about them at the link.

TL;DR

In summary: Bootstrapping finance is hard but absolutely *doable*. You just need to follow the priorities of work, understand your numbers, and use the strategic and measuring tools to track and monitor your progress on a set cadence.

Guess what's also necessary for the health of your business? The "soft stuff": your core values, culture, business philosophy, and so on. This is where we're going next. After all, a business can fail if it goes bankrupt, but it can *also* fail if there's high turnover and poor delivery. We don't want you to fail in either case. We want you to grow a Good Business.

The really important stuff is building your team and serving clients. But—you better not take your eye off the numbers! Ever!

Your business is scaling as an *ecosystem*. Keep it all healthy. Shore up your cash management —*and* strengthen the inner workings of the business through codifying your core values and culture.

Actions You Can Take Now

1. Audit your company against the ten rules in this chapter. Where are you struggling? Where are you knocking it out of the park?

2. List your priorities. What are some next steps to bring clarity to your financials? Do you need help with this? What advisors can you reach out to?

3. Spend time understanding and digesting the strategic tools. If those feel readily graspable and you want to dive into practical calculations, check out the measuring tools via the provided QR codes. If you take time to understand them, you will level up your mastery of the numbers and be able to apply them more predictability to improve the financial health of your business.

CODIFY YOUR CORE VALUES AND CULTURE

It's About Substance, Not Show

Narrated by Christian Hyatt

> *"Culture eats strategy for breakfast."*
>
> —Unknown (often attributed to Peter Drucker)

Initially, I meant it as a joke. "Hey, we should run a hundred-mile relay race."

Around 2018, we'd been bantering about doing a culture-building event with our small team, based around our core value of grit. We both had a history of being on teams that do hard things together—CW through his military experience, and me with my wrestling experience. We intuited that shared adversity would provide a fast track to building trust in relationships.

A 5K seemed too easy. A ropes course seemed like a cliché.

Hence, the hundred-mile relay. I expected CW to shoot it down, saying something like: "No way, man. That's too much."

But instead, he said, "Google it. Let's see if there's one in our area."

Sure enough, there was one happening in North Georgia in October—only twelve weeks away.

We signed up for it. Our risk3sixty team wasn't big enough to do the entire event ourselves, so we recruited some of our clients to join us. There were twelve of us, total: two teams of six. Each person would have to run three different legs with breaks in between, their average total mileage adding up to almost seventeen miles.

And thinking back on it now, frankly, it was awful. A *wonderful*, but awful, experience.

It was the hottest October in Georgia we could remember. Most days hit highs of ninety-five degrees or above. We tried to get ahead of that by renting an RV, thinking that the teammates who weren't running could enjoy A/C, take a cold shower after each leg, and have access to a bathroom.

But, as it turns out, an RV is not equipped to support the growing needs of twelve adults for thirty hours on ninety-five-degree days. On the day of the race, everything broke. The A/C didn't work. We couldn't figure out the shower. It was miserable.

We had to drive those hundred miles in a heated tin can, with hot air blasting at us through the vents.

I was sure that the clients who came along with us would fire us.

The upside, if there is one, was that the race started at midnight, long before the heat of the day reached its apex. I ran the first leg. I was drenched in sweat when I climbed into the RV. With no shower option, I resigned myself to sitting in my own sweat for the next twenty hours.

Everyone else suffered the same fate.

It was around 5:00 a.m. when everyone started to lag. The magnitude of what we had signed up for became real.

"We should not have done this."

"We're not going to be done for another *thirteen hours*."

"Why did we think this was a good idea?!"

"The logistics are bad. We don't have the right setup. Driving this RV around makes no sense."

We seriously questioned our decision to put our team—and our *clients*—through this ordeal. "Should we turn it around?" I asked.

But then, the sun came up. The first glimpse of daylight over the horizon. A hot cup of coffee.

Something about the sunlight hitting us and taking a rest together at dawn changed everything. We all ate some breakfast. Our humor returned. Everyone was reinvigorated and ready to continue.

I didn't know it at the time, but everyone in that RV would talk about that moment for years to come.

For the next nine hours, we ran. Mile after slow mile, we ran. The morning turned to afternoon, each hour getting hotter. We started learning about each other in new ways. Who could hold it together under pressure and who receded inside themselves. Around 2:00 p.m., we hit another low. Everything sucked again.

The heat of the day pressed past ninety-five degrees. A suppressive sort of heat and humidity in Georgia that none of us could escape.

But we pushed through it, each one of us managing to complete our third leg. And then— around 6:00 p.m.—the end was in sight. The finish line brought a type of relief that can only be understood after prolonged suffering.

Suddenly, euphoria arrived. The instant we crossed the finish line, the high was *so high* that everyone immediately began talking about doing it again next year. (And we did.)

All the misery was forgotten. What remained was the bond we'd forged. Now, years later, when we meet any of those guys now—even former teammates who no longer work with us—the conversation always turns to that crazy hundred-mile relay we all did together. It became part of our history, and it helped shape the ethos of our company.

The Annual Grit Event has become a risk3sixty tradition. We did the relay again the following year and eventually participated in a two-hundred-mile relay through South Carolina. We've also done Spartan Races and GORUCK events. As our team has grown, we've found ways for people of all skill levels and abilities to participate: Some act as the support team, bringing snacks and cheering runners on. We had one guy in charge of the photography who laughed at us crawling through mud while snapping our photos. Another one of our team members is known for working the grill and feeding the team.

The point is to do something hard *together*. It's a physical symbol of what we're all about: strange renegades, embracing grit, and forging bonds as a team. In this and many other ways, we codify our culture, moving our values from words on a poster to something we live, eat, and breathe.

In chapter 4, we talked about *setting the foundation* of your company's identity: forming a strong vision and getting clarity on your values and business philosophy.

But there's a difference between simply *identifying* values and *living* your values. Having "grit" written on a poster in our office was one thing; having our team run hundreds of miles together was another.

As we wrap up Part 2, we're going to talk about ways to incorporate your values and culture into every aspect of your business. Not only will this help you build a positive, high-performing team, but it will also help you attract star recruits. And—perhaps most importantly—it's a critical prerequisite to scale.

> There's a difference between simply *identifying* values and *living* your values. Codifying your culture and core values is a critical prerequisite for scaling the Good Business.

Living Your Values

Most likely, you've been part of at least one workplace culture where the values were posted on the wall, but the organization's leaders didn't live by them. For instance, you see a company leader berating his team in front of a poster that reads, "PEOPLE FIRST." Sometimes—maybe even often—the company's documented values go *against* the values that it embraces in practice.

It's not enough to document your values. You have to live them too, holding yourself and your team accountable to those values in a conscious, deliberate way. When you do, you'll achieve things you never thought possible.

> When your culture is informed by aspirational values and anchored in accountability mechanisms, your team can achieve things you never thought possible.

Core values always mattered to us, but as our company has increased in size and revenue, we've come to rely on them a whole lot more. Our values don't just live in our heads; they direct our decisions. They inform how we hire and fire, conduct performance reviews, and decide which opportunities to pursue. They have become a set of lasting principles that form the foundation of how we've scaled. Not only do the two of us genuinely prioritize them, but our other company leaders also steward these values.

How did we manage that? When I arrived home from vacation with a list of five values in 2018, CW said, "This is *exactly* what we've been talking about." Then he asked a very important question: "Now, how do we put them into action? How do we *do* stuff with these values?"

Grit

Tenacity, a relentless pursuit, passion, and persistence.

Craftsmanship

Master tradesmen who produce uncommon quality in work product.

Steadfast

Consistent, firm, and adherence to the code.

Freedom

Opportunity to innovate, take ownership, and stand by the results.

Team

Continuity in purpose and action.

How do you put your values into action? How do you *do* stuff with them?

That's what the rest of this chapter is all about.

Values in Action: More than a Slogan

If you want your core values to meaningfully shape the culture of your company, they need to drive things that *matter*. We're talking about decision-making, accountability, performance reviews—and yes, your own conduct as a leader. If your team sees that your organizational values are attached to career development and progression, used as a filter for important decisions, and consistent with *your* behavior, they'll learn to take those values seriously—even if previous work experiences have made them skeptical. However, when you incorporate your values into the areas below, even the most hardened skeptics will get the picture real quick.

Decision-Making

You want to scale? Deputizing your decision-making is a critical step in removing yourself as a bottleneck. This is not a step you can put off until you're a thousand-person company—or even a hundred-person company. This is a thirty- to fifty-person company issue.

As your business grows, the number of things you oversee directly will shrink. This is necessary—and a sign of *healthy* leadership—but it means you'll lose your span of control over time. Maybe you don't interact with the clients anymore. You're no longer the direct supervisor of any key business processes. And rather than *you* making all the decisions, you trust your leaders to make many of them instead.

Note that this isn't *blind* trust. This is about helping your leaders make decisions when you aren't in the room to guide them. When the situation is unclear and when there are many variables. This is how you decentralize decision-making to the people closest to the problem—to the people in the best position to solve them. Your leaders' decision-making will pull from your playbook: namely, the filters determined by your BHAG, annual plan, and *core values*.

Core values help you deputize decision-making—a crucial requirement for scaling.

We guide decision-making in the following three ways.

1. Train

We've learned that excellent company leaders don't just happen; they have to be developed. So, we train all company leaders to conduct themselves in alignment with our five values.

This training program is CW's baby. He and another West Point grad, Jessica, developed a six-month leadership development program called the Journeyman Program. Any team member who wants to seek career advancement opportunities and grow as a leader can apply. Then, once enrolled, program participants are guided in self-reflection, tactical skills, and leadership.

Our core values serve as a filter for making decisions that account for all the intangibles that are otherwise hard to build a process around. When things are otherwise unclear, we can always revert to: "Well, did that decision align with our values?" And that approach has proven to be helpful.

2. Equip

As part of the Journeyman Program, we offer two modules on decision-making that take our junior leaders through a framework for analyzing and making tough decisions. The framework begins with assessing the decision in the context of our core values.

This is how we decentralize decision-making and empower leaders to make the call. When this framework is followed successfully, our leaders are able to make decisions similar to (or even better than) the ones we would make, freeing up our time to operate in our best and highest use.

As you can see in the following example, this framework is guided by our core values and vision:

Decision Making Framework

Problem Statement:

The challenge we are facing is Client is potentially unethical, disrespectful, we are doing a lot of questionnaires. Could be a liability because they broke a contract with the customer. Big piece of our revenue. Is our role clear with the client?

Solution Analysis

	Option 1	Option 2	Option 3
Description of proposed solution			
What are the potential risks of this decision? Who is impacted?			
What steps can we take to reduce the impact or likelihood of the downside?			
What are the potential positive outcomes of this decision?			
What steps can we take to maximize the potential positive outcome of this decision?			
Does this match our core values?			
Grit			
Craftsmanship			
Steadfast			
Team			
Freedom			
Does this align to our strategy flywheel?			
Hire Strange Renegades			
Build Craftsmen			
Create Artisan Products			
Raving Fans			
Inimitable Brand			

First, leaders clearly state the problem requiring a decision at the top. Then, after analyzing three different possible solutions—noting possible risks and the potential benefits—company leaders run these solutions through the filter of our core values. How does each solution align with our commitment to grit, craftsmanship, steadfast, team, and freedom? Finally, leaders go through our strategy flywheel. How is the potential solution aligned with our key strategic goals to hire strange renegades, build craftsmen, create artisan products, build an inimitable brand, and create raving fans?

That's how the two of *us* make decisions, and the decision-making framework guides leaders through that same thought process. As a result, there's a high likelihood that they'll end up making the same decision we would, if we were in their shoes.

For example—let's say we're working with a client who verbally berates our team. We're going to ask: "Could we maintain our value of being *steadfast* with this client, building a lasting relationship based upon earned trust over time? Is keeping this client supporting our value of *team*? Does this client impinge on our team's *freedom*?"

We're likely to conclude from that exercise that this disrespectful client isn't a good fit for our company. At that point, we would give the client two options: Either they stop the behavior, or we'll fire them as a client. It might be a hard call if they're supplying a large portion of our revenue, but the values-based framework for our decision-making helps clarify the necessary next step. In fact, we *have* fired a few clients over the years—including our largest, at one point—due to this exact situation. We're proud to say that we made the tough calls, and our team and business are better for it.

When our leaders make enough decisions based on these principles, the values become part of the DNA of the organization.

3. Create Accountability

Leaders don't just have the *option* to use the decision-making framework. Accountability is baked in, because our values are directly written into our annual goals and our BHAG; one of our cultural goals is "maintain our core values."

What does that mean, practically? We could *try* to become a $100 million company in the next three years, but we're not going to sell our souls to do so. Instead, we'll set a more modest growth rate that enables us to maintain our values and healthy culture as we grow. The values impact our strategy at *every* level

In all these ways, our values, culture, and decision-making process are *scalable*, including in hiring.

Hiring

Our core values help us bring top performers to our company because we share what we're about during the interview process, ensuring we hire great people *who also align with our values.*

John Gordon, author of *The Energy Bus,* says the number one thing company leaders should focus on is getting the right people *on* the bus—and the wrong people *off* the bus. According to Gordon, you must harness your team's energy to accomplish an important mission. If you're hiring "energy vampires," you'll wreck your culture—especially if you're still in the startup phase. Even one person with bad energy on a team of ten people accounts for 10 percent of that team's culture. From my experience, this is accurate.

Don't fall into the trap of hiring for talent or skill over values and character. Values and character are foundational and developed over a long time, whereas skills can be taught through training. Don't underestimate how far you can get with the right person and good training. This has been a core philosophy of ours since we started and has worked well when we've stuck to it.

In the early days, we sometimes made exceptions for people we really wanted to hire, or we ignored potential red flags. Nearly always, we lived to regret it. If we had remained true and authentic in our criteria, we would have seen more consistent results with our hires.

But we didn't—which brings us to our next point.

Firing

We have not been great at firing, historically. Our weakness has been keeping people too long, wanting to give them another chance, hoping they could turn things around. Through these experiences, we've learned that your choices about firing serve as a loudspeaker for your company's values. Keep a toxic person too long, and your team quickly concludes your values are only lip service. Fire a toxic person, and the team learns you take your values seriously.

In a small company, especially in the startup phase, everyone's close. Hiring and firing decisions are personal. Even if moving someone out is the right choice for the business, it hurts. But postponing the inevitable hurts more.

The two hardest fires to make are (1) the people you're close to as friends and (2) the toxic high-performers—aka the "brilliant jerks."

I can speak to this personally. One of the first hires we made was one of my best friends. We'd met each other at eighteen and bonded over our similar rough backgrounds, and the friendship had lasted into adulthood. When we were recruiting some of our first team members, my buddy was top of mind.

Unfortunately, the red flags started popping up quickly.

First, my friend didn't show me much respect as the company's CEO. For a while, I wrote that off. We had a history together—I didn't mind that our professional relationship looked different from everyone else's. I also failed to set expectations and normalized the behavior myself.

Second, my friend made jokes and behaved in ways that were consistently off-color. Again, that felt like no big deal early on. We were a team of six guys, and it was easy to dismiss his jokes as crass humor.

But, as we sought to grow, we realized that we wouldn't be able to hire other capable leaders with this guy around—a point that our first female hire made clear. "Guys—his 'locker room' humor isn't funny. It's offensive," she patiently explained to us. "And you're not going to be able to create the culture or hire the team you want if he keeps doing that."

When I tried to address the inappropriate humor, my friend blew it off. Other team members noticed and began to express concerns. The stakes had become too high: There was a lot of revenue at stake, people's jobs were on the line, and the company couldn't wait for our relationship to evolve.

Even CW had begun to lose faith. "I like him as a person," he told me, "but it feels like he's uncoachable."

Six months later, we finally fired him. We kept him much longer than we should have. It sucked. It felt like a bad breakup.

Thankfully, the change ended up being healthy. We now have a culture where everyone is empowered as leaders in all areas of our business, and my friend found a new job where he could thrive. It was a necessary upgrade for our entire culture.

Then there are the brilliant jerks.

You know the type. You might even have one on your team: They're top performers, but they're dragging everyone else down. They make you the most money, and your clients love them, but they often undermine both the organization and their teammates—taking energy away from the company by causing problems and stirring up drama.

> The two hardest fires to make are the people you're close to and the brilliant jerks.

You might fear you'll fail without them, or that your clients will up and leave. They feel irreplaceable. But it's not true: they're absolutely replaceable. And they probably need to be replaced. Regardless of what they can produce, a person who spreads negativity can wreak havoc on an organization and limit its ability to grow.

My advice here is to avoid relying solely on your own impressions to make these decisions. My experience is that people often put on their best behavior in front of founders, so you can develop a skewed perspective. Gather data using 360 surveys and— more importantly—listen to other leaders in your organization when they express concerns. Every time we've parted ways with a brilliant jerk, their team has thanked us. The people in the trenches always know how bad the situation really is. Often long before you do.

Our track record of firing brilliant jerks has proven out how important it is for the business. Each time, when we eventually part ways with a brilliant jerk—usually years later than we should have—their replacement turns out to be *fantastic.* Firing someone is hard! But *waiting* to fire someone will stall your business. It will demotivate your best performers and undermine your culture. And tolerating them is a message to your team about what type of culture you are building. If you want to get to $10 million, it's your job to make those hard decisions.

We've learned to be confident in making those hard decisions—the right answer is usually obvious. And when you get rid of someone with bad energy, not only do you tend to see a cumulative increase in everyone else's performance, but you also open the door to promote or hire the next leader who *can* help deliver a team's full potential.

When you purge toxic people from your team, you allow fresh air to sweep in, creating a healthier culture. It's also one of the clearest signs you can make that your values are a code to live by.

Performance Reviews

In addition to hiring and firing, our core values also play an important role in how we conduct performance reviews. Twice a year, employees do performance self-assessments, and their managers do the same. Our performance reviews include traditional performance assessment criteria, as well as formal opportunities to highlight alignment with core values. Those conversations are useful as a springboard to discuss each team member's goals and ambitions—which we're eager to encourage. We've learned that the company will outgrow every person unless they actively seek to grow themselves.

The performance reviews are just one more way we reinforce the idea that core values *mean* something. We use them in all our big decisions, embed them in our strategic vision, and they guide us in our hiring, firing, and performance accountability checks. The expectation is that every person on our team doesn't just know and understand the core values—they live them.

Culture

In recent years, it seems that many organizations have reduced company culture to office aesthetics. When people think about culture, they will talk about company retreats or perks, like free food, a video-game room, or ping-pong tables.

I think too much attention has been paid to shaping *that* kind of culture: the flashy, polished, shiny kind that you might see in a magazine.

Personally, we think it's fake. Often, companies do this as a way to compensate for their lack of healthy and *real culture.*

That's not to say we don't do *some* of it. At this stage, we're established enough that we now have a cool office space. We give our team swag. We have great food and put on fun events.

But we also know companies that do all that and more, while having *terrible* cultures underneath.

That's because, without real values underpinning your culture, the physical stuff is just window dressing. The *meat* of a culture is how team members are treated, how they're compensated and incentivized, whether or not their bosses give them time to take care of their families, the nature of their work, and the *values* that root the vibes across the entire organization. Everything else is just perks. There's "show"—and then there's *substance.*

We prefer substance.

> Lasting, good cultures are shaped by substance, not show.

Granted, sometimes the perks can be physical manifestations of your values. For instance, we plan team events and have great office snacks because we care about our team. But if we *only* did team get-togethers, without the substance to back it up—no family leave policy, bad healthcare benefits, no flexibility—do you think our team members would feel supported? No way.

Perks without substance is hypocrisy. And that's what I'm getting at.

Take all the shiny perks away, and you could still have a great culture. My mother-in-law works for a manufacturing company. Their office spaces are boring. The leaders of the company are very frugal. But everyone *loves* working there, because the owners reinvest in their employees' benefits and wellness. They try to help every one of their employees max out their 401(k)s every year. People are encouraged to get home and see their family every night. The values are strong and collaborative. Where it counts, this company's got the right culture.

It's easy to throw money at a problem—and much harder to do the arduous work of establishing positive core values from the inside out and then living them. That takes a long time and a lot of effort.

And you know what might be the hardest part?

You.

Leaders Set the Tone

There's one glaringly obvious influence on your company's culture that we haven't discussed yet: *Your* leadership. *Your* behavior. *Your* demonstration of values.

People take their behavioral cues from their leaders. If the CEO cusses in the office, the whole staff follows suit. If a company leader constantly communicates with sarcasm, the culture will likely feel like a sharp-witted, snarky environment. If you cut corners, your team will cut corners. Ultimately, your team will come to mirror *you*, regardless of what your core values say.

This is also true for what you *tolerate.* For instance, you might not be a particularly negative person, but if one of your executive leaders has a reputation for brutally ripping apart their direct reports' work and making personal insults, your tolerance tells the entire company that such behavior is acceptable. That level of behavior then becomes the new standard.

> If you allow bad behavior to exist, your team will assume you *approve*, and it will likely spread.

Most learning happens through observation. As the old saying goes, "Actions speak louder than words." If you want to shape a positive culture consistently aligned with your company's core values, start with you. As your company's leader and foremost influencer, we encourage you to do the hard work of demonstrating these qualities:

- **Be professional.** We hear people say, "We treat each other like family," or "We're all friends." But that's disingenuous. There *is* a power dynamic. Family members don't fire each other, but you may need to fire one of your team members. Distinguishing a relationship as professional—through words, actions, clothing, and other signals—helps maintain healthy boundaries. Your team deserves a professional at the helm.

- **Be approachable.** Ultimately, you want your culture to have a balance of camaraderie and professionalism. We've been able to create that balance through our different strengths as partners. You can craft that dynamic as a solo leader as well, although it might take a great deal of intentionality on your part, depending on your natural tendencies. My biggest piece of advice when it comes to being approachable is to listen to people—*really listen.*

- **Consistently uphold values.** Our teams don't have to question whether or not they can trust us. There's no doubt about what the standards are, or expectations for good work. There's no playing one founder against the other. We live by the same values we ask our team to uphold.

- **Invest in your personal growth.** No one can fire you or give you a performance improvement plan, but all leaders need to grow along with their companies. If you're made aware of an aspect of your leadership that doesn't align with your core values, take action. As leaders, we need to look in the mirror and hold ourselves accountable to the standards we set. That's the only way we can realistically hold others accountable. If you're reading this thinking you have nothing to improve on, then we'd encourage you to make extra sure of that, using data.

- **Create checks and balances.** Have processes in place to maintain a clear-eyed view about how you're doing as a leader. We have a program called "Coffee with the Craftsmen," which randomly pairs people up to have conversations, increasing the circulation in the business, making it easier to get a general feeling of morale across the organization and identify any issues to address. We also do anonymous employee feedback surveys, allowing us to quickly surface and address issues, rather than letting them fester.

- **Control the pace.** One thing I have noticed over the years is that leaders have to control the pace of the company. For example, one way that manifests itself is that your team wants to make decisions quickly and move fast. Often, the same day. But as the leader, you have to slow things down and think about how decisions may impact the business for the next year, five years, or ten years. You have to consider second- and third-order effects. At other times, your team may be paralyzed by indecision and afraid to take risks. In those circumstances, you may have to light a fire under people, so they take a swing and go for it. Remember, set the tone for company speed.

All leaders need to grow along with their companies.

Bottom line: If you, as your company's leader, consistently live, hire, fire, and make decisions by your core values, people will take them seriously.

Leaders set the standard for a culture built on substance, not just show. If you can do that, you're well on your way to cultivating an uplifting workplace where people can thrive.

From Building to Scaling

The earlier you establish your core values, the better. As you enable other leaders to be stewards of those values, you can scale into a Good Business.

And speaking of scale, it's time to hit the gas. Part 2 taught you how to "Build the Good Business": niche down, hone your finances, and codify your core values. If you've done that, you're now in a position to grow rapidly. For the rest of this book, we'll teach you how to *expand* what you're doing: build out your leadership team, implement scalable systems and processes, and learn how to remove limits on yourself as a leader!

Actions You Can Take Now

1. If you haven't already, take some time to think about and define your core values. You don't have to nail this on day one, but it's good to have a working framework for how you want to operate as a business and treat others, both team members and clients.

   - What values do you hold true, believe to be timeless, want to live by?
   - If you had to choose five, what would they be and why?

2. Put your values into action. Consider: Where are there opportunities to bake your values into key processes, communications, and operations? When core values are part of how the business operates, it is much easier to live them out and teach them to others.

3. Take inventory of your team:

   - Are there brilliant jerks holding the team back? Ask your leaders what they think.
   - Have you avoided firing an underperformer because you're personally close to them?
   - Make the tough call. If someone needs to go, you likely already know. It's just a matter of having or building the courage to take action!

4. Define your leadership development plan:

   - How are you leveling up as a leader?
   - How are you inspiring your team toward growth and greatness?
   - The tone is set at the top. Make time to develop yourself!

3. SCALE

SCALE THE GOOD BUSINESS

SCALE YOUR LEADERSHIP AND TEAMS

Escape the "Black Hole" by Expanding Your Leadership Infrastructure

Narrated by Christian White

"You don't build a business. You build people, and people build the business."

—Zig Ziglar

We call it the Black Hole now, but at the time it was pulling us in, we didn't have the term—we just felt the effects. After we were well beyond it, Greg Crabtree shared the concept with us, and we knew exactly what it was and when in our journey we had fought it's pull: between $3 and 5 million in revenue.

Every small business hits this inflection point as it grows: You're more profitable than you've ever been, but you and your team are at your most miserable.

Why? Because you're completely maxed out. You can't personally take anything else on. Your customers want more—yet you have nothing more to give.

When risk3sixty hovered on the edge of the Black Hole, our profit margin was north of 35 percent—which is phenomenal. But everyone on our small team was operating with their hair on fire. It was completely unsustainable. We knew we needed to supplement our team with back-office support, but we also knew those hires would eat into our profits, profits we needed to build up our cash reserves and to sustain our growth.

If we only cared about making a healthy paycheck, we could have stayed small and continued operating at 35 percent profitability for as long as our cardiac health held out. We could have pushed our team to their max capacity without a break and accepted the inevitable turnover.

But we wanted more than that. We wanted to build a business with lasting value and grow a high-performing team. We wanted our team to love coming to work and to feel inspired by our shared mission. We wanted to scale. We wanted a Good Business.

So, we accepted that our profitability would have to decrease. We started hiring support roles, and then—more critically and more expensively—executive leaders. We defined a minimum target level of profitability at 15 percent and decided to reinvest the rest into team members and new software.

It wasn't easy, but *that's* how we got ourselves beyond the pull of the Black Hole.

It's *hard* to escape the Black Hole because it requires you to do three incredibly difficult things that will propel you beyond the force of the Black Hole:

1. Give up important responsibilities that you're good at.
2. Sacrifice profits to expand your team.
3. Put in time to train new leaders.

I watched firsthand as Christian struggled with these principles. He could barely bring himself to do the first of those three difficult things. He felt uncomfortable giving up *any* responsibilities. He liked being in control of the tasks he'd taken on—and besides, we'd experienced quite a bit of success doing it his way. Why would he want to delegate anything?

Well, because we both wanted to be around for our kids' childhoods.

Also, I twisted his arm.

I called Christian shortly after returning home from a business trip to Boston in 2019. "Christian, I've got our guy," he said. "I know him from the army. He's amazing. He'd excel at whatever we give him to do." Tim didn't have a deep background in business, startups, or cybersecurity, *but* he had a great reputation. "He's got his MBA. He's in a leadership training program right now. And he has a track record of success in everything he's ever done," I said.

"Yeah...but he's never done anything that *we* do," Christian countered.

"He was a world-class wrestler," I said. "He wrestled in college as an All American."

That got Christian's attention. As a former high-school wrestler, Christian suddenly felt he knew everything he needed to know about Tim: the dedication, the cutting weight, the scrappiness, the grit. If this guy was a world-class wrestler *and* I vouched for him, then perhaps Christian could surrender some of the work we desperately needed help with.

I suggested that Christian start by assigning the invoicing to Tim. He agreed—but on the inside, I knew he was kicking and screaming. What if Tim messed up our cash flow? What impact would that have on our financial viability—not to mention our client relationships?

Tim quickly proved he was way better at invoicing than Christian ever had been. He built a system to send the invoice emails that was *scalable* and persistent, but still very polite. We got paid on time more consistently. Our clients appreciated the reminders. Nothing broke. It got *better*.

In hindsight, it might seem silly to some that Christian struggled so much with delegating invoicing. I never thought it was silly. Giving away responsibilities is scary. Founders put a tremendous amount of pressure on themselves. If we were going to pay someone else to free up his time—then, suddenly, Christian and I both had to make *better use* of our time. But that's exactly the point. No company can scale as long as the founder is still trying to wear every hat. In order to grow, the operation needs new leaders.

> No company can scale as long as the founder is still trying to wear every hat. In order to grow, the operation needs new leaders.

In this chapter, we'll outline exactly what needs to happen in order to scale your organization *beyond* the Black Hole and into the stratosphere of the Good Business. What has to happen first? You're probably not going to like hearing it any more than I enjoyed doing it...

Step 1: Clarify Your Role and Delegate the Rest

In his reluctance to give up responsibilities, Christian needed to get a clearer sense of what his true responsibilities were. Together, we worked to define the highest and best use of his time:

    A.   Making sure the executive team is all rowing in the same direction
    B.   Leading "Mission to Metrics, as described in Chapter 5

C. Modeling and reinforcing culture by defining systems that promote our core values

D. Building brand equity by telling the world about risk3sixty through books, social media, interviews, and other visible platforms

Get very clear about how you should be spending *your* time so you can stop doing work that others can do better and accelerate the business in the ways only you can.

One of the most important leadership skills is understanding which work truly compounds the business vs. which work slows it down. Not all of your effort yields equal impact. Some work creates leverage far beyond the hours invested, while other work consumes your energy without moving the organization forward.

To bring clarity to this, we use our **Compounding Work Framework**, which evaluates work across two dimensions: how much leverage it creates for the business and how sustainable it is for you performing it.

At the top of the framework is **Compounding Work**: high-leverage work that is sustainable and energizing. This is where leaders create outsized impact. Time spent here strengthens the organization, brings clarity, and enables scale. This is where your role should increasingly live over time.

There is also **Stewardship Work**: high-leverage but draining work. These are the difficult decisions, accountability conversations, and judgment calls that come with leadership. This work matters, but is a burden; it should be time-boxed and intentional, not allowed to sprawl across your calendar. Competent leaders can increasingly take this type of work off your plate if you are willing to invest in them and develop their ability to steward.

At the bottom of the framework are two categories that deserve increasing scrutiny as the business grows. **Comfort Work** is enjoyable and familiar but produces little leverage. It often feels productive, yet doesn't materially move the business forward. **Friction Work**, on the other hand, is both draining and low leverage. It creates stress, bottlenecks momentum, and should be eliminated or delegated as quickly as possible.

The Compounding Work Framework

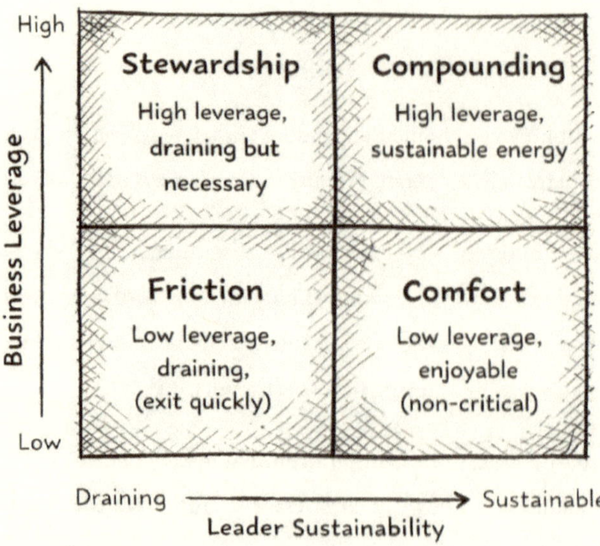

Early in a company's life, founders often operate in all four areas out of necessity. But once the business is profitable enough to solve problems with money, leaders must narrow their focus. Scale comes not from doing more, but from doing the *right* work and letting go of the rest.

Start by removing friction work from your plate. Then reduce and systematize stewardship work. Be disciplined about how much time you   allow comfort work to occupy. Protect compounding work aggressively.

Once your role is clear, delegate everything else. There is very little that cannot be delegated as long as your expectations are clear and you have the right people in place. Don't feel like doing this work means you are abdicating your responsibility (ultimately, you are accountable). The purpose of this is to create leverage.

As the organization scales, this same principle should apply to every leader. Imagine a company where each department head consistently operates in work that compounds their impact. That's a company with a competitive advantage.

Two tools borrowed from my military leadership experience have been critical in my ability to delegate effectively and move the majority of my impact into Compounding Work:

1. Commander's Intent and

2. Levels of Initiative.

Scan the QR code to learn more.

If you have a team of A-players, there's nothing you can't delegate. If you have B- or C-players, on the other hand, there may be nothing you *can* delegate.

Which brings us to step number 2: get the *right* people on your team. Build a leadership team with star recruits.

Step 2: Build Your Leadership Team

Here's one of the things we did right on our journey: we *anticipated* the Black Hole effect and built the infrastructure to get *out* of it ahead of time.

In the Army, I learned firsthand the value of a command team formation. When overseeing large numbers of troops, there were always three people who came together to coordinate decisions: a company commander, an executive officer serving as second in command, and the first sergeant, the highest-ranking noncommissioned officer in the formation. Those three individuals bore the responsibility for the entire 130-person organization.

As we looked to scale beyond the Black Hole, we wanted to set up a similar "command team"—an executive leadership team—to coordinate strategy and decentralize decisions.

We wanted a core team of leaders made up of people who could evolve along with the company and could serve as our trusted advisors on tough issues.

Today, our team consists of leaders in the areas of operations, people, revenue, product, and technology. We hired or promoted them based on their proven track records, and they each bring tremendous wisdom and diverse experiences from their various backgrounds. Collectively, this team represents every practice and function within our business, so that all aspects of the company have an advocate when we discuss strategy or make key decisions. Every one of them fuels a powerful rocket booster, giving us enormous momentum to carry the business forward, well beyond the Black Hole.

That's what a good leadership team does: it enables you to think *ahead* of where your business currently is and to create the conditions that will enable your team to move *past* a growth plateau.

But how do you get your leadership team right? Some seemingly perfect hires may not turn out to be a great fit, or you may get the balance wrong—too many managers, or an org structure that doesn't totally work. And then there's the manager conundrum: What are they supposed to do? Do they manage a function, a project, people? How should their role be defined?

> Strong leaders are your ticket out of the Black Hole.

Expect to work through some trial and error before you've optimized your leadership team. Every business and market is unique, requiring its own nuanced approach. That said, here are two guiding principles that have made our work significantly easier.

Prioritize Ethical Decision Makers

At West Point, I remember a professor asking, "What is the number one job of a leader?"

People answered in different ways, but he wasn't satisfied with any of their responses. "No," he said. "The number one job of a leader is *ethical decision-making*. Because if you do that, you're going to build trust in your organization and establish a reputation for doing the right thing. And you're going to have a team who gets behind your decisions and uses your example as a basis for *their* decision-making."

We've embraced that same philosophy. We absolutely want to gain a reputation for doing the right thing, building trust in our organization so that more and more people will want to do business with us over time. This is how you grow a world-class organization!

That's why ethical decision making is top of mind when we're interviewing a new candidate. In one nightmare interview, I asked a potential hire about his military leadership experience. "You probably had to do a lot of ruck marches," I prompted him. "Carrying heavy equipment."

"Yeah," he agreed.

"So, how did you train your troops for that? Did you have them carry even heavier weights during training marches?"

"No, actually." The candidate seemed to balk. "When we went on training marches, I'd have my guys stuff pillows in their rucksacks. That way, it didn't wear on them."

Immediately, I thought, *Outside of reeducation and leadership training, there is no way this guy can be a leader for us.* He was *unethical* in faking an element of his people's training, making them *less* prepared for battle.

The right thing is often the harder thing. We need leaders who can handle adversity—both their own and their team's.

Leaders need to set the standard for their organization. That's why ethical decision-making is the number one responsibility of a leader, regardless of function or role.

The best-case scenario interviews are with individuals who have done their homework. They've researched us and know who we are and what we're all about. They understand our culture and values and show up to those interviews excited. For them, this isn't just an employment opportunity; they want to be part of a team seeking to be the very best in the industry. They like our high standards and the prospect of working with an elite firm that makes a positive impact in their clients' and team's lives.

When we meet candidates like that, we can feel confident that they'll not only make great leaders, but also be a great culture fit. Which brings us to our next point…

Hire for Culture

We take the old business adage "Hire for culture; train for skill" seriously.

Our culture is our pride and joy. We've invested enormous amounts of time, energy, and effort into building a strong culture, and we believe it is a huge factor in our success as a company.

However, as our business has grown, our direct influence over our people has become increasingly limited. While we set the tone from the top, the people with the biggest influence over our team members are the day-to-day managers. To keep our culture strong, those managers *must* be fully bought into our core values.

That's why we look for executive leaders whose core values align with our own. Signs of a good culture fit include:

- **Player/coach attitude.** Fast-growing companies typically need individuals who can do the work *and* lead a team. In other words, you need people who can coach *and* pitch. When you hire a leader, you're also hiring the team they'll eventually build. You want a player/coach who understands the work and can lead those individuals effectively.
- **Positive energy.** Find leaders who will enjoy all the elements of your culture, contributing positive and upbeat energy.
- **Appreciation for accountability measures.** Leaders need to exhibit high performance and accurately track it on their teams, following KPIs based on the BHAG.

Remember, as your business grows, your teams will be taking culture cues from other leaders and managers far more than they'll be taking them from you. If you want to maintain that pristine culture that you worked so hard to build, a little extra effort here will go a long way.

Hire for culture; train for skill.

Make Your Business Irresistible

We make a point of taking excellent care of our people. That might sound altruistic, but it's actually motivated by considerable self-interest. To hire cream-of-the-crop "strange renegades," we need to present a strong case as to why they should choose to work with us, over any other firm.

We also embrace Zig Ziglar's maxim in the epigraph of building the people who will help build the business. Every dollar we spend on one of our team members is an investment in their well-being, satisfaction, development, performance, tenure, and yes—our own Good Business. Our people build that business. If we want their best work, then *of course,* we should build them up.

Here's how.

Job Descriptions

Providing clear job descriptions might seem like an odd place to start with this topic, but we've learned the hard way that team members are *hindered* without clear expectations.

When you're a small startup, job descriptions may seem less important. After all, everyone needs to wear many different hats. But if you want to build scaling infrastructure, you must formalize things like interviews and job descriptions so that others can follow the same process.

Christian is the perfect example of someone who thrives at agile companies. It was a big jump for him to formalize something like a job description, which historically he would have rolled his eyes at. "What's your job description? Um, do whatever needs to be done!"

This mindset works when your business depends on you to be flexible. But it doesn't land well with the kind of A-player you will need to hire to take your company to the next level.

As you scale, get crystal clear on what you need and why. Then, communicate those expectations to the person you're hiring, along with a clear description of what success looks like in that role. In brief, provide:

- An overview of the role as it relates to the company's overall vision
- Role-specific responsibilities along with measurable KPIs that will help them track their progress toward their objectives
- Relevant company-wide information
- Any compliance details

We've provided a job description resource where each point is spelled out more clearly at the QR code below.

Money

We have historically paid our leaders a lot—probably more than what most CEOs at a company of our size would pay. We also give them significant freedom over their practice areas and how they shape their careers.

Most CEOs that we've talked to believe our approach is risky. We disagree. It has consistently paid off.

Take Jessica, for instance, our VP of People. She is paid very well and has a ton of freedom. We know several other CEOs who only have one or two people in HR, and they function as generalists at the bottom of their salary grid and don't have a voice in the organization. They're good at admin tasks like running payroll—but they're not asked to think about strategy, leadership, or push the envelope in any way to support the company's growth. Our culture looks radically different than theirs, and we think it's in large part because of how we've invested in people like Jessica. Because of that investment, we also *ask* a lot of her—and she delivers. A strategic thinker in the People department of a company wields enormous impact, provided you've got an A-player in the role with sufficient latitude to innovate and lead.

We know this is hard to do. For a growing company with lean profit margins, it's hard to *actually* put your money where your mouth is and believe it's going to pay off for you. Getting out of the Black Hole will cost you money—a *lot* of money.

But if you're working with A-players, we've found it *does* pay off.

> Getting out of the Black Hole will cost you money—but that's strategic. You're investing in the future potential of your business.

However—in the spirit of scrappy bootstrapping—we found a way to make this process a bit more affordable. When we brought on Tim, and later Jessica, we couldn't pay for them to serve exclusively in support roles. We just didn't have the cash for that. Instead, we started them in hybrid roles that were partially billable: doing 50 percent billable work for clients and 50 percent back-office work. This created an affordable on-ramp for their salaries because their billable work was covering most of their cost.

After a transition period of six to twelve months, we started moving their focus more exclusively to their strategic roles. By then, we had full confidence in the value of their contributions and had continued to build up our own revenue. As an added bonus, Tim and Jessica's work "in the field" gave them understanding of how we tactically deliver services, resulting in empathy for the people they eventually led and helping them build relationships across the team.

Also, the two of us weren't running around with our hair on fire anymore. Their contributions made an immediate positive impact on our quality of life.

If and when you hire leaders for your business, pay a salary generous enough to secure A-players. The level of your compensation is a sign of your support for them—*and* an indication of the value you expect from them. If you've hired the right person, you won't regret the investment. There will be a healthy ROI over time.

Benefits

Your benefits package should be another selling point in attracting star recruits. Not only do you need to *have* a good benefits package, commensurate with your industry, but you must also *articulate* what those benefits are.

Again, this is probably going to require a shift for the startup business looking to scale. No one wants to spend time writing an employee manual when you have a team of four people—but when you've got a team of fifty to sixty, suddenly that manual becomes incredibly important. What's the leave of absence policy? No one cares until someone needs it—and then you *need* it.

This is the kind of stuff we used to roll our eyes at, but now that we have a large team whose families' well-being relies on our benefits packages, we've realized it's important to have a clear understanding of the support we offer. Over the years, we've continued to expand our benefits, including family leave and profit sharing.

You may have noticed by now that getting beyond the Black Hole requires changing almost *everything*: your own responsibilities, the level of formality throughout the business, your profit margins, the people on your team, and even the benefits package. That's par for the course: You've got to evolve to grow.

And speaking of evolution, remember how we guided you to niche down in Chapter 6? You want to take a similar approach with prospective hires: Communicate to them exactly what makes your company so special.

Your UVP

To attract the top talent in the industry, we had to offer potential employees *more* than just good pay and benefits. We had to somehow show ourselves to be the *best* company they could choose to work for.

We're proud of the culture we've created, and we believe it's a major selling point. But it's also harder to convey to a candidate in simple words. So, we've worked to develop our "unique value proposition" (UVP) as an employer so that we're truly and totally irresistible:

- We've got all the expected stuff—401(k), PTO, and health benefits.
- We've added a sabbatical program for all employees, once they've worked a certain amount of time.
- Employees get a gadget budget and a training budget.
- We've increased paternity leave from four weeks to six weeks and increased maternity leave from six weeks to three months, not an insignificant commitment for a company our size.
- Since hitting our BHAG, we've added short-term and long-term incentive plans that enable team members to share in the short- and long-term success of the business.

Any one of those on their own is probably not an incredibly strong UVP, but taken together, they create an exciting package for a potential hire. To generate this list, we've asked ourselves, "What are the best-in-class companies doing? How can we do better?" We know those companies are trying to recruit the same candidates we are.

The UVP you generate for your own recruits will probably be unique to your business and maybe your industry. Keep in mind, not all perks need to be expensive. In any industry, there are things you can do that cost your company nothing but add huge value to your employees. For instance, flexibility over schedule and freedom to work from home cost nothing monetarily but might be hugely important to people on your team. Training is another major value-add that doesn't need to cost you a lot (more on that soon).

By getting creative and considering your team's quality of life, you can market your company with a UVP that gets them truly excited to come on board.

Recognize Excellence

Once you've got star recruits on board, don't stop taking care of them. Provide your leaders with support and recognize excellence when you see it.

Although it's not my natural inclination to go searching for excellence and giving "attaboys," I've realized a handwritten thank-you note makes a huge impact on someone's day. We're blessed to work with people who put a ton of effort into what they do. When we recognize and call out their excellence, they feel validated and affirmed. Their energy is renewed because their efforts are *seen*.

> People's energy is renewed when their efforts are seen and validated.

In the past, this had been a blind spot for me, so I've asked some of my leaders to help me proactively recognize excellent performance. We've even worked it into some of our company's rhythms. Every Monday morning, we gather as a company to share "wins and lessons learned." During the "wins," people give shout-outs to team members who did something great. "Lessons learned" offers us the chance to share how we're iterating our work and growing by identifying areas for improvement.

It is *so powerful* for someone's excellent work to be shared, to broadcast a shout-out from a client, or to highlight a team member's embodiment of a core value.

If you've done the hard work of recruiting and securing A-players to join your team, make sure they know how much you value them. Words of affirmation and shared celebrations are powerful ways to validate your stellar people.

Now that you now know how to get yourself out of the way and attract star recruits, here's the final step in firing up those rocket boosters: become a training organization and equip your leaders to excel.

Step 3: Be a Training Organization

Why is it important to train people? Couldn't a true A-player just figure things out on their own?

We're going to answer that with a story.

When we first interviewed Sawyer, he told us, "I'm happy to be an individual contributor. I'll give you everything I've got, and I'll do a great job. But I never want to be a manager."

That surprised us, because Sawyer had listed managerial experience on his CV. "Why don't you want to be a manager?" we asked.

"Well, I've had bad experiences," he admitted. "I feel like I didn't do a good job."

When asked to explain more about his experience as a manager, Sawyer said that it was a high-pressure environment. His boss told him what to do, and when his team didn't get the demanded results, he had to be the one to tell his people they were being let go. He had no authority of his own to form strategy or make decisions, and yet he was stuck delivering the bad news to people he'd built relationships with.

"Did they give you any training?" we asked. "Any support?"

He shook his head. "No."

"And you couldn't go to bat for your people or make decisions on their behalf?"

He shook his head again. "It felt like my hands were tied. So, *that's* why I don't want to be a manager."

Yeah, no wonder, we thought. Clearly, he'd felt burned by the experience. At the same time, we could tell that Sawyer would probably be a great leader, provided he had the right support.

Over time, as Sawyer got used to the culture of risk3sixty and learned about the kind of strategic freedom we give our leaders, he began to realize being a manager with us would look very different than his past experience. His level of responsibility gradually increased, and he seemed to thrive. Eventually, he raised his hand to be a manager.

Now, Sawyer is one of the best leaders we have and a member of our executive leadership team. It's a testament to the effort he's put in, but it's also a byproduct of the culture we've established, where leaders are trusted to make decisions and supported and coached when they make mistakes.

None of that support just "happens." It's cultivated through deliberate training.

The best organizations in the world consider themselves training organizations. Think of the military, or GE back in the day—these big institutions place a huge emphasis on training, because without it, companies outgrow their people. If you don't help your team level up, they won't have the necessary skills to keep pace.

> Without training and helping your people level up, your company will outgrow them.

The alternative to turnover is *employees who can level up* to the increasingly complex challenges that arise. Provided you give them the right support, you'll see plenty of your people rising to those challenges. Consider that many team members probably *want* to be promoted; they *want* upward momentum. If you give them the chance to develop and grow, they'll take advantage of opportunities to become better versions of themselves and help drive the organization forward—instead of leaving to find those opportunities elsewhere.

We've built learning and development infrastructure to support training throughout our organization, at the company-wide, department, and individual levels:

Company-wide

- We provide **company-wide training weekly** through our "Lunch and Learns," which encompass everything from semi-annual security training, to benefits, to effective communication and leadership training.

- We bring our entire team in for **quarterly team meetings** during which we present the state of the business to the team and provide training opportunities to teach them about our different departments.

- We've created **training infrastructure**, like an HRIS platform that enables our department leaders to set up customized training programs for their people, based on their roles.

- More generally, company leaders also set training **strategies** and **policies**, and they bring in the **tools** to facilitate training.

Department

- Department and practice leaders create **department-based training plans** for their people based on their roles. For example, one of our technical developers will have a different training plan than a marketing associate.

- We also have **team-based training plans** that are even more specific to what someone might do day to day. If an associate joins our offensive security team for instance, there's a training plan in place to help that associate skill up.

Individual

- Each individual also has their own **personalized goals and development plan.**
- Employees interested in growth opportunities can also go through our **leadership development program**, which we'll say more about in a moment.

These various training programs ensure there are constantly people leveling up their skills and rising into leadership so that as we grow, we have people ready to take on new challenges.

What happens if you invest in training your people and they leave? As the saying goes, what happens if you *don't* train them and they stay?

This prospect has never felt like an issue for us. Training craftsmen is one of the blades of our flywheel; we know that we have to train our team to be great if we hope to become a great organization. If they leave, they can go be great somewhere else. They may eventually become customers some day! We can't control that. We just know that if we want to be a world-class organization, we need to provide world-class training.

Leadership Development

A few years ago, we realized something puzzling: Our very competent consultants weren't magically transitioning into very competent managers. In fact, they were struggling.

"This is on us," we said to each other. "We can't expect people to make this leap on their own, from being an individual contributor to a skilled leader. If we want to grow our organization and keep the culture strong, we need to come up with a leadership training program."

Our goals for the program were threefold: help future leaders in the company develop personally, help them develop professionally, and ensure the quality of leaders at our company remained in line with our vision.

I took on developing this program along with Jessica, our VP of People. We both are Army vets and West Point grads who have participated in many different leadership training programs. Based on our combined experiences, we put together the Journeyman Program for our consultants.

"Journeyman" riffs on the craftsmen term we've embraced at our company. In ancient times, a master craftsman was someone who had worked in the craft for a long time and had proven expertise in producing uncommon quality. A person studying the craft was known as an apprentice, but once they had demonstrated enough skill and understanding, they became known as a journeyman. That title signaled their commitment to pursuing the still-higher title of craftsman—and eventually master craftsman.

We liked the notion of a journeyman program sitting in between "apprenticeship"—what we would call the individual-contributor level—and "craftsman." It implied a transitional time of learning, with a focus on growing into a higher level of expertise and leadership.

The Journeyman Program runs for six months, with a new cohort starting every January. Our directors nominate people they see demonstrating leadership potential to participate, but ultimately, every individual must volunteer to do it themselves. We want our future leaders to have a personal interest in being educated on leadership and desire a change in mindset. We tell people, "Step one of being a leader is you *want* to be a leader."

Not everyone who completes the program gets a promotion; in fact, probably only 30 percent become managers within twelve months of graduating. However, the program *is* a prerequisite for anyone who hopes to be promoted from within.

The lessons participants learn will help them develop as leaders in every area of their lives. We explain at the start of the program that anyone who wants to be a leader can be, whether of themselves, their peers, their clients, or their families. No one needs to bestow that title. Becoming a leader starts with a shift in mindset: *I am a leader because I choose to be a leader and choose to bear the responsibility of leadership going forward.* By the end of the program, they've learned a lot about leadership and also about themselves. That's not just good for our company; it's good for our people—moving us out of the Black Hole and into that Good Business stratosphere.

If you are interested in developing your own leadership development program and need a place to start, we make our Journeyman curriculum freely available on the risk3sixty website. We could go on and on about the different ways we work to build up our people—but we know that, to some extent, you'll need to discover your own best practices. One thing we can tell you confidently: Without finding, elevating, and training great people, we would never have grown beyond the Black Hole; we couldn't do it alone.

Good Fruit of the Good Business

When we sought to scale up and build our team, we wanted to build a place where people could start a good life. We wanted to enable them to build a launch pad for their thriving—to find stability, experience an oasis of positive culture, and be able to invest in their futures. Well, we are now seeing the fruits of that work.

Our team members are buying homes. We have less than 5 percent voluntary turnover. We're even experiencing a risk3sixty baby boom. Some bosses might balk at the prospect of 25 percent of their staff going on parental leave in the same year—but the two of us couldn't be more delighted.

We can say that for two reasons. Number one, we're *able* to do it. We're not going to die as a business. As we'll explore in the next chapter, thanks to our leadership team and all the systems and processes we've worked hard to implement, we're going to manage just fine.

But more importantly, *this is what we wanted.* We wanted to provide a bigger and better future for our team and a high quality of life for everyone involved—not just financially but also personally and qualitatively. We wanted *the Good Business.*

These signs of our team members' thriving seem like confirmation that we've built it. We've sought to build up our people, and now they're building the business.

Best of all, they're building up their lives as well.

Actions You Can Take Now

1. Step 1: Clarify your role and delegate the rest!

   - Consider our Compounding Work Framework to clarify your highest and best use.
   - What are you currently doing that you should be delegating and not be doing?
   - What are the key requirements of your role?
   - If you hired someone else to fill your role, what would you stop doing?

2. Step 2: Build your leadership team. Consider:

   - What are the key roles needed now?
   - Can someone be coached and promoted into that role, or do you need an external resource?
   - What are your hiring criteria for key leaders?

3. Hire A-players. Develop a UVP for future team members:

   - What's in it for them?
   - What are the multiple points of value that, when packaged together, create something truly unique and hard for competitors to replicate?

4. Set your organization's training priorities:

   - Top organizations are training organizations. Where can you create business impact through training?
   - Who is responsible for training in your organization? What are the standards?
   - How are you developing leaders?

CHAPTER 10

IMPLEMENT SYSTEMS AND PROCESSES

A Manual for Going on Vacation Without Everything Falling Apart

Narrated by Christian Hyatt

> *"The best companies have documented systems and processes which enable you to hire ordinary people and empower them to do extraordinary things."*

> —Christopher Johnson (CEO, The Johnson Group, Inc.)

My work has taken me to some interesting places. Once, I was visiting a town off the Mississippi river, doing a security assessment for a new client...who happened to have a *mine*. Traveling to the center of the mine wasn't originally on our agenda, and it had little to do with our work helping the company's security team. However, I am a firm believer that if someone asks you if you want to see the inside of a mine, the only proper answer is a resounding "yes!"

My guide talked about the intricacies of blasting rock for maximum utility. Holding up a small amount of C-4, no larger than a quarter, he explained, that depending on how it was applied to the tunnel wall, it could have wildly different results.

Applied superficially, it would barely make an impact. Applied strategically in the form of a shaped charge, it could do an incredible amount of damage to the rock. Why?

Focused energy.

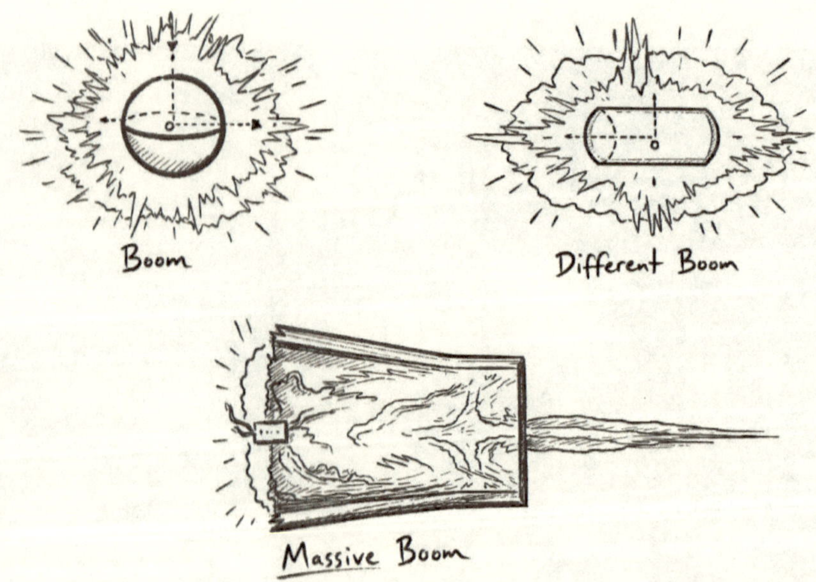

The same goes for your team. You can either let them run in different directions, or you can carefully harness their energy to accomplish a clear mission. With that focused energy, anything is possible. But many organizations lack systems to create that focus and execute the vision.

That's the problem, isn't it?

As leaders, we often have a vision for what we want, but we rarely take the next step and design systems for people to help us. We've had the same problem as risk3sixty has grown. To help, we invented a five-part Management Operating System (MOS). Each part requires the leader to clearly define and put into action critical elements of the vision.

Why You Need a Management Operating System

Recently, we heard thought leader Dan Martell, author of *Buy Back Your Time*, say, "Your first $100,000 is from skills; your first $1 million is from hiring, and your first $10 million is from systems." That is true, in our experience. In order to grow the Good Business and scale ambitiously, you eventually must shift from relying on raw talent to establishing strong systems.

If the business depends on a group of rock stars pulling off completely unique and stellar performances day in and day out, it can't grow beyond them. Somehow, you need to empower others to grow into leadership positions and create systems with baked-in expertise.

In other words, make yourself replaceable.

Everyone should be replaceable.

That sounds harsh, but it's simply pragmatic. Let's say one of your employees goes on maternity leave or gets sick and needs to take PTO. Who's stepping up? If your business relies upon any single strand or person, it's unstable. It works while that rock star is operating. But in their absence, you need other people who can do the same work at a comparable level. Basically, everything for every single function needs documentation so that another team member can slide into that role and take over for someone else.

> If your business relies upon any single strand or person, it's unstable.

Creating repeatable systems and processes is part of building long-term sustainability and continuity for the business. It also increases your *enterprise* value: No one wants to buy a business where the CEO still sends invoices. A healthy, self-managing business operates just fine even when a key individual steps away.

In our own efforts to move in this direction, we started by trying to make ourselves less important.

Now, I actually feel worried if I'm the only one who can do something. Even though one of my current focuses is building brand equity, I don't want to be the only one doing that! We're working to promote other voices from risk3sixty to speak on public platforms as well.

Think of your business as a living organism. Ideally, it will be self-healing, rather than healed by external parties. When everything you do flows from good processes and systems, people naturally pick them up. Even if a key employee were to exit without warning, your processes should be so embedded into your business operations that the next person has no choice but to pick up where the departing employee left off. That's sustainability.

One way of building redundancy is to automate what can be automated. Generally, tools and technology are less expensive and more predictable than people. For example, we implemented a low-cost HRIS system early on, which helped us automate things like payroll and tax payments. Without that technology, we would have needed to hire outside vendors or consultants to help with HR tasks or hire an in-house employee. But with that automated system, we scaled to over $10 million in revenue with just a single person, Jessica, heading up our HR department. That was possible because we had an amazing leader in that role, adopted the tools and technology to assist, and equipped other leaders to take an active role in supporting and supplementing her.

As our company evolved and our HR needs became more complex, we upgraded our license within the HRIS platform to get consulting hours. That way, if Jessica ever ran into an issue she didn't know how to solve, she had experts to consult. That was an incredibly low-cost, high-value way to scale most of our HR functions.

On the finance side, QuickBooks provided similar automation. For a long time, we used it for everything from invoicing to bookkeeping at a very low cost. Eventually, we hired bookkeepers on a fractional basis.

You still want rock stars, but you also want those rockstars to be able to go on *vacation* without your business falling apart.

So, what's required to build systems and processes that coordinate efforts and enable someone to step away? Specifically:

- *Who* will do the work?
- *How will it* be done?
- *When will* follow-up happen?

Those points are all answered by building a Management Operating System.

Components of the MOS

One of the hardest jobs as an entrepreneur is mustering the courage to clarify a vision for your team and give them tools to act on it. Think about it: It takes courage to tell your team, "This is the strategy, here is the plan to execute the strategy, and I'm holding you all accountable to it." But that kind of clarity, courage, and conviction is exactly what people want from their leaders.

And, believe us, the people around you are begging for leadership—even if you don't realize it. They want someone to paint a clear target, encourage them to hit it, manage conflict head on, establish an ethical standard, and make hard decisions.

If you haven't taken the steps to be clear with your team, that is exactly what the MOS provides. After we implemented ours, it propelled us to double in size every two years. It also helped us reduce turnover and adapt more nimbly to industry changes and our fast growth.

The MOS begins by identifying a shared **purpose**, moves on to aligned **values**, and then clarifies individual **roles**. Those three points cover *who* and *why*. From there, we get into the **rhythms** of coordinating information, and then we end with **goals**: that's the *when*, *what*, and *how*.

Here's how I guided leaders to reflect on these five points in my book, *Security Team Operating System*:

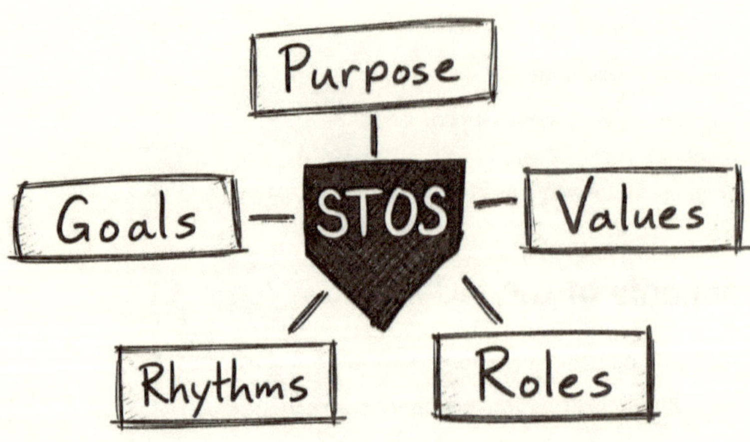

We've already covered purpose and values extensively in this book. If you've stayed with us this far, you know to set a BHAG, clearly define your values, and ensure that every member at every level of your organization is operating accordingly. Now, let's take a closer look at each of the other points.

Roles

Narrated by Christian White

"Hey, commander, you're dead."

That's the kind of thing I heard in a "Next Man Up" drill during military training. The facilitator would announce an untimely demise, saying, "The commander's dead. Continue the mission."

The exercise is meant to test the team's resilience if their leader is suddenly gone. Do they know who's second in command? Does that executive officer know how to step up and take over leadership? Have they been sufficiently prepared and equipped with the mission's strategy and planning?

In battle, these were very real scenarios. If we hoped to succeed, we needed to know our own responsibilities inside and out, but we also needed to know how to flex when others were taken out of commission. The Next Man Up drill could easily become our reality, and no one wanted to be caught unprepared if it did.

The roles element of the MOS takes some of that same philosophy on preparation and continuity and applies it to business: Ensure the *right* people are doing the *right* job to accomplish the mission.

> **Roles:** Leaders ensure the right people are doing the right job to accomplish the mission.

These are the necessary elements:

- Clarify key functions, processes, and owners. *Who is doing what?*
- Clearly define each person's role, along with the KPIs to measure their work. *How will you know the job has been done well? Define what success looks like in each role.*

- Provide team-wide transparency. *Make sure everyone's on the same page.*

We use a tactical tool called a RACI to communicate these points to our team. Spelled out on a chart:

Responsible: the person doing the thing

Accountable: the person who will answer for the thing being done or not done

Consulted: the people who have a say in the process

Informed: the people who need to be made aware of any changes or updates in the project's completion

As our business has grown, we've created RACI charts to help people understand who does what within the business. The charts also help us plan ahead for assignments if we know someone will be out: We clarify the "next person up" if the primary person is absent.

Rhythms

Rhythms refers to our cadence of sharing data and having regular meetings to coordinate strategy, ensuring everyone's on the same page.

Rhythms: Make sure everyone's on the same page.

Here are some examples of our regular company rhythms:

- Weekly tactical all-hands meeting
- Weekly department-level and team-level tactical meetings
- Weekly executive leadership team meeting
- Weekly company-wide training
- Bi-weekly one-on-ones
- Quarterly on-sites

We also have a cadence of data sharing and updates that facilitate clarity and accountability. Between our roles and rhythms, there's a regular and predictable flow of communication.

Here's how Christian stressed the importance of rhythms in *Security Team Operating System*:

> Rhythms create flow. They create predictability for teams. The best teams use rhythms to ensure every team member has the right information at the right time on a predictable cadence. This reduces the need for ad hoc meetings and constant information gathering, and it creates an environment where every team member knows exactly what to expect. Rhythms are the heartbeat of your team.

Keep the lifeblood of your organization pumping. Use regular rhythms of information sharing throughout your organization to make sure everyone stays on the same page.

Goals

We've talked about harnessing the team's collective energy to accomplish a clear objective. That's *exactly* what you're able to do with strategically nested goals. Here's how Christian made the case for goal setting in *Security Team Operating System*:

> *Goal setting is most powerful when the leader can rally the entire team around a single objective. Often, team members will set great goals, but the goals are often ad hoc and chosen on a member-by-member basis. The result is a jumble of disjointed efforts that fail to help the security team accomplish its most important team objectives. To practice goal setting successfully,*
>
> 1. *Understand the company's biggest objectives.*
> 2. *Align the security team's objectives to the company's objectives.*
> 3. *Set team level goals to help accomplish the security team's objectives.*
> 4. *Set individual goals to help accomplish the team's objectives.*

The best security leaders get these four priorities right.

We devoted Chapter 5 to teaching you how to do this, because you want to start this process of nested goal setting as soon as possible, even in your startup phase.

As you evolve into a much bigger company with multiple practice areas, departments, teams, and so on, communication can easily break down, causing a diffusion of energy as people work on unrelated initiatives.

Think of that kid's song: "The shoulder bone's connected to the backbone. The back bone's connected to the hip bone. The hip bone's connected to the leg bone..." That's how you want your goals to stack up.

As you scale and dial in your systems, your accountability measures need to get even tighter and more consistent. To do that, we follow a simple maxim: inspect what you expect.

Accountability isn't just about hovering over people and making sure they're getting their work done. It's a way to *honor* and *validate* the work our people do. We want them to trust that if they do great work, they'll be recognized and rewarded for it. And yes—we also want them to be aware that if they're bringing our organization down, they're going to get a "C-" on their report cards.

> Accountability mechanisms ensure you *honor* and *validate* the work your people do.

So, what do we base our accountability mechanisms on? At this stage in our company's growth, we've dialed it in:

1. **Everyone has a number.** In other words, each person knows what KPI they're being held accountable to. This starts at the top with the executive leaders, who report on the KPIs that they own monthly. That holds *them* accountable to those numbers, and in turn, they're holding their team accountable to the numbers they're responsible for.

2. **Hold twice-yearly performance reviews.** We have formal reviews baked into our annual calendar every six months, which serve as consistent reminders that clarify each team member's priorities and maintain accountability.

3. **Align incentives.** People aren't just held accountable to their goals verbally; their variable compensation and bonuses are also tied to whether or not they hit their goals. They have skin in the game, motivating them both professionally and financially. When they succeed, they're rewarded for it. That keeps our team members happy and our steady growth humming.

Because of the coordinated elements of the MOS, there's no mystery about hitting these goals. The roles piece of our operating system ensures that each person's job description has a description of what success looks like. Our rhythms ensure there's regular quarterly review and tracking.

We've talked about our coordinated Management Operating *System*; now, let's talk about some of the *processes* that ensure everyone has the information they need, exactly when they need it.

Knowledge Management Processes

In a small company, knowledge management doesn't need to be a thing. It's not a big deal if someone does their job intuitively or carries most information about their role in their head. Client files are easy enough to keep track of because there aren't many of them. If a particular piece of information needs to be found, a small team can quickly resolve that issue.

But once an organization gets bigger, it's a major problem when everyone does things their own way.

> When everyone in the organization does things their own way, a minor issue for a small company becomes a major issue for a big company.

As your company, team, and client work grow, you need processes to keep track of everything. *Organize* knowledge so that everyone knows where to find necessary tools and documents. *Communicate* knowledge so that everyone stays on the same page.

By developing knowledge management processes, you ensure clarity and efficiency among leaders, the team, and clients. Here's the way we think about organizing our knowledge management.

Organizing Knowledge

There are three main categories of knowledge your company needs to organize.

1. Policy

Yes, policy is boring. People almost never read the fine print, and it usually lives in some rarely accessed company manual or shared drive. But, when you need it, *you need it.* Policies enable your firm's governance through clear standards. They're not worded tactically but rather articulate your intent to the rest of the team. For instance, "Team members are expected to conduct themselves with professionalism when dealing with clients."

2. Procedures

Procedures define *how* to do something. They're more granular and specific than policies. For instance, if we were to write procedures for professional conduct with clients, we might state:

1. During a video meeting with a client, have your camera on.
2. Wear professional attire (dress to the level of management) during all client interactions.

Your language around procedures should provide specific guidance on successfully implementing the policies.

3. Standard Work Instructions

These are the detailed instructions necessary for successfully executing a task. For instance, a team member preparing to host a video client meeting should be able to open that task on your project management software and see a link: *Meeting Agenda Template*, which provides specific instructions for planning and execute a successful meeting:

1. Email client meeting agenda in advance of the meeting. (Click here for an email template.)
2. Review notes on previous meeting with this client; follow up on any relevant notes.
3. During the meeting, address [A, B, and C....]

Standard Work Instructions should be housed as *close* to the relevant task as possible, so that they're easily referenced at the relevant moment. **Templates** should also be used as a key support for these instructions. No one needs to reinvent the wheel; just reference the template.

Communicating Knowledge

When it comes to knowledge management, effective communication also deserves its own hierarchical flow. Here's how we structure ours:

- **Executive leaders** should be informed about decisions related to firm strategy and organizational structure.
- **Department-level leaders** need to know how strategy decisions specifically impact their department.
- **Firm-wide announcements** address changes that impact everyone.
- **The outside world** receives marketing updates or any information that highlights the quality of work you do.

Our **training procedures** reference our procedures and standard work instructions, but the training process takes that information from the page to the person. For example, if one of us was coaching someone—let's say on a consulting engagement—we'd go through a three-stage process:

- **Do for:** The first time around, the manager does the task, letting the new staff person observe and ask questions. Working through the task checklist, the trainer models how to find the relevant information to complete the engagement.
- **Do with:** The second time around, the manager and new team member do the task together. The new hire takes the lead, with heavy coaching from the manager, practicing until they get the hang of it.
- **Observe while they do:** The new hire "graduates" when the manager observes them successfully doing the task on their own, allowing the trainer to step away and stop supervising, though they might still offer feedback as needed.

Any growing organization needs to formalize the "tribal" knowledge inside the head of a single person. To equip ordinary people to do extraordinary things, your extraordinary people need to distill their knowledge into an ordinary checklist.

If you want to equip ordinary people to do extraordinary things, get your extraordinary people to distill their knowledge into an ordinary checklist.

When our rock stars build a process, then coach others to do what they're currently doing, they're able to elevate in their own role. A wonderful byproduct of this baton-passing is increased trust throughout the team. The leaders have actively invested in the people coming up behind them, creating shared understanding and camaraderie. The newer hires see examples of what it looks like for a leader to pass the torch. When it's *their* turn to serve as a coach and pass on information, they'll remember how they were invested in and follow suit. In this way, we've watched our culture collectively strengthen.

"The Most Relaxed I've Ever Been"

Narrated by Christian White

I used to sit at the dinner table every night with my family, but I wasn't really there. My mind would be thinking about work: tomorrow's to-do list, people issues, worries. The same thing happened when I went on "vacation." Maybe my laptop wasn't open, but I'd still be working remotely. Then, the guilt came in. I was missing precious moments with my family. We'd built this business to be free, but sometimes it felt like an inescapable prison.

Have you ever felt like that?

A lot of entrepreneurs we speak with say they can't escape the business they've built. We felt the same way—until we implemented the systems we've described in this chapter. Since then, I've been able to clock out for a month-long sabbatical.

And the sabbatical was *fantastic.*

My wife and I road-tripped with our kids down to Florida. We rented a house near the beach for three weeks. It was the longest stretch I'd ever had with my family where I was completely removed from the business and wasn't worried about it.

We spent a lot of time at the beach. There was a waterpark that the kids loved. I took the boys out kayaking on one of the lakes. Rachel and I got a lot of one-on-one time, going on dates and grabbing coffee. I woke up early every morning to go running on the beach.

Around the third week, it really hit me: I didn't need to be anywhere, at any time, or do any particular thing.

It was the most relaxed I'd ever been.

I returned to work feeling incredibly refreshed. And—one unexpected benefit—I held off on jumping back into all my old responsibilities. I delegated the duties permanently. Prior to the sabbatical, most of my work was with clients. I was very much working *in* the business, rather than *on* the business. And to be honest, it was creating a bit of a bottleneck with client service.

But with all those old tasks delegated, I had the chance to rethink how I could add the most value. I began doing more work *on* the business, focusing especially on coaching leaders and empowering others to problem-solve, rather than doing all the problem-solving myself. The sabbatical was transformative. Not only did it help us scale; it also prompted me to evolve and become a more effective leader.

Every risk3sixty employee gets a sabbatical after they've worked with us for five years. As founders, our five-year marks came first. But every year since, we've watched other key leaders do the same. It's amazing to watch how those leaders tighten up their systems and processes to prepare for their absence. They train other people to take over the work, write things down, and shore up continuity with even greater thoughtfulness, because they want to fully embrace the sabbatical benefit.

They want to clock out and know everything's going to be fine.

Because of the team, systems, and processes we have in place, it is.

When we started the whole thing, we wanted *freedom*—over strategy, over our finances, and especially over our time.

That's what we've found, on the other side of the Black Hole: *freedom* to leave work at five o'clock, go home, and be present with our families. *Freedom* to turn off our phones and shut down our email. *Freedom* to go on vacation.

We've also found *freedom* to pursue opportunities for our own growth. If there's a great mastermind group we want to attend for a week, no one misses us. We can go to leadership development sessions and bring back tons of new ideas to the company, because we're *able* to step away. In our next chapter, we'll explain how targeting your own growth as a leader is the next step in helping your company level up.

As a result of these freedoms—*freedom* in trusting our leaders, *freedom* to get out of the way—we also now have the *freedom* to scale way beyond $10 million.

And that is exactly what we want for you.

Once you have the infrastructure of a strong leadership team and coordinated systems and processes, there's no limit. Forget about the Black Hole. You've rocketed far past it.

Now, you just need to make sure your rocket stays intact.

Actions You Can Take Now

- Document your MOS. Download and complete the template using the link provided.

- Review your knowledge management. Where do can you tighten things up? How can you organize knowledge more effectively?
- Schedule a sabbatical! Get it on the calendar, even if it is a year or more from now—you won't regret doing it. Enjoy the freedom your systems and processes provide and allow your team to step up. The experience will not only give you a break; it will also enable you to level up as a leader.

CHAPTER 11

UNLIMIT YOURSELF

Elevate Yourself to Elevate Everyone Around You

Narrated by Christian White

"Your level of success will rarely exceed your level of personal development, because success is something you attract by the person you become."

—Jim Rohn

"How many of you think you deserve to be happy?"

That was not the question we expected Gino Wickman to posit at his Entrepreneurial Operating System conference.

We expected the author of *Traction* to discuss nested goals, quarterly rocks, or meetings—anything that lined up with the content of his books. Instead, he got all *deep* on us.

"Seriously. Raise your hands. Who here thinks you deserve to be happy?"

There was an uncomfortable silence. A few hands tentatively rose, but the vast majority of the audience kept their hands down—including us.

Gino shook his head in disbelief. "I feel bad for all of you. Why would you *not* deserve to be happy? That's a self-limiting belief."

My brain easily supplied a few answers: *Not worthy. Don't deserve it.*

"If you're not getting therapy, you need to." Gino nodded decisively, then doubled down. "Every entrepreneur needs *seven* years of therapy." Several of the other featured speakers were sitting near the front, illuminated by the stage lights—all of them huge successes in their own rights. They nodded emphatically.

"Do you think you need therapy?" Christian whispered to me.

"Maybe? I mean—I guess so. *Gino Wickman* is saying this."

"I bet I need therapy," Christian said. "We might have self-limiting beliefs."

"That we don't even *know* about," I added.

Both of us left the EOS conference with new ideas to level up risk3sixty. But one of the biggest takeaways was that we needed to level up *ourselves.*

Despite any misgivings we may have had about "self-care," we concluded that investing in our own leadership was the *un*selfish thing to do because of the positive impact that would ripple out to our family, friends, community, and business.

After that 2021 conference, we began a multiyear journey of investing in mastermind groups. I joined YPO (the Young Presidents' Organization), Strategic Coach, and Chad Willardson's Platinum ELEVATED group. Christian joined Vistage, a monthly CEO group. We both joined the Simple Numbers Mastermind. Not only have these groups helped us grow as leaders; they've also provided a critical source of community among other CEOs and founders, easing the loneliness that often comes with being a senior leader.

And yes—I invested in therapy, which has been game-changing. In fact, I'll say it's the *single most significant factor* in my growth as a leader and human being. It is the hidden work, the inner work, that manifests in the output. It's changed every aspect of my life for the better.

There's a common understanding in business that every growing company will eventually outgrow every person on its team, unless they intentionally grow, evolve, and level up along with the business. We've talked about this concept with regard to your employees—but not as it applies to *you.*

In a bootstrapped company, there's no one telling you—the founder—about your limitations as a leader. Nobody will point to the CEO and say, "The business has grown beyond you, and you need to move on." But the truth is, if you don't take action to develop *yourself,* the company will outgrow you. Or, perhaps even worse, you will limit the company's growth.

> You must evolve yourself if you hope to continue growing your business.

We've given you a number of key strategies to scale beyond the Black Hole and accelerate your growth. Even so, no company can grow beyond an immature leader.

Has your growth plateaued? Ask yourself the following self-assessment questions:

- Does your company have a coordinated system of nested goal setting?
- Have you niched down your company's offerings and amplified your message to the marketplace?
- Do you have a strong leadership team in place?
- Are your company leaders starting to build out and create more structure for their own teams?
- Do you have systems and processes in place that are working, including for sales and marketing, even if they're still rudimentary?
- Do your numbers show relatively predictable growth?
- Do you have rhythms for effective communication?

That's just a short list, but in many ways, those are the easy boxes to check. They describe impersonal, strategic levers.

The harder boxes are the ones that require *you* to evolve:

- Have you built intentional self-awareness around leadership shortcomings?
- Who is mentoring you? Do you seek out help and wise counsel?
- How have you invested in your personal growth and development?
- Have you invested in therapy and/or mindset coaching?

The two of us have tried to grow personally since we started our business, but we struggled to make it a priority in our early days. There was so much to do just to get the business operational. It didn't feel like we had the space to think about anything beyond getting risk3sixty off the ground.

But once we began scaling, a bit more space opened up. We'd established a great management team, and we had systems and processes in place. At that point, we began asking ourselves, "What's next? How do we level up from here?"

And Gino was ready to supply an answer: "Get therapy."

In other words, the continued evolution of our company started with *us*. Christian needed to envision an even bigger and better future for our team. I needed to initiate elevated conversations around our operations and leadership development. There was *more* required from the two of us.

Which meant we needed others to help us find it.

The first piece of outside wisdom to permeate was simply that we *needed* wisdom. We're not sure either of us would have had the self-awareness to recognize independently that we might be holding the business back. It was only by hearing the message enough times, from enough respected people that we concluded, "Huh. I guess maybe I *do* have some growing to do...even if I can't necessarily perceive how."

As we've leaned into our personal growth, so many lightbulbs have gone off. When we have a self-limiting belief or a dysfunctional habit, it trickles down to others. But productive beliefs and habits spread too. By investing in ourselves as leaders, we elevate *every* conversation we have with the people around us. We can help others on our team identify their own self-limiting beliefs, because we've done work on ourselves and have tools to share. We also have more internal space and awareness to navigate emotionally fraught conversations.

> When you invest in yourself as a leader, you elevate every conversation you have.

Leaders have a *tremendous* impact on the people in their orbit. We owe it to our teams, families, and wider communities to become the best leaders we can be. And your continued development is essential for your business to scale.

Grow Beyond Self-Limiting Beliefs

A well-known entrepreneur in Atlanta gave a memorable "fireside chat" about his leadership journey, and it made an impression on us.

"We were running the business so fast, and growing even faster. I was trying to do everything at once. I was down in the weeds, but also trying to lead from above," he explained. Then he paused.

"I ended up putting myself in the hospital—for months," he admitted. "My body forced me to slow down. It just stopped functioning properly."

His story was shocking—all the more so because we recognized aspects of his pace in our younger selves.

"The tank is bottomless!" we used to claim. We took pride in our 4:45 a.m. founders' meeting. Couldn't we go forever? Couldn't we grit our way indefinitely? Maybe, except we began noticing cracks and fissures forming. The early meetings took a toll on our bodies—and on our families. We struggled to maintain the energy to be present with our teams and then go home and be present with our kids. As much as we hated to admit it, the grind was becoming too much.

We started hearing stories about other entrepreneurs who—like this Atlanta CEO—put themselves in the hospital due to burnout, anxiety, and running their bodies into the ground.

His story took a positive turn, though. He ended his talk by explaining, "That's when I started getting help. I began exercising regularly. I changed my schedule. I began *taking care* of myself so that I could continue to lead my business."

That's the answer—not just personally, but professionally. Self-care is integral if you want to grow to $10 million and beyond. You can't grow the business past your own limiting behaviors and beliefs.

> You can't grow a business past your own limiting behaviors and beliefs.

Here are just a few ways your self-limiting beliefs can manifest:

- You hesitate to invest money in your own growth unless you can clearly see an ROI. If you invest $25,000 in a mastermind, you feel like you need to get *more* than $25,000 out of it. You struggle to trust you're inherently worth investing in.

- Self-care strikes you as selfish and unnecessary. Why would you get 8 hours of sleep, make time to work out, or take a vacation?

- You're not able to help other people on your team identify self-limiting beliefs, because you haven't learned to recognize your own.

- You tend to self-sabotage. When things start going really well, you don't trust the success—and sometimes, you wreck it. It's hard to believe you deserve success or happiness.

- You function with an "upper limit." You have an idea in your head of what your limit is or what's good enough, and it feels scary to venture beyond that. You feel more comfortable when things are still a little chaotic or dysfunctional.

- You're "successful"—financially—but you hate your life. You might even take pride in your misery, stress, and fatigue, as a hardened "gritty" person.

- You work constantly. Any time you're not working, you feel anxious. You experience disconnection with your family and friends because your head's always in another space. You also feel guilty taking time off.

Think about the ripple effect of any one of these scenarios. You could implode, taking everybody down with you. You might have an explosion in the office and lose trust with people. You might make a rash decision that leads to major damage. These self-limiting beliefs impose constraints on everything you touch—and even destroy things.

That's why self-care is your *responsibility*, not a luxury. It's an imperative for healthy leadership. And self-*investment* is fundamental for scaling up to your Good Business. By 10X-ing yourself, you pave the way for the business to grow up behind you.

> Self-care is one of the most important responsibilities of your leadership—it's an imperative.

Granted, we know prioritizing self-investment is a challenge, especially if you're still in the earlier stages of running your business. But there are ways to incorporate rhythms of self-care, even when there's not a lot of breathing room. Start by orienting yourself toward sustainability, instead of the triage room.

Play the Long Game

Rule number 1 in the Entrepreneur's Self-Care Playbook: If you're going to bootstrap the $10 million company, you need to play the long game. Live in a way that's sustainable, with rhythms that you could maintain indefinitely.

The concept of the "business athlete" drives this home, which relates the stress of corporate leadership to pro sports. Think of some of the all-time great athletes, like Tom Brady or LeBron James. These guys were so good, *for so long*. They maintained an incredible level of athletic mastery, even when they were considered "old men" by professional sports standards. LeBron, at age forty-one, is the oldest active professional basketball player in the NBA, and he's still killing it. Tom Brady was the starting quarterback in Super Bowl LV when he was *forty-three*—and his team won.

How did they do that? They were disciplined in taking care of themselves. Tom Brady is famous for eating well, getting massages, and doing everything possible to help his body perform at the peak of success. LeBron sleeps *ten* hours a day. Not six; not eight—*ten*. These guys knew that if they wanted to outpace and outlast their competition, they had to do things differently.

The same is true for you. If you want to perform at your best and stay in this for the long haul, you've got to think about what's sustainable. What are good *practices* that you can implement, which will give you an edge over time?

Here are some healthy practices you can incorporate into your routine, even when things feel crazy:

- **Practice energy management.** Figure out how your energy flows throughout the day, then structure your day accordingly. For instance, if you think best in the morning, shoot to reserve that time to do your deep work.

- **Schedule thinking time.** Maybe this is only an hour during your hair-on-fire seasons; maybe it's an entire day, once a week, that you devote to thinking strategically. As a leader, if you are not doing the deep thinking to drive long-term strategy—no one is.

- **Build in recharge time so you can best serve others.** One of the most exhausting aspects of leadership is creating space for other people who have emotional needs. If you don't create space to refuel, you won't be able to show up for others. Take mini breaks to restore your equilibrium, so that you're not losing your temper during a meeting or shortchanging people.

- **Take a "recharge" day at least once per quarter.** Fill your tank by taking a day to go on a solo hike or head to the driving range. Give yourself permission to take time to rest. In doing so, you'll be reinforcing the healthy mindset that *you are worthy* of happiness and self-investment.

Early on, you probably won't be spending five or six figures on masterminds or professional development opportunities. But scheduling a think day, meeting with a small group, or taking vacation time is available to anyone. Know that the time invested will pay back dividends of renewed clarity and better energy.

Building the Good Business is a marathon, not a sprint.

Building the Good Business is a long-term endeavor. You need sustainable habits that will fuel a marathon, not just a sprint.

We're going to spend the rest of this chapter sharing our own methods of self-investment. These practices enable us to show up at our best, so that we can be the leaders, family members, and "elite business athletes" our communities need.

The 5-F Model

Narrated by Christian Hyatt

"Christian, you're the most coachable guy on the team," my wrestling coach told me one day.

Talk about a backhanded compliment. In other words, *Christian, you're not bringing a whole lot of natural talent, but you're good at receiving coaching and applying it.*

I always thought this remark was funny, mostly affirming, and the tiniest bit insulting. But it's true. I wasn't naturally the best wrestler, but I worked hard, listened to people, tried to discern their wisdom, and then applied the good advice. This discipline got me to the state championship in high school, and it's helped me build a Good Business as an adult alongside CW, who has the same "coachable" attitude that I and many other successful entrepreneurs share.

After absorbing around four decades' worth of coaching, I have found that life and leadership work best when leaning into five F's: faith, family/friends, finances, fitness, and fun. I've used this method of evaluating my life and goal setting for the last ten years, and I convinced CW to adopt it too. Let's unpack each one together.

Faith

For some people, faith relates to philosophy; others call it spirituality. CW and I are both Christians and belong to wonderful church communities, respectively, and faith is a big part of our lives. Whether you're a religious person or not, there's power in believing in something greater than yourself, allowing us to reflect on and strengthen the principles that guide our lives. My faith, for instance, has given me clarity around my principles and guides me to live with humility and gratitude.

> There's power in believing in something greater than yourself.

I have found this mindset to be a difference maker in the business world. Quite frankly, many business leaders seem unhappy. They're over-indexed on activity and ambition but often underinvested in faith. Perhaps that's because there isn't an obvious monetary return. Spending the day on a business-related strategy session feels like time well spent, whereas spending the day thinking about one's philosophy, faith, or beliefs feels more nebulous.

The problem is, when we neglect tending to the core of our lives—our inner selves—we end up empty.

Like me, many business leaders may also fall into the trap of being control freaks. Fierce independence and self-reliance may not sound like bad things, but if you can *only* believe in yourself, that becomes a breeding ground for anxiety, egotism, or emptiness.

Whether you're willing to admit it or not, some things *are* out of your control. Faith can interrupt the pull of extreme self-reliance in a very freeing way by giving you something bigger to believe in. Anchored by this understanding, we've been able to find a much greater sense of peace and happiness in our lives.

Family and Friends

Your "why" for starting your business might have had a lot to do with the kind of life you wanted to create for you and your loved ones.

So, don't accidentally sacrifice your family or friends in the process of making your business successful.

If you hope to *enjoy* success and scale up your Good Business over the process of several years, it's important to find rhythms that prioritize the closest relationships in your life. In fact, the main reason the two of us finally moved our 4:45 a.m. meeting was to better accommodate our families.

As a friend of CW's likes to say, "No success that you can have in business can compensate for failures in the home." It's such a great reminder. As entrepreneurs, we can easily grind so hard and get so preoccupied with work that we forget why we're doing it in the first place—for the people we love.

> "No success in business can compensate for failures in the home."

As the founder of your business, you get to make the rules. Ask yourself: *Why am I doing this?* As seasons change, we change the rules.

Think about all the ways your business intersects with your family's lifestyle. You have the power to make adjustments that are good for your family:

- You can move meetings around to better align with your family's schedules.
- You can ensure your spouse approves of your business partner.
- You can adjust your take-home pay to ease financial stress.
- You can be considerate of the level of risk you expose your family to.
- You can choose to be unavailable when you get home. Silence your phone and stick it in a drawer. Don't open your email.
- You can discuss travel requirements with your spouse—how long you stay away, how often you go.

Keep your marriage happy, show your kids they matter, and remember that they spell love T-I-M-E. Make decisions as a family about all the things that *affect* your family.

Friends are a key piece of this relational category too—and this is another area where many entrepreneurs find themselves underinvested. Who has time for friends? A lot of friendships can simply drift away when you're in the intensity of the startup phase. My wife, Lauren, used to tease me about this, saying, "Oh wait—that's right. You don't have any friends."

"I have friends!" I'd protest.

"Do you have any friends *outside* of work?"

She'd have him there. "No..."

But guess what?

You can make new friends!

Even better, your friend-making efforts can dovetail with other aspects of your self-investment. When you level up your network and join professional organizations, you'll often form friendships with people who share similarities in your stage of life and professional journey. Or you can form friendships through hobby groups, rec sports, book clubs, or church.

It's refreshing to have trusted relationships where you're not the boss. Forget about strategy; forget about deliverables or outcomes. Friendships outside of work mean you can get real with people about the *other* aspects of your life that are equally important.

Audit Your Inner Circle

One of the best ways you can invest in your own growth is by elevating your inner circle. If the people around you are negative and pulling you down, those voices will influence you. To get to the next level, you may need to change your influences. This is one reason we've endorsed masterminds and positive communities like those you might find at church. But consider that you may need to *leave* one community to plug into a better one.

Level up your network, your advisors, and the people you associate with. Sunset relationships that steal your joy and take your energy. This is easier said than done—sunsetting even a mediocre relationship is difficult. I approached this by making myself less available, politely declining invitations when I knew the environment would be negative. It was hard to work through, but on the other side, it's felt completely liberating.

A courageous conversation can lift you up in ways you couldn't before. Build relationships with the people who inspire you and shift away from those who want to keep you in the dirt.

Finances

Narrated by Christian White

I have read *a ton* about personal finance, and all that reading has yielded one major takeaway: The way you handle your personal finances has to work for *you*. Everyone has an opinion on how you should do it, but at the end of the day, if a personal financial plan doesn't align with your goals and values, you won't stick with it.

Keep that in mind as you read our tips. They've worked well for us, but you may decide you want to adjust them to better suit your preferences.

As a successful entrepreneur, you have two choices when it comes to handling your money:

1. Be the expert.
2. Hire a good advisor and understand how they get paid.

If you're incredibly knowledgeable about personal finance and have a calm demeanor, you may not need an advisor in this area of your life. But if not, a good advisor can significantly add to your well-being.

What should you look for in a financial advisor? You want them to be a good fit—ideally, you'll get along and feel confident in their advice. But even more importantly, you want a *fiduciary* advisor who is on the same side of the table as you—someone whose compensation and legal obligation are tied to giving you financial advice in *your best interest*.

Surprisingly, many so-called "advisors" in the financial world are not fiduciaries. They may appear to be knowledgeable about personal finance, but they get paid a commission for selling you a financial product. They're *salespeople* with financial certifications that enable them to do what they do. Rather than being incentivized to do what's best for you, they're incentivized, through commissions, to get you to invest in one of their products.

A fiduciary advisor, on the other hand, usually gets paid by a fee, based on assets under management. Their interests are more aligned with your own, because their compensation increases as your assets increase. We'd recommend getting expert advice from a fiduciary financial advisor if you feel any insecurity about your personal finances. They'll help you build your financial strategy and discipline.

With that said, there's plenty of room to build your financial strategy on your own.

Whichever path you choose, we'd *discourage* any bootstrapping entrepreneur from building a lifestyle and budget around anticipated company earnings or dividends, which are based on business profitability. This can put you at odds with the business, encouraging you to *under*invest or make short-term decisions that run counter to building a Good Business over the long haul.

If you're trying to build the Good Business, you need to be patient, take care of the business, and in doing so, take care of your family all along the way. If you are prudent and live off your *salary*, rather than relying on dividends for consumption purposes, you'll live more modestly and better protect the business and your family at the same time.

We'd also recommend bootstrapped entrepreneurs consider something we call "The Founder Protocol."

The Founder Protocol

Both of us practice what we've coined "The Founder Protocol," based on some of the unique needs that founders have related to personal capital allocation. This is an idea intended to shore up your personal financial health and wealth.

Here's the protocol:

Save 4x months of operating expenses outside the business to de-risk and complement the 2x months of operating expenses within the business. Keep these funds in low-cost liquid securities, cash and/or cash equivalents. This provides liquidity and optionality, both of which are extremely important for the bootstrapped entrepreneur.

Use your dividends to do this. If your journey is like ours, it may take several years to build this initial permanent capital base. As you continue to grow the business, your permanent capital base will need to increase along with the operating expenses of the business.

We recommend this to entrepreneurs for the following three reasons:

1. Learn personal capital allocation and the discipline of not living off or relying on dividends to fund your lifestyle. This is a very boring exercise in patience and is like watching paint dry. But, this discipline will help you make better business decisions that prioritize long-term value creation over short-term cash distributions. As Thomas J. Stanley describes in his classic *The Millionaire Next Door*, rich is what you see; wealth is what you don't see.

2. De-risk the business by building up cash reserves outside it. Remember, as a founder, you are the lender of last resort.

3. Build out a mechanism to achieve a form of personal financial independence. You took and shouldered risk to build a bigger and better future that benefits your whole team and all of your clients. This is the personal benefit to you and your immediate family for that risk taking and value creation.

We're not advising you to pinch pennies like Scrooge. You want to *balance* prudence and saving with thoughtful spending. That's why we encouraged you to pay yourself a market rate, back in Chapter 7. If you think of how your money can help you *solve problems*, often, that mentality will guide you to spend or invest money wisely, without falling into the trap of "flaunting riches."

> Use your money as a tool to solve problems; don't just hoard it.

Beyond the Founder Protocol, which has a defined purpose to it, we don't advocate hoarding your money in a bank account, where it won't even keep up with inflation. Make it pay for itself. Money will constantly depreciate in value, so use it as a tool to solve real problems, like your child's education, or getting a personal trainer or a therapist.

Finally, as Gino Wickman says, "If you want to make six figures, don't do $25-an-hour work." As the years have gone on, I've calculated my hourly rate. If a task is below that hourly rate, I delegate it. If it's *above* that hourly rate but there's risk involved (e.g., tree and chainsaw) or special expertise needed, most likely I'll still delegate that to someone better qualified.

Fitness

Fitness is both physical *and* mental. If you want next-level growth, find someone to push your fitness beyond your perceived ceilings. The most elite entrepreneurs we know have therapists, personal trainers, or both.

I want sustained energy throughout the workday, able to engage in hard conversations with gas in the tank. For those reasons, I makes physical fitness a priority—and I know I'll make way more progress if I have someone holding me accountable, so I works with a trainer three times a week.

I don't have to think about what exercises to do; I just show up at the gym. Over time, years, my whole body composition has changed. This expert has enabled me to get beyond my own plateaus, and in turn, upped my mental resilience as well.

Working on physical fitness also helps mental fitness. They work together holistically. I tend to think more clearly after a good workout, and I'll often feel an increase in positive energy after a breakthrough in therapy.

Yes, therapy. The idea of going to therapy would have made me cringe during my crawling-through-the-mud-days as an infantry officer in Ranger School. Growing up, I always thought therapy was a bad thing. It was stigmatized; if you needed therapy, that meant you were crazy or weak. But as we've explained, the most successful entrepreneurs endorse it for a reason. It's a game changer.

By electing to put yourself in a context like therapy or a mastermind group, you *open* yourself to challenging your thinking. You might have gotten the same advice in a passing conversation and ignored it. But when you've paid good money to receive counsel, you're more receptive to wisdom. If you do that frequently and regularly, you're in a constant state of refinement and growth—and that's going to give you an edge.

> By electing to put yourself in a context like therapy or a mastermind group, you *open* yourself to challenging your thinking.

Fun

Narrated by Christian Hyatt

Create space that will allow you to enjoy yourself.

And yes—you need to give yourself *permission* to do that. Does that feel hard? Here: We're giving you that permission. It's on your "Five F's To-Do List": Learn How to Not Become a Miserable Bastard.

I literally plan fun into my life. I don't accidentally enjoy things. I have to consciously and forcefully plan to have fun. If goal setting works in our business, why wouldn't it work in our personal lives? Here are some of the ways I take fun seriously:

- At the start of every year, I set goals exclusively concerned with having fun.
- I plan vacations.
- I bookend my workday with things I like, helping me look forward to every day and maintain positive energy all the way through.
- I remind myself not to live life in silos. Fun should infuse every other "F." When these categories overlap, like a Venn diagram, life feels more balanced and meaningful.
- If something feels like work, I try to figure out a way to make it fun. When I felt too tired to play with my kids after work, I went to Target and bought the best Super Soaker guns they had—ones that *I* wanted to play with. *Now,* I was excited to have fun with the kids, even after a long day!
- When I'm stressed, I make little lists of ways to change things up. One recent list had things like "take a day off and go hiking"; "go to Rosemary Beach, rent a house, and stay for two months"; and "work somewhere off the wall for a day."

Take fun *seriously.* Leading a business is draining and stressful. If you're not having fun along the way—what are you even doing it for?

We want to share one final thought from our experience to unlimit yourself and invest in your personal growth and development.

Elevate

Do you think you deserve to be happy?

Back in 2021, we didn't raise our hands. We didn't even know *why* we had that self-limiting belief. But if someone were to ask us that question now, after the years we've invested in personal growth—we'd absolutely raise our hands. We wouldn't need to think twice.

A lot has happened between then and now. In many positive ways, we are not the same people we were before.

The limit of your success will be your investment in yourself. We know that may not seem obvious, especially in the earlier stages of your business. You think there are so many other things you should be doing—but what will eventually help your business grow is developing *yourself*.

Consider this short story, shared with me by an entrepreneur friend of mine, who was in Denver recently, trying to fly home, and the weather was terrible. He was sitting on the plane, wondering if they were going to be able to take off. His phone was pinging with texts from friends whose flights were getting canceled. Out the window, he could see workers trying to de-ice the wings, getting pelted with snow and blown around by the wind.

Eventually though, they were given approval to take off. The plane taxied forward. It sped up—and then they were airborne. It was a *rough* flight climbing up through the storm. But after climbing for a few minutes, suddenly, they got above the cloud cover. Up there, the weather was beautiful. It was clear. He could see the sunshine on the tops of the clouds. At cruising altitude, the atmosphere and the ride was different.

He shared that his experience on the plane is like the life of an entrepreneur. Sometimes, your perspective is just what you see in front of you, and you can't see the way out. But if you're willing to go through the effort of de-icing the wings, taxiing down the runway, and battering your way through a turbulent climb—you're going to get to a much better place. The whole time, that much better place existed, but it existed above the cloud cover. You were on the ground, stuck in the snow. You couldn't see it—but that's where you're going.

If you're stuck on the ground in the snow, or getting hammered on the turbulent climb, find the support you need to get yourself above the clouds. When you elevate yourself, you elevate everyone around you to a much better place.

Actions You Can Take Now

- Take an inventory of your five F's over the past twelve months. How are you doing in each of these categories, and how do you want to drive change over the next twelve months?
- Audit your inner circle.
    - Who is part of your inner circle? Who has access to you, and who can influence you, your mood, mindset, and energy on a regular basis?
    - Of those, who are the negative influence bringing you down, seeking to keep the status quo, not supporting your wildly successful progress, or killing your energy and vibe? Write down a plan to sunset those relationships if you truly want to level up your life.
    - Who do you want to *add* to your inner circle? Why? Document a plan to bring them into your inner circle.

WORK *ON*, NOT *IN*

Make the Highest and Best Use of Your Time

Narrated by Christian Hyatt

> *"If you're going to apply higher levels of teamwork in your life, you'll need to relinquish control over how things get done."*

> —Dr. Benjamin Hardy

I had been down in the weeds all day, doing work I knew I probably shouldn't be doing. I got back to my office and shut the door, feeling stressed and anxious.

I woke up my computer and opened my inbox. There were fifty-eight unread emails.

I minimized my inbox and opened up Google instead. I needed some source of inspiration—something that could help me zoom out and remember what was important.

I typed: *What should a startup CEO be doing?*

A list of results populated the screen. I read the first couple of articles, which were lame. Then, I landed on one titled "The Second Job of a Startup CEO" by Ali Rowghani.[5] It had been published by Y Combinator, a famous incubator for startups.

It was good. *Really* good. As I read through it, I began to feel a burden lift. *This* was clarifying.

"A CEO's first job is to build a great product and find a small group of people who love it and use it enthusiastically," the article stated.

Okay—we've done that, I thought. *We have great product/market fit.* "A Phase 1 startup CEO is the Doer-in-Chief," the author wrote. That was validating. I *had* been the "Doer-in-Chief" until we had a great product and a stable, growing client base.

But we'd crossed that threshold a while ago. Now what?

The article continued:

> As a Phase 2 CEO, you need to transition from "Doer-in-Chief" to "Company-Builder-in-Chief." This is how you scale as a CEO, and CEO scaling is the first step in company-building. For most founders, this is very difficult. When you've been a successful Doer-in-Chief, it's hard to stop. It's

---

[5] Ali Rowghani, "The Second Job of a Startup CEO," YC Startup Library, accessed September 9, 2024, https://www.ycombinator.com/library/3k-the-second-job-of-a-startup-ceo#footnoteid2.

hard to stop coding, designing product specs, and interacting with customers on a daily basis.

I thought of my morning: I'd been interacting with customers. Reviewing contracts. Designing product specs. *Yes*, I agreed. *It is very difficult to stop DOING.*

> "You need to transition from 'Doer-in-Chief' to 'Company-Builder-in-Chief.'"
>
> —Ali Rowghani

Rowghani proceeded to lay out three jobs for the "Phase 2" startup CEO (paraphrased here):

1. Hire a great leadership team and make sure they're rowing in the same direction. *Okay, we've done that*, I thought. *Check.*
2. Create purpose and alignment. *Mission to Metrics, nested goal setting, and the Management Operating System*, I thought. *We're clear on where we're going, and we've got the metrics to achieve it.*
3. Build a strong culture based on shared values. We were in good shape on culture and values too, both having invested in codifying our values throughout the company building up our leadership team.

The article wrapped itself up, but mentally I added a fourth job for myself:

4. Brand equity—tell the world about risk3sixty.

That meant white papers, blog posts, LinkedIn articles, podcast interviews, working on a book... I mentally affirmed spending time on those things.

Then, I brought myself back to the day at hand. As a "Phase 2 CEO," what did the company need from me most, *today*? With these four jobs clearly identified, my responsibilities suddenly seemed tangible. Doable. Clarified.

THAT'S what I'm supposed to be doing, I thought.

On days when I find myself back in the weeds—because those days still *do* happen, despite the best intentions—I reread that article as a good reminder of what I should be working on.

"Working *on*" is exactly the point, in fact. At this stage in your company's evolution, you should be working *on* the business, not *in* the business. It's no easy mental switch for the CEO who's spent years bootstrapping from the ground up.

As you graduate from a "Phase 1 startup CEO" to a "Phase 2 CEO"—leading your company's scaling journey into the Good Business—here are some specific pointers for thinking above and ahead of the rest of your company to lead its continued evolution.

> Think above and ahead of the rest of your company to lead its continued evolution.

Prerequisites to Working ON the Business

It's easy to pontificate about "working *on* the business"—we hear other entrepreneurs throw that phrase around at masterminds all the time. But it's not always clear what that means. When do you make the shift, and what needs to be in place for it to happen?

There are some prerequisites to take care of. As the "Second Job of a Startup CEO" article implied, there's a first job. Until your first job is satisfied, you'll still function as Doer-in-Chief.

That first job is figuring out your product/market fit. This was the focus of Chapter 6. Even for companies that have already nailed the niching down process, as the market landscape shifts, products or services may need to evolve too. Think of all the ways the worldwide pandemic in 2020 forced businesses to rethink their approach to the market. Whenever your product/market fit gets off track, it's time to shift your attention back *into* the business.

We didn't need a pandemic to force a shift in the product/market space. In our case, the issue was a predictable and boring one: plain ol' market competition.

We used to do a lot of simple compliance audits, but two of our major competitors worked to automate the process and ended up driving prices into the ground. We realized we shouldn't try to compete in the simple compliance audit space anymore. That meant turning our attention back *into* the business and revamping our offerings to clients.

We spent the better part of a year rethinking our product suite and how to go to market. We also rebranded and identified a new ideal client profile (ICP). Our focus as a company turned to helping sophisticated and complex organizations <u>comply</u> with any security framework, <u>optimize</u> their program through AI, and <u>secure</u> their program through proactive security services. Even though it meant working *in* the business instead of *on* the business, we had to do it.

Hold this prerequisite in mind: If your product/market fit is off, your first priority as CEO is to straighten that out. And yes, this may involve getting into the weeds with your team.

> Your first priority as CEO is to ensure strong product/market fit. That may require getting into the weeds with your team.

Speaking of team, that's the second prerequisite before becoming a "Phase 2 CEO": You need a strong leadership team in place to take over the "doing" throughout your organization. That's why we devoted attention to building up leaders in Chapters 9 and 10. It's theoretically possible to get beyond $10 million without a leadership team you can trust, but we don't recommend it. We know another CEO who runs a $35 million business—but he still doesn't have confidence in his leadership team. No surprise: He is overworked and stuck in the weeds.

Once you have a great product/market fit and a strong leadership team, it's time to evolve to Phase 2.

A Phase 2 CEO Needs a Different Set of Skills

Narrated by Christian White

When you started your business, you were an excellent practitioner. You were the *expert* at doing the particular thing your company is known for.

Now, you have to give up a piece of your identity. Your company doesn't need you to be a subject matter expert anymore; it needs you to be the leader and visionary. We've heard it said, "You've got to give up to go up."

> Give up to go up.

But how? You either learn to love things you've never done before, or you just have to hate it for a while.

But listen—haven't you done that already in the process of building your business? When we were battling the sleet in Pittsburgh, doing contract work in the shadow of Mordor, we were miserable. But we loved it at the same time! We built camaraderie through the adversity, and the level of suckiness was almost funny.

You've hustled. You've been flexible. You've practiced positivity. You've evolved yourself as your company has grown. *You know how to embrace the discomfort* required to develop new skills.

> You know how to embrace the discomfort required to develop new skills.

Expect to be bad at first. You will hate delegating. You will feel awkward putting together leadership development programs. You will try nested goal setting and then discover all the mistakes you made at the end of your first quarter.

But you're in this for the *long haul*, and you will get better with time. The other day, I was talking to my son, who wants to get better at soccer. "Put ten cones out in the yard every day," I instructed him, "and then dribble between the ten cones. Do that ten times. Then, go out the next day and do it again. Every day, get your ten times."

It was one of those parenting moments where you hope your kid realizes the lesson is about life, not just soccer. "You know what? Most people will do that for one or two days, and then they'll stop," I said. "But the people who do it every single day, rain or shine, *those* are the people who become elite at what they do."

There have been seasons when we had to embrace the suck of learning new skills. When we first started our company, I had expertise in military leadership but none in cybersecurity. I had to grind and learn about being a cybersecurity practitioner for around three years, until the business had grown enough that I could shift into working within my highest and best use.

For Christian, it was almost the opposite. He *was* the subject matter expert in our early years. His painful evolution came when he had to learn to delegate responsibilities he enjoyed and was good at. But as he stuck with it, he discovered new strengths. It turns out he's an even better leader than he is a practitioner. He just needed some time to develop those skills.

Show up every day and do the work. The growth will seem almost invisible; it's like winning in the dark. Nobody pays attention to your backyard dribbling, until one day when you tear down the field and someone asks, "Whoa—how'd you get so good?" They are surprised, but you are not. You were there putting in the work when no one was watching.

As the saying goes, any "overnight success" is usually ten years in the making.

For us, it's been a decade and that feels about right.

> You win in the dark. Any "overnight success" is usually years in the making.

So, let's talk about these new skills you need.

Do Less, Not More

Entrepreneurs often assume they need to do *more* to get to the next level.

Actually, you need to do less.

Embracing grind-culture undermines your impact by preventing you from showing up as the best version of yourself. If you can effectively manage your energy, on the other hand, giving your team the best of what you've got to offer—you'll make the most of your leadership.

You don't have to enter into every problematic scenario. In fact, if you've hired well, your leaders will do a better job solving those problems than you would.

"The Second Job of a Startup CEO" ends with this succinct advice:

> **Reaching the point of having a lot of unscheduled think time is perhaps the clearest sign of success for a Phase 2 CEO.** It suggests that you have hired a leadership team, delegated the day-to-day activities to them, and codified Mission, Strategy, and Metrics well enough for them to operate effectively without your daily involvement. Your reward is the bounty of time to think and plan the future of your startup. (Our emphasis)

By stepping back, we ensure our business is self-managing and open up more space for our own creative thinking. It's unstructured and deeply productive.

"But who has *time* for that?!" If you're still running around with your hair on fire, or if you're used to leading a funded company functioning on someone else's timeline, that's a fair question.

Remember, though: The bootstrapping CEO has more freedom over their time. Our growth horizon is indefinite. Even our next BHAG is four years off. That means we're not functioning with an artificial sense of urgency, frantically trying to achieve overnight success. *Steady*, sustainable progress is okay.

Are you doing less, with greater impact? Have you opened up space in your schedule for deep thinking and unstructured creativity? That's a clear sign you're evolving into a Good Business CEO.

Lead, Don't Manage

We operate based on a model of three levels of initiative, which you'll remember if you scanned the QR code from Chapter 9. The first level of initiative is "wait to be told what to do"; the second is "ask for permission and then take action." Those are largely the people that *managers* are working with: team members functioning on the first or second level of initiative.

Managers must inspect what their direct reports do. Alternatively, they model the correct work and then have their direct reports repeat their example. They may need to supervise work more closely to ensure it's done to satisfaction.

The third level of initiative is "act and then report it's done." People at this level can absorb your intent and complete the mission. *Leaders* work with people who have achieved that third level of initiative. They cast vision and ensure people know their intent, enabling others to internalize the overarching mission and then problem-solve in alignment with it.

You are free when you have a leadership team that allows you to lead in that way.

There may be times when you step back into *managing* for a time—for instance, during a restructuring period as people learn new roles. However, you should ideally be moving toward *leadership*, exclusively. You're coaching managers, guiding directors, and tightening up systems, but you're not actually *managing* anyone.

When you lead rather than manage, you increase the enterprise value of your company by guiding it toward *self*-management. A business will be more attractive to a buyer if they recognize the CEO can step away for a time, and everything can still function smoothly.

Do Not "Do"

Working within your highest and best use should be your number one goal, and that should be what everyone else in your company is moving toward too. This is a defining characteristic of an elite Good Business: You don't have people trying to wear sixteen hats anymore.

Remember the Compounding Work Framework? When working to offload tasks from your plate or your top leaders' plates, those tasks should define the requirements for the new job posting. Don't hire someone just because you think you need a person. Hire someone whose skills and abilities and passion is doing a specific set of tasks, further freeing you to focus on Compounding Work.

Let's say the number one thing you want is uninterrupted focus time. When you block off time for deep thinking or to lead a meeting, you want protection from interruptions and pinging notifications.

So, that becomes priority number one for your executive assistant. They're answering your phone, sorting through your emails, and protecting your calendar. As a result, you can now spend just ten to fifteen minutes at the end of the day reading your emails, rather than sorting through one hundred as they flow in.

Many entrepreneurs fall into the trap of thinking, "I'm so busy—I just need *someone* to help me. I don't even know what I need help with." They'll hire someone and hope it works out—but that's a gamble, at best, and could result in wasted time and money.

Instead, find the "who" to do what you do, giving you the freedom to evolve into the best possible leader you can become.

Drive the Vision

What *can't* you delegate?

If you break apart the "who, what, where, when, why, and how" of your company's work, you, as leader, determine the why and the where. Everything else can be delegated—the right "who" can easily carry out the what, when, and how.

But *you* determine the purpose of your organization, and where you're going to go as a company. Only the founder can drive the vision. As you evolve into that "Phase 2 CEO," casting vision is perhaps your primary responsibility.

From there, you can empower your other leaders to carry out the mission. *They* can manage the methods for implementing the vision and help shape the timeline for its achievement.

> Only the founder can drive the vision.

Take the Hardest Problems

If empowered to do so, your team will become increasingly good problem-solvers. Any unscheduled problems that get boiled up to your level should be the most pressing and challenging ones.

We sometimes get called in to solve client issues, especially if there is a misalignment issue for some reason. We're looking to untangle the disconnect and find opportunities to get the relationship back on track. Beyond problem-solving, we also validate the client as a valued customer. Typically, if a founder gets involved, a frustrated client is likely to feel respected and seen. That's the type of bigger challenge worthy of your time.

Train your team to solve issues at their level. Show them they have your trust to make decisions, which will help protect your attention and time.

In addition, provide guidance for when they should escalate a problem to your attention. The military uses a filter called Commander's Critical Information Requirements

(CCIR), clearly stating when information should be immediately shared with the highest level of leadership and how to handle less urgent problems.

What would that filtering system look like for your organization? Providing this sort of clarity for your team will increase efficacy and trust across the organization.

Weigh in on the hardest problems and trust your team to handle the rest. If you can dial in your focus, you will have a greater impact in everything you do.

> Water can cut through steel, but only if it's laser focused. Work on fewer things, but with greater impact.

Time Management

Christian's problem was with how to allocate his time. That's the issue that drove him to the Google search bar one anxious afternoon.

This question haunts many business leaders. There's only so much time, and we want to make sure every minute counts—but that's easier said than done. Even in this book, we've charged you to make "the highest and best use of your time."

So, what does that actually *look* like?

We're going to get granular as we take a deeper dive into time management. As executives and entrepreneurs, we've found it helpful to block time-bracketed tasks into our calendars. This has helped us intentionally plan to do the majority of our work with compound impact, and practice smart energy management.

Our calendars look different. For instance, Christian likes to work out at the end of the day, but I exercise in the morning. Christian tries to block off one or two entire days during the week to do "deep thinking." I, on the other hand, know that my mental energy starts to trail off after noon, so I reserve my mornings for all my high-impact stuff: deep mental work, or key meetings requiring skillful collaboration. My afternoons open up to meetings that are less cognitively demanding, or admin tasks.

We've tailored our calendars to work with our different energy needs, preferences, and the needs of our business and families. But both of us practice time bracketing by breaking our calendars down into four categories: self-investment, coaching leaders, revenue-generating and/or scaling activities, and "battlefield circulation."

Breaking up your time into categories is certainly not the only way to structure your time, but we've found it to be both efficient and flexible. It ensures we're functioning in the highest and best use of our time, while still giving us freedom and flexibility. Let's break our bracketing process down:

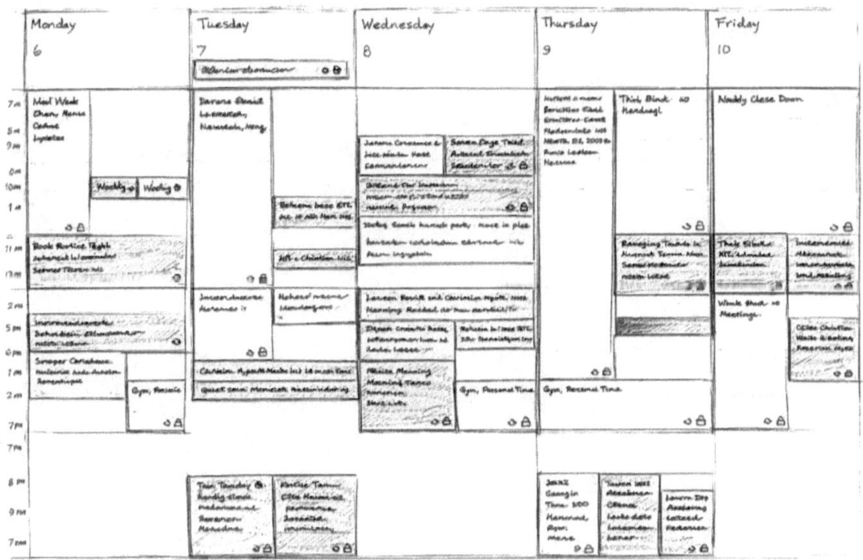

20 Percent Developing You

Narrated by Christian Hyatt

Twenty percent of your time should be devoted to self-investment: developing *you*. We made a case for this in our previous chapter, but we want to get into the specifics of how that might translate to your calendar.

Self-development time includes anything that either (a) helps you *maintain* mental and/or physical fitness, or (b) helps you *grow* as a leader, thinker, visionary, and founder.

Here's how I have labeled some of my "self-investment" activities:

- (On Monday mornings) "Ideal work plan"
- Think block—no meetings
- Personal brand: LinkedIn, newsletter, writing
- Gym, personal time
- (On Friday mornings) "Weekly close down"

You can customize your self-development time however you'd like. In general, we recommend prioritizing the following three development areas:

- **Generate new ideas** through CEO networks, masterminds, think time, coaching, and reading.
- **Gain clarity** through reflecting, writing, processing, and goal setting.
- **Meet new people** through attending lunches, networking events, and/or speaking events. Building your network will help with idea generation and can also turn into new prospects, clients, future team members, etc.

More on the "generating new ideas" piece—as an entrepreneur, I can't overstate how important this is. Most people spend their days doing a lot of the same activities over and over. Their tasks are familiar, which means they're not doing a lot of new thinking; probably 80 percent of their days are spent doing the same kind of thinking they did the day before. But an entrepreneur should be seeking to *flip* that ratio: Ideally, 80 percent of your time should be spent engaging with *new* ideas, and only 20 percent would be "same thinking."

To be clear, "thinking differently" is no small challenge. Pushing yourself to constantly think in new ways is *hard*. That's why we recommend this time allocation. If you don't devote the time, who else on your team will bring the new thoughts?

30 Percent Coaching Leaders

Narrated by Christian White

Thirty percent of your time should be devoted to coaching leaders. On Christian's calendar, this category includes tasks like:

- One-on-ones
- Executive team meetings
- Communicating the vision meetings
- Skip-level meetings

Anything I do with our Leadership Development program would also fall into this category.

By this point in the book, we hope you can recognize "Coaching Leaders" as one of the highest and best uses of your time. *Only* through your team of leaders can you ensure everyone keeps rowing in the same direction.

Not all "coaching" will occur in meetings, by the way. One of the most powerful tools you have at your disposal for incentivizing your team is compensation. If you tie an incentive plan to some of your coaching goals, you'll see people work toward them with increased motivation.

When we sit down with our leaders, we help them think through ways to spread that motivation ripple effect. We discuss ways they can implement incentive plans, carry out delegation, elevate their own development, and grow as leaders.

Highly competent leaders will always have opportunities to go elsewhere. Invest good time developing your leaders and helping them achieve their goals. Not only will this enhance their efficacy, thereby strengthening the team as a whole, but it will also keep them happy, which is part of building a Good Business.

40 Percent Generating Revenue and/or Scaling Business Operations

Forty percent of your time should go toward generating revenue—and/or helping your business scale, so it can make more money.

That might sound crass, but "making money" isn't about greed. It's about creating the bigger, better future for every person on your team, enhancing the value you bring to the market, and building financial freedom for yourself.

Since we have two founders, I focus on scaling business operations, while Christian devotes more of his time toward revenue-generating activities. On our calendars, those time blocks might be labeled:

- Speaking engagements
- Recruiting leaders
- Allocating capital
- Strategy sessions
- Working on our unique value proposition to the marketplace

Many of the big business decisions we need to make fall into this category. If it relates to revenue, that's part of this 40 percent. If it relates to team building—and, therefore, scaling—it's also part of this 40 percent.

Another time commitment we'd put in this category is creating strategic partnerships. As company founders, we have access to other business leaders whom most other people on our team wouldn't. For instance, Christian as CEO might be the only person who could get a meeting with another CEO—and that meeting could lead to a valuable strategic partnership.

It's a common saying that you should *only* do the things that *only* you can do. Our time in this category should be devoted to *high-level* strategy and operations—as should yours.

10 Percent Battlefield Circulation

We've got 10 percent left. What's it for? Battlefield circulation.

That's another military term, which describes being available to your team. If you're a military leader, there's crucial information you'll only absorb by circulating among your soldiers. You'll get a sense of their morale, hear their questions, reinforce the mission, and clarify your sense of how everything is going.

We prioritize this use of our time in our business as well. Talking to associates, conversing with people about their projects, getting to know new team members and hearing about what they observe—this is a hugely valuable use of time. Doing this circulation is like taking the pulse of the organization.

The Good Leader

It's not easy to be the founder of a bootstrapping company—especially one that needs you to evolve faster than it scales. But there are specific steps you can take to set yourself up for success. Invest in yourself; invest in your leaders. Do the things that only you can do, especially when it comes to revenue generation and scaling operations. Stay connected to your people through battlefield circulation. And make sure you're surrounding yourself with other elite players who can offer you resources, new ideas, wisdom, coaching, and camaraderie.

When you care for yourself and strategically move into the highest and best use of your time, you're living your identity as a Good Leader.

And that's the *final* piece of building the Good Business.

Actions You Can Take Now

- Are you currently in Phase 1 or Phase 2 as a leader and founder? Where does the business need you most? Let your answers guide your actions today and inform your continued evolution as you seek to meet the future needs of the business.

- Write down the top three things you should stop doing, based on your role; document a simple plan and timeline to delegate those tasks to a competent person who can take them to the next level.

- Audit your calendar. Document how and when you spend your **time** and your best **energy**. Consider:
    - What are the most important four buckets for where you create maximum impact?
    - What are the best time blocks of the day and best days of the week to lean into your highest and best use?
    - What do you need help with, or could you delegate if you had the right "who" for it?
    - Draft the job description for the next hire who will free up your time to focus on your highest and best use.

WHEN YOU KNOW YOU'VE ARRIVED AT THE GOOD BUSINESS

Narrated by Christian Hyatt

"You, your demeanor, this place. I don't know for sure. But I get the feeling you're doing exactly what you want to be doing. I assume you asked the question at some point, and this place is the result."

—John Strelecky, *The Cafe on the Edge of the World*

The Reverend Fred Craddock was a remarkable preacher from my home state of Georgia. And while he may have been imagining things, he says that the following story is true.

Dr. Craddock was visiting his niece. There was this old greyhound dog there, just like the ones who race around a track chasing those mechanical rabbits. His niece had adopted the dog to prevent it from being euthanized because its racing days were over.

Dr. Craddock strikes up a conversation with the dog:

"I said to the dog, are you still racing?"

"No," he replied.

"Well, what was the matter? Did you get too old to race?"

"No, I still had some race in me."

"Well, what then? Did you not win?"

"I won over a million dollars for my owner."

"Well, what was it? Bad treatment? Were you abused?"

"Oh, no," the dog said, "they treated us royally when we were racing."

"Did you get crippled?"

"No, I'm healthy."

"Were you starved?"

"No!" the greyhound said proudly. "I was fed like a king!"

"Then why?" Craddock pressed, "Why?"

The dog answered, "I quit."

"You quit?"

"Yes," he said, "I quit."

"Why did you quit?"

"I just quit. Because after all that running and running and running, *I found out that the rabbit I was chasing wasn't even real.*"

And that about sums it up, doesn't it?

Often in life, we work ourselves to the bone, neglecting the things in life that matter the most. Things like faith, our family, and our community. We watch our marriages fall apart, our kids become adults, we miss good meals, deep conversations, and opportunities for connection and warmth with the people we love.

We are distracted. Physically present, but absent. And then one day, often far too late, we wake up from the trance and realize that we missed it all. We missed it all.

Chasing rabbits that aren't real.

But that doesn't have to be you. You can choose to do things differently. To make a life for yourself, for your family, and for your team that is truly meaningful. That is built on real things. You can truly enjoy the gift of life throughout the process of building.

And if this book offers one thing, besides a look behind the curtain on what it takes to bootstrap a Good Business, besides opportunity to pause and consider what you are setting out to build, we hope it is the encouragement to keep going and a reminder to enjoy the journey along the way. I hope we have planted this seed and offered a roadmap for how you might approach the adventure of business building in a better way.

The Day We Hit $10,000,000

Seven years after launching risk3sixty, we hit $10 million in annual recurring revenue. It came on a warm autumn day the first of October 2023. We sent a scheduled batch of invoices to clients like we always do, and then our revenue tracker quietly ticked past the $10 million mark. There were no fireworks. No fan fair. But we did it.

Our first BHAG.

As I was leaving the office at the end of the workday CW surprised me with a gift to memorialize the event. A watch made by hand by Nashville-based watchmaker Cameron Weiss—one of the only Swiss-trained American watchmakers building watches independently in America. The watch has become one of my most prized possessions. On the back is engraved the inscription *"Time loves the good business."*

Indeed, it does.

Your Next Step

Throughout this book, we've provided you with "Actions You Can Take *Now*."

We've created a library of resources and templates to assist you in your leadership journey. Once you've identified the areas where you want to focus your action, check out the relevant materials by scanning the QR code below.

More Good Leaders and Good Businesses means more integrity, thriving, and prosperity in the world—and we're all about that.

ABOUT THE AUTHORS

Christian White

Christian White (CW) is the president and cofounder of risk3sixty, overseeing strategy, operations, and people. CW is a steward of the business, working with an exceptional executive leadership team to guide the company's strategic vision, grow its culture, mentor leaders, and oversee client and team health. CW enjoys building high-performing teams, investing in people, and being a part of his team's and clients' growth journey.

A native of Connecticut, CW received his BS from the United States Military Academy at West Point and served in the US Army as an Infantry Officer. After more than six years of service, CW transitioned to civilian life and received his MBA from the Georgia Institute of Technology, where he met Christian Hyatt and founded the risk3sixty we know and love today. CW calls Atlanta, GA home; he and his wife Rachel are raising three wonderful children, Christian, Noah, and Mikaela. Favorite activities outside of work include supporting his kids' sporting endeavors, coffee and adventure with Rachel, conducting mental and physical training with Bret, engaging with mastermind groups and his church family, and enjoying the deliberate practices of gratitude and of being present: here, now, at this time, in this place.

Christian Hyatt

Christian is the CEO and cofounder of risk3sixty, responsible for setting the vision for the team, ensuring the leadership team is "rowing in the same direction," creating purpose and alignment across the firm, and nurturing company culture. He is also the bestselling author of the critically acclaimed cybersecurity leadership book *Security Team Operating System.*

With experience overseeing more than two thousand cybersecurity engagements, Christian is one of the most experienced experts in the nation. Under Christian's leadership, risk3sixty has been named to multiple prestigious lists, including *Consulting Magazine*'s Best Firms to Work For (three times), Atlanta's Fastest Growing companies (seven times), and Atlanta's Best Places to Work (three times), as well as a HIRE Vets Platinum Honoree (twice). Christian has been named as one of Atlanta's Top CEOs.

Christian has an MBA from Georgia Tech and a BBA from the University of Georgia. Christian is a Georgia Tech Technology and Management (T&M) corporate partner and Advisory Board Member for UGA's Management Information System Advisory Board.

Christian lives in Atlanta, GA, with his wife Lauren and their three children: Lily, Benjamin, and Sonora. Outside of work, he enjoys church and community involvement, traveling with his family, speaking and writing, running, and pursuing new adventure activities.

ACKNOWLEDGMENTS

Christian White

As a man of faith, I want to first thank my Lord and Savior Jesus Christ. He has guided my steps throughout my life to this day, and my faith in Him is my foundation.

Second, I want to thank my wife, Rachel, who is my life partner, fellow adventurer, and best friend. She has supported us through two army deployments, enthusiastically gave me the green light to start risk3sixty with Christian Hyatt, and has been the emotional rock of our family. Rach, you are the best, and I love you!

I also want to thank my children, Christian, Noah, and Mikaela, for being the wonderful people they are and for keeping what matters at the forefront of our lives. I'm so proud of you kiddos and the blessing to be your dad. Love you!

Thank you to my parents, who gave me unconditional love, introduced me to Jesus Christ, and gave me the permission to pursue my own path from a young age. What more could a son ask for?

Special thanks to Greta Myers, who labored with us on this project and, without whom, we would not have been able to bring this book that was in our heads into reality. Thank you to Chas Hoppe and Nicole and Timmy Bauer – it took a team to get this into print!

Lastly, I want to acknowledge that no one is self-made, and I have a whole host of people to thank who have made a lasting impact on my life. These people have taught me, encouraged me, picked me up when I was down, and invested in me. I'm humbled and grateful to have had these people in my life along the journey: Rob Campbell, Rebekah Hicks, Jason Alford, Henry Dolezal, Daniel Livolsi, Christian Hyatt, Timothy Palmer, Jessica Andree, Kevin Ketts, Ryan McGowan, Philip Brudney, Sawyer Miller, Cal Supik, the entire risk3sixty team, Rob Swartwood, Chip Daniels, David Gray, Brandon Gray, Greg Crabtree, and Chad Johnson.

Christian Hyatt

God. Your will is a mystery. But, over time I hope that I do a better job listening. Listening as much with my heart as with my head. Thank you for every experience in life required to get to this point.

Thank you to my family for giving me the time, space, and encouragement to write this book: Lauren, Lily, Benjamin, and Sonora. Building the Good business is for you. Thank you.

The ideas in this book aren't just ideas. They are put into practice every day at risk3sixty. Thank you to my business partner and risk3sixty co-founder, Christian White, for the brainstorming sessions, the encouragement, and the partnership over the last decade.

To my mother, Sonya Hyatt, who instilled in me an unreasonable confidence as a child. That confidence set a foundation to take shots like starting a business and writing a book. Unconditional love is a rare thing, but I have that gift from you. Thank you.

Harry and Becky. I love you guys and thank you for always being there. There is a certain comfort in knowing someone will always be there for you. For over twenty years you guys have been that for me.

Our amazing team at risk3sixty. Anything we have accomplished as a business was due to the efforts of an amazing team helping us get there. Thank you!

Many of my beliefs about business have been shaped by guides and mentors. Thank you to my unofficial mastermind group, most of which I have only met in books, who have had significant influence on my thinking to this point: Gino Wickman, Verne Harnish, Patrick Lencioni, Jack Stack, Rob Campbell, Jason Fried, David Maister, Dan Sullivan, Felix Denis, and many more.

We could not have completed this book without the partnership of the team who helped us with this book: Greta, Chas, Timmy, and Nicole. Thank you for the help getting this over the finish line.

APPENDIX

Chapter 7: Bootstrapping Finance, 101: Measuring Tools

Welcome to the nerd-out on numbers section! Use these tools to level up your financial bootstrapping prowess.

For further reading, we recommend Greg Crabtree's books, *Simple Numbers* for businesses under $5m in revenue and *Simple Numbers 2.0* for businesses greater than $5m in revenue, which provide an even deeper look at all of these concepts. We've mentioned Greg Crabtree and his Simple Numbers advisory team several times when discussing small business finance. There's a reason for it—after reading hundreds of books on personal and business finance, we think his approach to small business finance is "noise-free" and applicable to any small business intent on scaling. If you enjoy nerding out on the numbers and getting more into the weeds, beyond the high-level concepts we are presenting, definitely check out Greg's books.

Rule 6. Obsess Over Your Cash Flow

Measuring Tools: P&L Statements

Your Profit and Loss statement (P&L) is a great tool to help you understand your economic model and obsess over your cash flow effectively. And really—to have a full financial picture, you're going to want one in each hand: the **Accrual Accounting P&L** and the **Cash Accounting P&L**. That sounds jargony, so we'll explain why you need both.

Let's say you have a landscaping business, and you mow a neighbor's property. When you're done, you put an invoice in their mailbox that tells them they owe you $150. That invoice is a sign of *performance*: you've done $150 worth of work. That's great! But the homeowner may not pay you right away. They might wait thirty days. Or sixty. Or even *ninety* before they finally pay up.

See, that invoice is not the same as cash. That's why you need these two P&L statements:

- **Accrual Accounting P&L** provides a *clearer picture of the company's financial performance* over a specific period of time by recognizing revenues and expenses when they are earned or incurred, regardless of when cash is actually exchanged. In other words, it tells you what money you have *coming* to you: "$150 due from Joe Neighbor, by September 1st" for the work that you did this week.

- **Cash Accounting P&L** provides a *clearer picture for understanding cash flow*, as it records revenue and expenses only when cash is actually received or paid. For example, it tells you what cash you have received in your bank account *this* month, regardless of when the work was actually done, e.g. *last* month.

We are not CPAs, but we do understand our numbers and our financial statements because we have studied them relentlessly for years. We recommend that you do the same and meet with your own CPA advisors to coach you on anything in your P&L statements that you do not understand as well as how to utilize these statements to both manage the business as well as optimize financial levers that can make a real impact.

In the early years, you will likely file taxes based on your Cash P&L, but once you achieve a certain size, you will need to transition your financial reporting to be Accrual-based. Again, assessing that, the benefits and requirements of each is beyond the scope of this book. The point that we want to convey is that to truly understand your business, you need to understand the numbers, the flow of the numbers, and how they are related. Mastering the P&L statement is a key part of that.

Measuring Tool: Cash Flow Report

Okay, let's say you're looking at your Cash Accounting P&L, but you're still trying to do math in your head: *It says we have $100,000 profit, but we had to take $40,000 out for taxes,* *and we did an owner's distribution as well... How much increase in cash did we realize over this period once we account for those items?*

That's what the **Cash Flow Report** (e.g. Statement of Cash Flows) tells you. The *Cash Flow Report* shows the change in cash over a defined period of time.

> The Cash Flow Report tells you the net change in cash over a defined period of time after all your expenses have been paid and distributions allocated.

This number does more for you than simply provide reassurance that you'll still have money in the bank. This number also tells you if you can *grow*. For instance, if you consistently have increases in *Cash Flow*, you are more confident in hiring your next employee.

We report on *Cash Flow* for the month ending. (Basically, once the books are closed for March, which would happen the first week of April, we look at what our free cash flow was for March. That's helpful data that gives us a sense of our trends.) We also project the next thirty, sixty, and ninety days. By making these projections, we protect ourselves from running out of cash or committing to a new obligation that could put us in a negative cash flow position.

P&L statements and the Free Cash Flow report: those are some of the tools that are going to help you measure and track your cash flow, enabling you to properly obsess over your cash numbers. The Balance Sheet is also very important; we recommend Greg Crabtree's writing to understand the following key insights from the Balance Sheet: 1) Return on Invested Capital, 2) Core Capital, 3) Trade Capital.

Rule 7. Get Paid

Pro-Tips: Optimize Your CCC

Here are some thoughts on ways to optimize your Cash Conversion Cycle (CCC):

- Tighten your inventory levels, if you carry inventory. You can do this in several ways: reduce inventory; enlist the services of a fulfillment partner to reduce inventory costs; or, optimize inventory levels and timing of delivery based on your data. (This is known as a "Just-in-time" inventory method.) Note that carrying inventory—which you often have to pay for upfront—coupled with giving credit terms to customers is the worst of both worlds, as this creates a very long CCC.

- Do faster invoicing: invoice more frequently instead of waiting until the end of the month.

- Some businesses get paid upfront *before* rendering a service; others get paid at the point of sale but may have to stock inventory. Consider those variables when you're doing your own CCC calculation.

- Ask customers for upfront payments or a portion of payment upfront, or offer payment discounts for upfront payments. This may work in some industries and with clients who value this. Sometimes, all you need to do is ask.

- Tighten credit terms with customers: we like to start with 15 days and negotiate from there.

- Optimize collection procedures: discussed in Chapter 7. (This is a big needle mover!)

- Negotiate better payment terms with suppliers. Explore supplier financing.

- Streamline operational efficiencies.

- "Measure & Manage": use a cash flow management software or monthly calls with a financial consultant or your internal team to help you move the needle on CCC.

Measuring Tool: Aging A/R

"A/R" stands for Accounts Receivable. In other words, you've invoiced somebody, but they haven't paid you yet. With just a handful of clients, it's easy enough to keep track of who still owes you money—smaller businesses or those in other industries (e.g. direct to consumer) may not even use Accounts Receivable. But as your business grows, and your number of clients grows, your Accounts Receivable is going to become a big ol' thing.

Ten clients have thirty-day terms; eighteen clients have sixty-day terms; another client has sixty-day terms but regularly pays thirty days late. Keep track of all those due dates, terms, and payments with your Accounts Receivable spreadsheet or software (e.g. QuickBooks).

Your *Aging A/R* spreadsheet is exactly what it sounds like: it's for those invoices that are *past due.* They're getting wrinkled and old! They need your prompt attention!

You need to **actively manage your *Aging A/R***; there's no room for passivity here. Some clients may genuinely forget to pay you and need your reminder. Some clients may play games, trying to get sixty-day terms instead of thirty by simply not paying you until they're thirty days past due. These wayward clients can affect your cash conversion cycle if you don't stay on top of them, hindering your ability to grow the business.

Measuring Tool: Days Sales Outstanding (DSO)

One handy little tool works with your *Aging A/R:* the Days Sales Outstanding number. The DSO tells you the average number of days it takes for your company to collect payment after a sale has been made.

> The Aging A/R lists all the past-due invoices.
> The DSO measures the average number of days your clients take to pay you.

If you're using an accounting system like QuickBooks, your *Aging A/R* will have data on every customer who's late, along with how many days they're late. QuickBooks can run a report, aggregating all that tardiness data:

DSO: 60 days

What?! Your clients take 60 days to pay you, on average? That's a sign you need to be a whole lot more fierce following up on those invoices. Get those payments in the bank!

DSO: 32 days

Ah, now that's better. The lower your DSO, the better able you are able to grow confidently and not be at risk for growing faster than your cash. For non-retail-based businesses, under thirty days is best practice, in our opinion. However, if you work with bigger clients who command longer terms—say, Walmart-type with ninety plus day terms—that will extend your *DSO*. Use this number to measure performance and stay on top of your *Aging A/R*.

Can you see why implementing financial cadences is so helpful? Regularly checking in on these numbers is a critical practice for the bootstrapping entrepreneur. If you don't religiously monitor invoices, some customers may pay you ninety days late. Other customers would be happy to *never* pay. In any case, that puts a major strain on your cash. And—have we said this enough?—*cash is the lifeblood of your business.*

Not only do these cadences help keep cash in your bank account; they also help drive discipline and accountability. For instance, in our start up days, monitoring cash was a team effort. Christian did the invoicing and a lot of the follow-up cash collecting, while I did the bookkeeping. Our joint review of these numbers prompted regular meetings that helped us make solid thirty-, sixty-, and ninety-day forecasts on our cash flow and accounts receivable. That kept *us* accountable with handling finances, and it also kept us accountable to our business plan, ensuring we were playing off the same sheet of music. That's Good Business.

As a final point from experience here, *proactively managing A/R is **one of the top ways that we have been able to confidently and predictably bootstrap fast growth**.* It is so important that we have often tied compensation incentives for the person responsible for managing our A/R. We consistently operated at sub-30 days DSO for years, and though it felt like a good number, we didn't realize that it was three times better than typical firms in our industry until a financial consultant told us. Small tweaks like that, in aggregate, help to form a hidden back-office competitive advantage, and that enables other parts of the business to operate better. These small things add up over time!

By doing a little numbers-crunching, it's possible to see just *how much* it adds up. Check out the impact to cash flow in reducing DSO from ninety to thirty days on a $10 million annual revenue business. You can use these same formulas to calculate the impact on *your* business' cash flow—just swap out the variables with your actual numbers:

Impact on Cash Flow:

1. **Annual Revenue**: $10 million

2. **Initial DSO**: 90 days

3. **Reduced DSO**: 30 days

Step 1: Calculate Average Accounts Receivable at 90 Days DSO

- Formula:

$$\text{Accounts Receivable} = \left(\frac{\text{Annual Revenue}}{365} \right) \times \text{DSO}$$

- Calculation:

$$\text{Accounts Receivable at 90 Days DSO} = \left(\frac{10,000,000}{365} \right) \times 90 \approx \$2,465,753$$

Step 2: Calculate Average Accounts Receivable at 30 Days DSO

- Calculation:

$$\text{Accounts Receivable at 30 Days DSO} = \left(\frac{10,000,000}{365} \right) \times 30 \approx \$821,918$$

Step 3: Determine the Cash Freed Up

- Cash Freed Up:

$$\text{Cash Freed Up} = \text{Accounts Receivable at 90 Days DSO} - \text{Accounts Receivable at}$$

- Calculation:

$$\text{Cash Freed Up} = 2,465,753 - 821,918 \approx \$1,643,835$$

Look at that impact on cash! It's a pretty big deal for growing a bootstrapped business!

Rule 9. Invest Strategically

Measuring Tool: Key Ratios

Here are a few more numbers that can help you make confident decisions about hiring. I geek out on these next few numbers, but for Christian, these numbers were more of an acquired taste. The words—**Direct Labor Efficiency Ratios (dLER)** and **Management Labor Efficiency Ratios (mLER)**—as defined in *Simple Numbers, Straight Talk, Big Profits!*, were hard to interpret, at first. But when I actually conceptualized what they were, the numbers became meaningful and quite helpful. They're both numbers that can help you invest strategically, make smart tactical decisions about people, and ensure health in your business as it grows.

Let's talk about the **Direct Labor Efficiency Ratio** first. This refers to the people actually *doing* the work and is calculated by their productivity (revenue generated or delivered) divided by their salary cost. We can apply this to a landscaping situation: "direct labor" describes the folks out there mowing the grass, directly executing the service. Specifically, it describes how *efficient* each one of those people are at performing their tasks.

> The dLER describes the efficiency of the people who are actually carrying out the work with clients—the "direct labor."

So, if I'm running my landscaping business and I want to know if I can hire more mowers, I need to look at this number. One of my mowers can do forty lawns in a week. His *dLER* is really good! But another guy can only mow twenty lawns in a week. His *dLER* is bad. Until I understand what good output is and consider average costs of my labor, I don't know what a realistic efficiency ratio range *should be*. I'm not out there doing the work. I'm in my office looking at financial statements. Is 100 lawns per week crazy-town? Is that a sign the guy is mowing lawns badly? Or, is four lawns per week ludicrous? Is that a sign the gal is sleeping on the job? What should I realistically be expecting of my employees?

Once I start measuring everyone's *dLER*, I can start to see what a healthy range is. Maybe I determine that the best mowers are consistently hitting fifty-five lawns per week, so that's generating a dLER of 3.0—in other words, they are producing 3x their salary cost. The *dLER* becomes a tool to manage, both in how I hold employees accountable and in the workload that I assign. Once the *dLER* starts creeping up past a healthy threshold—say, to 3.25—I probably need to hire more people to help.[6] If I don't, I may be asking my employees to do too much, and their quality may be dropping or they may burn out.

That's why the *dLER* is ultimately about the right, healthy number for *your* business. You want it to reflect a high level of efficiency, but not *so* high you're sacrificing service quality or team member quality of life. But if it floats down too *low*, say 2.5, that signals something else: perhaps this department isn't executing efficiently; maybe they are overstaffed; do we need to update our pricing? The number gives us a vantage point to manage the business and set realistic targets.

However—that number doesn't take into account the people who *aren't* executing the direct labor. What about all the back-end folks that are key to making the business engine run? The accounts receivable person, the office manager, the HR director? How do we measure them?

This brings us to term number two: **Management Labor Efficiency Ratios (mLER).** This number is going to help you evaluate the back-office team. They're not the ones executing the work, but they're still vital to help the whole business run smoothly. You want to know, "Am I too bloated in my back-office team? Do I have too many managers? Or are we actually stretched too thin, and I need to hire someone else?"

> The mLER measures the efficiency of your back-end office staff.

Here's why these numbers get us so excited: by understanding your Direct Labor costs and your Management Labor costs, you can make confident forecasts and decisions that

---

[6] The ideal number for your dLER will depend on your industry. If this concept intrigues you, we'd encourage you to read Greg Crabtree's books for a deeper dive.

impact the future of the business in a scientific and healthy way. Without these numbers, you're just guessing—doing beer math. *With* these numbers, you can invest strategically!

The key to running a profitable business is keeping your *d/LER* high and managing your back-office costs. You could look at any profitable company in the entire world and their ranges for the *d/LER* and the *m/LER* would be similar to what we've described, adjusted for industry specific attributes. And based on their revenue numbers, you could guess how many people they have delivering the work, and how many people they have in the back office.

That's just the physics of business. It may be nerdy—but it's super helpful for that bottom line!

Rule 10. Confidently Forecast

Measuring Tool: Rule of 40

Allegedly, the term "Rule of 40" was originally popularized in 2015 by venture capitalists Brad Feld and Fred Wilson, but we heard about it first in a Mastermind group.[7] The speaker ran a company that invests in startups. In the middle of his speech, he mentioned the Rule of 40 in passing: "Everybody in investing knows the Rule of 40. Take the *profitability number* and add it to the *growth number*. If it adds up to 40 or above, it's investor-worthy. That's a great company."

> The Rule of 40: if your profitability margin and your growth rate percentage add up to 40 or above, you've got a great company.

---

7 SaaS Metrics Board. "Net Revenue Retention (NRR) | SaaS Metrics Standard Board," n.d. https://www.saasmetricsboard.com/rule-of-40.

Remember: growth sucks cash. Anytime you're spending money to grow, you're reducing your profitability. The trick is to keep those two numbers in balance. If your numbers equal forty or above—you're doing Good Business.

We're not a venture backed company, and the Rule of 40 was largely intended to benchmark SaaS companies to assess whether they were investment-worthy, but the metric still piqued our curiosity. Were *we* a great company, according to the Rule of 40? We went back and did the math with our numbers:

- *Growth rate percentage:* Our first year, we made $176,000 in revenue. The second year, we made $650,000. That gave us a growth rate of 269 percent. The third year, we made $1.2 million, giving us an eighty-four percent growth rate.
- *Profit margins:* For our first two years, we managed a thirty percent profit margin.

These numbers prompted us to give each other some pats on the back. When we added those two numbers together, we were way over 40! Our growth has become more steady and predictable as we've grown, but we're still benchmarking against the Rule of 40 every year.

How might the Rule of 40 apply to you?

- You might have zero percent profits, but you managed forty percent growth. 0 + 40 = 40. You're a great company on paper—but without profit, you are at risk of running out of cash, without outside capital
- Maybe you did twenty percent profits, and twenty percent growth. 20 + 20 = 40. *You're* a great company, and that may be a sustainable pace for years to come!
- You were forty percent profitable but didn't manage any growth. 40 + 0 = 40. The profitability is great, but without growth, you won't be able to help your team realize their bigger and better future.

This odd little law of business physics is a good reference point to think about. You can also use it as a guide to benchmark your success, build budgets, do your annual forecast, and so on.

Measuring Tool: Trade Capital

Trade Capital is an extremely important forecasting metric for a bootstrapped company. We learned this concept through our work with Brandon Gray and the Simple Numbers team, and it has made bootstrapping finance much easier for us to conceptualize and execute confidently. Why is this number so important? This number is going to tell you:

A.   If you *can* self-fund growth through bootstrapping

B.   How *fast* you can grow

C.   The *approach* you need to take to grow—i.e. Can you grow at a continuous rate? Or do you need to save, then grow, then save, then grow?

In essence, Trade Capital is the decisive number that reveals whether your business can thrive on bootstrapping alone or if you need to seek outside funding. Though the concept may seem complex, we will break it down.

To calculate Trade Capital, you need to find out the net of your current assets and liabilities; you will find these numbers in your balance sheet:

- Figure out the number of your *assets*: your Accounts Receivable, your inventory, and your work in progress. This is all the money you have coming *in*.
- Figure out the number of your *liabilities*—i.e. The amount you're responsible to pay *out*. This might include Accounts Payable, accrued expenses, and deferred revenue.

Let's start with that, using small, easy numbers.

- *Assets:* You've got...

    ○ $10 in Accounts Receivable
    ○ $10 worth of inventory
    ○ $10 in Work in Progress
    ○   *Equaling $30*

- *Liabilities:* You owe...

    - - $5 in Accounts Payable
    - - $5 in Accrued Expenses
    - - $5 in Deferred Revenue
    - *Equaling - $15*

To figure out your Trade Capital Dollars, put those numbers together:

- $30 - $15 = $15 Trade Capital Dollars

Beautiful! Now, let's get some context for this number. Take your Trade Capital Dollar amount and compare it to the dollar amount of revenue over the past twelve months. Use those two numbers to get a percentage:

- Trade Capital Dollars: $15
- 12-month revenue: $100
- 15 / 100 = .15
- *Trade Capital percentage: 15%*

Boom! You've got your Trade Capital percentage. Now, let's make that number *useful* for confident forecasting.

In order to forecast, you need to compare the Trade Capital percentage with your Profit Margin percentage (aka your Net Income percentage). Ideally, your Profit Margin percentage will be *bigger* than your Trade Capital percentage; when that's the case, you have cash coming in faster than you are spending it, which means you can continue to bootstrap your growth.

Let's figure out our Profit Margin percentage:

- 12-month revenue is $100
- Net income was $20
- 20 / 100 = .2
- *Profit margin: 20%*

Now, you have all the numbers you need to strategically forecast with the Trade Capital measurement. The rule is this: If your profit margin percentage is *higher* than your trade capital percentage, then you can continue to bootstrap your growth without any additional capital infusion from external sources; that's very good news! That means you're in what Greg calls a *Free Growth Zone.* When you are able to forecast your trade capital, you are also confidently able to forecast your ability to self-fund, which is the peace of mind all entrepreneurs need!

> If your Profit Margin is *higher* than your Trade Capital percentage, you're in the *Free Growth Zone.* In other words, you can continue to bootstrap your growth indefinitely.

What does it mean if your profit margin is *lower* than your trade capital percentage? Well, that's not great news. That means you're burning cash to grow and will be *limited* in your growth by how much cash you have on hand and how much debt you can draw upon. Maybe your profit margin is too low, and your liabilities are too high, and your terms are too long. You're giving customers ninety days to pay you. When you put all those numbers together, you're going to end up with a *high* trade capital percentage that may exceed your net income percentage. In that case—you're going to run out of cash at some point if you keep growing *without* pausing growth to build up cash reserves. You don't have enough money to pay employees to do new business, because it takes so long for you to get paid.

That doesn't necessarily mean you *need* to take external capital—you could take out a bank loan instead. You could even continue to bootstrap and fund your own growth, just at a slower rate. You'd want to use a "stair step" approach: save up, then fund growth; save up more cash, then fund more growth.

Here's a real-world example. Let's say you run a company that builds residential homes. You need to put down a lot of money to buy the property and materials and pay for labor—that's a great big number in your *Liabilities* column. But once the home is built and sold, you get a hefty paycheck: add that to your *Assets* column.

Now—do you need to grow your business slowly, building one house at a time? Do you need to get paid for the house you built *before* starting the next project? That's a slow model of growth. Do you have to keep taking out bank loans or investor money to fund your growth? That's no longer a self-funding model.

Or, you might find that your system works so efficiently, you're able to build and sell houses faster than the bills come due. You're in the Free Growth Zone! You're able to sell the homes so fast, you can use the profits to start your next project over and over again. You can bootstrap forever!

The Trade Capital percentage can be a challenging number to wrap your head around, but once you do, you'll be amazed at the assurance it gives you in bootstrapping your growth. Trade Capital can help you predict your cash flow from operations, helping you make confident strategic decisions.

Chapter 9: Scale Your Leadership and Teams

Commander's Intent & Levels of Initiative

Bottom Line Up Front:

To truly delegate and decentralize decision-making to the people closest to the work, leaders must provide **clarity of intent, not control of execution**.

A simple, shared framework from the US Army Mission Command doctrine, including Commander's Intent —*Mission, Purpose, Key Tasks, Desired End State*—creates the context required for autonomous, high-quality decisions without micromanagement.

When paired with clear **Levels of Initiative**, this becomes a force multiplier for building and sustaining a high-performing organization.

Give me a high performing connected team where trust is implicit and Level 3 initiative is business as usual, couple it with clearly stated **Executive** (Commander) **Intent**, and you've got the formula <u>to grow the organization beyond you being the bottleneck</u>.

Note: In Army doctrine, the mission is deliberately separate from Commander's Intent. In business, where such formal separation rarely exists, I include mission explicitly to ensure shared understanding before intent is exercised.

1. Executive Intent: The Delegation Framework

Assuming a foundation of trust (a critical and non-trivial prerequisite), Executive Intent provides the specificity needed for alignment **without prescribing the how**.

The Four Elements

1. **Mission** — What must be done?

    o The assignment or outcome required.

2. **Purpose** — Why does this matter?

    o The logic that allows intelligent adaptation when conditions change.

3. **Key Tasks** — What must go right?

    o A short list of essential priorities or constraints.

    o Not exhaustive; deliberately incomplete.

4. **Desired End State** — What does success look like?

    o Clear, observable conditions that define completion.

Together, these create a <u>shared framework and context</u> within which teams can determine the best execution path.

Why Executive Intent Works

- Provides alignment without rigidity through shared understanding.

- Enables speed and judgment at the level best suited to make decisions.

- Reduces escalation and decision bottlenecks, increasing organizational speed.

- Prevents micromanagement while maintaining accountability.

Leaders define <u>direction and boundaries</u>. **Teams own** <u>execution and adaptation</u>.

2. Levels of Initiative: Trust + Empowerment

High-performing people do not want to be micromanaged—and effective leaders do not want to micromanage them. The solution is not tighter control, but **higher initiative enabled by trust and empowerment**.

Organizations and individuals naturally operate at different Levels of Initiative based on culture, norms, standards, experience, and personality. To grow an organization beyond the leader as a bottleneck, leaders must intentionally create an environment where initiative can grow and where people are coached upward over time.

This progression requires mutual trust, psychological safety, risk tolerance, and deliberate empowerment.

New hires will not operate at the highest level of initiative on day one. They must first be onboarded, trained, and grounded in the organization's culture, values, and expectations. As mutual trust is built and good judgment is demonstrated, initiative should expand accordingly, until, at maturity, individuals and teams consistently operate at Level 3 initiative.

Level 1 — Directed

Wait to be told what to do.

- Appropriate for new hires, low trust, or high-risk situations.

- Slow, leader-dependent, and definitely non-scalable.

Level 2 — Permission-Based

See what needs to happen and ask permission to act.

- Better situational awareness than level 1, but still inadequate for high performance.

- Still takes too long to act, creating drag and decision congestion.

Level 3 — Intent-Driven Initiative

*See what needs to happen and **<u>take action within Executive Intent</u>**, while keeping leadership informed during or immediately after execution.*

- Fast, adaptive, and empowering.

- Where high-performing teams operate.

How the Two Fit Together

- **Executive Intent** sets direction and boundaries (<u>clarity</u>).

- **Levels of Initiative** determine how decisions are made within those boundaries (<u>action</u>).

As trust increases, leaders should deliberately move teams toward **Level 3**, where initiative is exercised confidently within shared intent.

This combination is the secret sauce:

- Leaders stop approving tactics.

- Teams stop waiting for permission.

- The organization gains speed, ownership, and resilience.

<u>**The Leadership Test**</u>

If your team regularly surprises you with decisions you didn't make, but that you fully support and that fall within your intent, you are delegating effectively.

Intent + Initiative = rocket fuel for a high-performing organization.

Job Descriptions

Clarity: that's one of the best ways you can support your team. A strong job description will ensure that you attract the right people to your company and provide them the clarity they need to excel in their role. Here are our tips to write a great one:

Start with an overview. A job description should open with the big picture. At risk3sixty, we do that by naming the different categories of a person's role, which all connect back to the company's vision:

9 Jobs: Practice Leader Responsibilities

Understand, support, and communicate the firm's vision and core values as articulated in the firm Management Operating System (MOS)

1. Vision
2. Culture
3. Economics
4. Develop Leaders
5. Product and Packaging
6. Delivery Methodology
7. Marketing and Thought Leadership
8. Sales Engineering
9. Client Relationship Ownership

risk3sixty

So, for a practice leader (think: director or manager), they have responsibilities in the areas of cultivating vision, culture, driving positive economics, developing leaders, and so on—all geared toward understanding, supporting, and communicating the firm's vision and core values as articulated in the firm MOS.

From the overview, we shift to **role-specific responsibilities.** This looks like clarity around how each of those responsibilities should play out in a given role, along with KPIs (key performance indicators) which will measure their success. Here's an example of how one of our practice leaders might be directed to cultivate culture in their leadership role:

Job 2: Culture

The Job:

- Work with the CEO and ELT to define the culture of the Practice as part of your Management Operating System (MOS)
- Document (in writing) the Practice culture
- Live the culture by example
- Communicate the culture to the team on a regular basis
  - Ensure vision is understood and shared by all

KPIs:

You will know you were successful if you can retain your team. A world class retention rate is somewhere around 90%.

risk3sixty

There's a description of how their responsibility will play out, notes about the support they'll receive, and—*this is crucial*—information about how their performance will be measured. For a Culture responsibility, the practice leader will be successful if they retain around 90 percent of their team.

An Economics related goal will have even more specific KPI measurements:

Job 3: Economics

The Job:

- Manage economic viability of the Practice in alignment with targets (Revenue, Contribution Margin)
- Hiring Decisions and request for resources
- Execution of projects on time, with quality, and on budget

KPIs:

- Profitable growth
  - Managed Revenue
  - DLER

risk3sixty

After detailing the role-specific responsibilities, a job description should then relay any **company-wide relevant information**.

By the way—AI can help you with this so you are not reinventing the wheel. Often, you'll get a helpful baseline that you can then edit and massage as needed.

In short: a good job description should provide an overview of the company's vision and core values, a list of role-specific responsibilities, a breakdown of each responsibility, and key performance indicators that will measure progress in each area.

www.ingramcontent.com/pod-product-compliance
Lightning Source LLC
Chambersburg PA
CBHW031444160726
47994CB00005B/1872